5-23-10

Given to me, by our beautiful daughter
Barbara as a gift! After reading
the stories, inside this beautiful book,
I have decided to gift it to you;
I hope you find the stories in this
book as inspirational and comforting
as I did!
   I wish you;
      Strength of spirit
   Peace of mind,
   The freedom to be
and love ever-lasting!
              God Bless you
              Always
         With love
            Jori

DAILY
GUIDEPOSTS
2010

Guideposts
New York, New York

Daily Guideposts 2010

ISBN-13: 978-0-8249-4783-5

Published by Guideposts
16 East 34th Street
New York, New York 10016
www.guideposts.com

Distributed by Ideals Publications, a division of Guideposts
2636 Elm Hill Pike, Suite 120
Nashville, Tennessee 37214

Guideposts, Daily Guideposts and *Ideals* are registered trademarks of Guideposts.

Acknowledgments

Every attempt has been made to credit the sources of copyrighted material used in this book. If any such acknowledgment has been inadvertently omitted or miscredited, receipt of such information would be appreciated.

All Scripture quotations, unless otherwise noted, are taken from *The King James Version of the Bible*.

Scripture quotations marked (GNB) are taken from *Good News Bible: Today's English Version*. Copyright © 1966, 1971, 1976 American Bible Society. All rights reserved.

Scripture quotations marked (MSG) are taken from *The Message*. Copyright © 1993, 1994, 1995, 1996, 2000, 2001, 2002 by Eugene H. Peterson.

Scripture quotations marked (NAS) are taken from the *New American Standard Bible*, copyright © 1960, 1962, 1963, 1968, 1971, 1972, 1973, 1975, 1977, 1995 by the Lockman Foundation. Used by permission.

Scripture quotations marked (NEB) are taken from *The New English Bible*. Copyright © The Delegates of the Oxford University Press and the Syndics of the Cambridge University Press 1961, 1970.

Scripture quotations marked (NIV) are taken from *The Holy Bible, New International Version*. Copyright © 1973, 1978, 1984 International Bible Society. Used by permission of Zondervan Bible Publishers.

Scripture quotations marked (NKJV) are taken from *The Holy Bible, New King James Version*. Copyright © 1997, 1990, 1985, 1983 by Thomas Nelson, Inc.

Scripture quotations marked (NLT) are taken from the *Holy Bible*, New Living Translation. Copyright © 1996. Used by permission of Tyndale House Publishers, Inc., Wheaton, Illinois 60189. All rights reserved.

Scripture quotations marked (NRSV) are taken from the *New Revised Standard Version Bible*. Copyright © 1989 by the Division of Christian Education of the National Council of the Churches of Christ in the U.S.A. Used by permission. All rights reserved.

Scripture quotations marked (RSV) are taken from the *Revised Standard Version of the Bible*. Copyright © 1946, 1952, 1971 by Division of Christian Education of the National Council of Churches of Christ in the U.S.A. Used by permission.

Scripture quotations marked (TLB) are taken from *The Living Bible*. Copyright © 1971 by Tyndale House Publishers, Wheaton, Illinois 60187. All rights reserved.

"Reader's Room" by Marilyn Tumminia, Monna Perrenoud, Rebecca McAlindon, Phoebe Barber, Judith Harmon, Florence Compher, Tiffany Klappenbach, Cathy Wiszowaty, Joni Dintelmann, Bonnie Pula, Lyle Archer and Mary Jo McCarthy are reprinted with permission from the authors.

Brian Doyle's photo by Jerry Hart. Oscar Greene's photo copyright © 2001 by Olan Mills, Inc. Edward Grinnan's and Rick Hamlin's photos by Nina Subin. Roberta Messner's photo by Jan D. Witter/Camelot Photography. Elizabeth Sherrill's and John Sherrill's photos by Gerardo Somoza.

Cover design by The DesignWorks Group
Cover photo by iStock
Interior design by Lorie Pagnozzi

Monthly page opener photos by Getty Images
Indexed by Patricia Woodruff
Typeset by Planet Patti Inc.

Printed and bound in the United States of America

10 9 8 7 6 5 4 3 2 1

INTRODUCTION

G od's gifts are all around us. Sometimes they're obvious, like our daily sustenance, our family, our friends, our faith. Sometimes they fly under our mental radar: the Bible verse we can't remember memorizing that got us through a sleepless night; the casual conversation that led to a new job; the chance meeting that led to marriage. And sometimes they seem to us, at first, anything but "good" and "perfect": the illness, the difficult parent or child, the financial squeeze that, as we look back over the course of our lives, turned us away from ourselves and drew us closer to God.

Our theme for *Daily Guideposts 2010*—our thirty-fourth edition—is "The Gifts We Are Given." We've asked our family of writers to share the gifts God has given them, through Scripture and prayer, through the hands of the people around them, and through the challenges that sent them deeper into their hearts and deeper into the Word. You'll meet our newest family member, Jeff Chu, an editor from Brooklyn, New York, who'll share some of the gifts he's received in his upbringing as a pastor's grandson and in his travels from Africa to Alabama. And you'll greet such longtime favorites as Fay Angus, Oscar Greene, Marion Bond West, Daniel Schantz and Isabel Wolseley.

We have a really special gift in store for you this year—a new, more open and readable design that fits each day's devotional comfortably on one page. We hope you'll find it adds to your ease and enjoyment in reading.

There's no denying that all of us have been through a lot this past year. We've felt the pinch here at Guideposts, but we've also experienced the encouragement and support of our whole Guideposts family. And we know that, as always, God has good and perfect gifts prepared for us throughout the coming year. Come join us as we walk these days together.

—ANDREW ATTAWAY
Editor, *Daily Guideposts*

DAILY GUIDEPOSTS DEVOTIONALS IN YOUR IN-BOX
Receive each day's devotional in your in-box or read it online!
Visit DailyGuideposts.com/DGP2010 and enter this code:
DGP2010

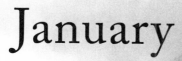

January

*The Lord will give strength
unto his people; the Lord will
bless his people with peace.*

—Psalm 29:11

Fri 1 *May God give peace to you, my Christian brothers, and love, with faith from God the Father and the Lord Jesus Christ.*
—EPHESIANS 6:23 (TLB)

E arly in the new year when I take down the tree, the garlands and the Christmas cards, it's become a tradition for me to prayerfully choose one of the greetings on a card and make it my inspirational focus for the year. This had been a somewhat nostalgic and sad Christmas, as I dearly missed my son Ian, my daughter-in-law Melissa and the grandkids. This was their first Christmas in Colorado; they phoned to tell me of the first snowfall with squeals of delight! Lovely for them but, oh, how I missed their hugs and cuddles.

The focus I chose for this year came by way of a letter from a pastor who has been one of my spiritual mentors. He reminded me of the wish sent by our mutual friend, the late Dr. Lew Smedes, who during his tenure as professor at Fuller Theological Seminary was always a great encourager: "We want you to be blessed with joys deeper than any sadness, gratitude happier than any regrets, hopes brighter than the shadows of any discouragement, and the vitality to make of every day what God on Christmas Day made for all days."

Joy, gratitude, hope and vitality for every day of this new year.

The glow of Your grace warms my heart, Lord Jesus;
the power of Your love sustains me.
—FAY ANGUS

Sat 2

Jesus Christ is the same yesterday and today and forever. —HEBREWS 13:8 (NIV)

Oma, you're wearing the same thing!" my three-year-old grand-daughter Karis observed as we sat on the couch, watching family pictures slide across the screen of her mommy's laptop.

Karis was delighted with her discovery that I was sitting next to her wearing the same light blue hoodie sweatshirt I wore in a picture taken more than a year ago. In fact, it had become part of the comfortable, pre-dictable uniform she saw me wearing way too often.

Her comment seemed to sum up the state of my life in the last year. So much seemed the same. When I'd written our Christmas card mes-sages a month earlier, I'd had less to share than in years past. No exciting adventures, no amazing accomplishments, same house, same spouse, same jobs and pretty much the same life circumstances.

As for New Year's resolutions, I could make the same ones I made last year: to walk a 13.7-mile half marathon and to train Kemo, our golden retriever puppy, so we could visit cancer patients in hospitals. Kemo is almost two years old, and surely he'd create hospital havoc in his eager-ness to greet patients. He needs more training; so do I. The closest I got to a half marathon was walking a six-mile event.

Meanwhile, the pictures kept sliding across the computer screen. "Oma, that's when you didn't have hair," Karis said, looking at another picture of me wearing a hat while still on chemotherapy a couple of years ago. Her comment reminded me that my husband Lynn and I continue to have good test results in our cancer checkups, which means more hair and more hope.

As I sat there reviewing photos with Karis, I realized that while some "sames" are good and some "sames" make me feel like I'm stuck in a rut, every new year brings the same opportunity to identify the good ones and stretch myself toward new adventures.

*Lord, when my life seems "same old, same old," show me where
to find some new possibilities.* —CAROL KUYKENDALL

January

Sun 3   *Follow me. . . .* —MATTHEW 8:22

L ast January I was ordained as an elder at Hillsboro Presbyterian Church. I've attended Hillsboro since my father became its minister when I was nine months old. To be an elder alongside him and to serve the church that is my extended family has been my lifelong dream. Now my opportunity had finally come.

Soon it was time for the annual elders' retreat. I'd always wondered what my father did when he was gone from us for this weekend event and now I'd find out.

The retreat combined devotions with thoughtful reflections on our faith and on our responsibilities as Christians. "Let's talk about God's way," my father said on the final morning. "How would our world look if we actually lived as Christ taught?"

As the discussion picked up, the distinction between the world's way and God's way took on a vivid meaning as it became increasingly clear that what we are urged to do as a church and as elders and members differs wildly from the way the real world works. Imagine taking God's way into the world where we work and play and live together—loving people regardless of our differences, forgiving quickly and without reservation, caring for the sick, feeding the hungry, welcoming the stranger, being thankful for the day at hand.

I wondered if God wanted us all to be His elders, whether ordained or not, and to take His teachings seriously. Maybe He's counting on us to make His way and the world's way one.

Dear God, help me to reflect Your way in everything I do.
—BROCK KIDD

Mon 4

His compassions fail not. They are new every morning: great is thy faithfulness. —LAMENTATIONS 3:22–23

New York City is a Christmas-tree graveyard on these January mornings, the curbsides lined with discarded Scotch and Norway pines, some still trailing bits of tinsel and the occasional ornament, waiting for collection. For our dog Millie on our predawn walks, it's an olfactory paradise. She treads carefully down the salted sidewalks with me in tow, sniffing the brown branches, requiring an occasional tug on the leash as a reminder that we can't spend all day out here.

It's strangely peaceful, this sidewalk forest, dreamlike and soul-soothing. The snow drifts muffle the city's sounds in a soft silence. People move slowly, hunched against the chill. It is the calm after the storm, I suppose. The end of the year comes in such a frantic rush—we're trying to get done everything we wanted to get done, see our families, celebrate the holidays. Who isn't exhausted by the time New Year's rolls up on us?

Yet these early days of January feel slow and purposeful, as if we're catching our breath and gathering our strength, an opportunity to reconnect with God, especially at this time of the morning. The sun is coming up just a tiny bit earlier, but you wouldn't notice unless you are like Millie and me, out at dawn every day.

Millie veers toward another tree lying on its side. I let her inspect it briefly and then give her a little pull. It's time to move on.

Father, let me begin my new year connected to You.
—EDWARD GRINNAN

Tue 5   *Every man that striveth for the mastery is temperate in all things. . . .* —I CORINTHIANS 9:25

A lmost everyone I know has been affected by the recent economic downturn. My family is no exception. This became clear on New Year's Day, when my wife and I went over our budget and realized that we would have to drop some of our dream projects. Most of them didn't matter very much; that vacation to Hawaii could wait. There was one cutback that hurt, however: We could no longer afford to convert our garage into a home office. Instead I would have to continue to work in a corner of our small den, already crammed with a couch, TV set, chess table, and countless books and DVDs.

I was angry and then depressed: Good-bye to all those dreams of a new workspace with floor-to-ceiling windows and beautiful built-in bookshelves, a quiet oasis in the hubbub of family life. Hello to messy, noisy reality!

Fortunately Carol refused to let me dwell in fantasies of might-have-been. Instead she suggested we give thanks for what we had and make the most of it. It was hard to argue with that. So we rolled up our sleeves and refashioned the den. We cleared out years of clutter, turned the computer around to face our lovely backyard garden, set up a new printer station and relocated our bulky old television far away from my work area. Lo and behold, I had a new workspace without spending a penny! I hadn't lost my dream office; I'd gained the serenity that comes with making do.

Lord, teach me to give thanks for what I have
rather than pine for what I don't have.
—PHILIP ZALESKI

Wed 6

Arise, shine; for your light has come, and the glory of the Lord has risen upon you. —ISAIAH 60:1 (RSV)

My niece Aimee and I visited an exhibit of watercolors—landscapes, cityscapes, interiors—by local artist John Bryans. "Which is your favorite?" Aimee asked.

I walked to a desert scene titled *Waiting for the Wisemen*: three riderless camels sitting on sand, each in its own world. Their feet were tucked under their bodies; colorful blankets covered their backs. "This reminds me of how I feel in the winter sometimes," I said. "It's easy to hunker down and let the dark and cold blow through till spring comes."

A week later, while attending meetings at a rural retreat center, I noted a similar tableau just yards outside our first-floor window. For nearly a full day, three rackless deer lounged on a grassy perch, legs tucked under like the painted camels, contentedly chewing their cud. I imagined the deer waiting, but for what?

Before leaving the grounds, I pulled out my camera, hoping for a close-up. As I approached, one doe jumped to her feet. Her quick movement drew my mind to Isaiah's command: "Arise, shine; for your light has come." Every year it's the first line of the Bible readings at our church for the feast of the Epiphany, commemorating the day the wise men found Jesus.

This morning I unearthed the photo of the three deer, one standing, alert, at the ready. As I studied the picture, Isaiah spoke to me again. Is this the time to host a midwinter ladies' tea? What am I waiting for? It's time to draft a guest list.

Lord, teach me that I don't need to wait till spring to serve You and others.
—EVELYN BENCE

🕉 GIFTS FROM ABOVE

Thu 7   *That they which come in may see the light.* —LUKE 11:33

A GIFT OF LIGHT

We took down the star today: a hanger-on, the last Christmas decoration. I hated to see it go.

The star was nothing special, just a piece of plastic with a few strings of lights twined around its edges. We had used duct tape to fasten it to a long wooden pole and then tied the pole to the highest limb of the dogwood tree at the entrance to our house. Some might call my star shabby, but I thought it was glorious. Its blue and white lights were a welcome sight when I returned home on those cold, pre-Christmas nights. And what a delight it was to look out the kitchen window and see the star shining in the darkness. All through the season, when guests were expected, my directions were simple: "Just come to the house with the star."

After we cut the rope and freed the tree of its burden, I walked through the house holding the pole with the star affixed, as if I were leading a parade. But I was far from festive; I felt as though something was ending. The nights would be darker without my star. My landmark was gone.

I found a snug place in the corner of my Christmas closet for the pole and pulled the door shut. As I walked back upstairs, I was already missing the star and ready to look for new ways to mark my home and my life with a light that dares the darkness.

> *Father, give me Your starshine so that I may be a welcoming light to someone every day of this new year.* —PAM KIDD

EDITOR'S NOTE: *We'd like to know what God is doing in your life this year. You can jot down your reflections on "The Gifts I've Been Given" journal pages at the end of every month.*

Fri 8   *"Ask and it will be given to you; seek and you will find; knock and the door will be opened to you. For everyone who asks receives; he who seeks finds; and to him who knocks, the door will be opened."* —MATTHEW 7:7–8 (NIV)

"A rrr," my niece Ella grunted. Unanswered, the grumble grew louder as she strained to reach the book on the corner of the table. "*Arrr . . .*"

When she was about nine months old, Ella, frustrated when something was out of reach, would grunt and grumble until someone came to her aid. It's no surprise that her mother Kristi quickly taught her the first word in her vocabulary.

"Ella," Kristi asked, "what do you say when you want something?"

"Help, help, help," Ella replied, her face going from a tense red to a cheery pink.

"That's right," Kristi replied. "If you just ask, anyone will be happy to help you."

Kristi's words struck me deeply. How often do I cry out in frustration, straining to reach for something just out of my grasp instead of dropping to my knees and simply asking for it?

The Bible tells us, "Ask and you shall receive," and yet so many times and for so many reasons I don't ask. Whatever I'm seeking is too big or too small, too minor or too important. But God doesn't say, "Ask me for the big stuff and get the small things on your own." He simply tells me to ask.

Now, when I find myself on the verge of tears, I remember my sweet niece and stop to say, "Please God, help me."

> *Lord, how wonderful that I can come to You with all my prayers,*
> *big or small, and that Your help is often all I need.*
> —ASHLEY JOHNSON

Sat 9 Be cheerful no matter what; pray all the time;
thank God no matter what happens.
—I THESSALONIANS 5:16–18 (MSG)

I woke up in a hospital bed, needing to go to the bathroom. The digital clock glowed a green 4:02 AM. "Growing old is getting a little irritating," I muttered.

The nurses had told me not to get up without help. An IV stand held a bag of the saline solution dripping into my vein. Pushing the nurse's call button brought no response; everyone seemed to be occupied with other Saturday night emergencies. Finally, I decided to try to get to the bathroom myself.

As I put weight on my feet, I almost slipped and fell. All I could see in the semidarkness was a shiny liquid puddle beside the bed, spreading silently toward the edges of the room. Carefully standing, I held on to my rolling tower for balance and shuffled toward the door where the light was better. There I could see the huge puddle was blood and then remembered that the IV tube had a Y-shaped shunt with two connections, the second to hook up a blood transfusion bag, if necessary, without sticking another needle into my forearm. Somehow that shunt had malfunctioned; the pump was pumping the blood out of my body!

I saw a nurse passing by. "Pardon me. I have a little problem in here." Seeing my situation, she stifled a scream and started to run into the room.

"No, don't run," I warned. "It's very slippery in here!" As bad as things looked, I couldn't help chuckling.

Later, lying in the dark, praying prayers of gratitude, I realized that if I hadn't awakened needing to go to the bathroom, I might have bled to death. Since that time I've pretty much quit complaining about the inconveniences of being old.

> *Lord, I'm very grateful that You will use even the infirmities*
> *I complain about to wake me up and save me.*
> —KEITH MILLER

❋ THE GIFT OF SIGHT

Sun 10   *Strength and beauty are in his sanctuary.*
—Psalm 96:6 (rsv)

god's smile

One of my earliest memories is of sitting in St. Alban's Episcopal Church in McCook, Nebraska, gazing at the stained glass window above the altar. I must have been three or four years old and bored by a sermon I couldn't understand. That was when I started gazing at the colorful window. The sun was at exactly the right height to shine directly through the glass, radiating stunning blues, emerald greens and deep maroons onto the white choir robes and even onto my lap. The colors were so jewel-like, they seemed magical to me.

Pulling on Mother's sleeve and pointing to the window, I said in a loud whisper, "Look! God is smiling at us from heaven!"

She put her finger to her lips and whispered, "No, dear. It's just the sun shining through the colored glass." But with preschool certainty, I was sure I was right. I had no doubt that those beautiful colors came from God and that He was smiling at me from heaven, just on the other side of the glass.

For the first of many times to come, I breathed in beauty and breathed out gratitude. Whether Mother knew it or not, I felt sure that beauty and the eyes with which to see it were special gifts from God—my favorite of all His presents.

Great Creator, thank You for painting our world with such heavenly colors.
—Marilyn Morgan King

Mon 11
The steps of a man are established by the Lord, And He delights in his way. —PSALM 37:23 (NAS)

My wife Beth and I are thrilled that our son Drew is engaged to Katie Alice. From the day Drew was born twenty-six years ago, I began to pray for the little girl whom he would one day marry. I never dreamed that he would meet his bride-to-be in Monroe, North Carolina, in the nursery of the first church where I served as a pastor. Three years later we moved from Monroe, and Drew and Katie Alice seldom saw each other over the ensuing years. Two years ago, however, they were both running in a road race in Charleston, South Carolina, and happened to meet each other afterward. The rest is joyful history.

God guides us down the paths of life in mysterious and wonderful ways. We can't know now how the events of this day might shape our tomorrow. But God does. From birth to death, God weaves the grand tapestry of our life. And it's exciting to watch as His design works itself out with faith and great expectation.

*Father, thank You for using whatever happens to me today
to shape my future for good.* —SCOTT WALKER

READER'S ROOM

I sat down at my kitchen table with my prayer list in front of me. There were a few people on the list I hadn't seen for a while, and I thought I'd remove some of them. The phone rang; I picked it up, but there was no answer. Five minutes later the same thing happened, and again a few minutes after that. When it rang a fourth time, I was really angry. But this time a voice came over the phone: my former pastor, who now lives in Nigeria. He was calling to thank me for a Christmas card I'd sent him. I told him about my thoughts of shortening my prayer list. His call was like a call from God saying, "I don't think so!" —*Marilyn Tumminia, St. Louis, Missouri*

⧗ COMFORT FOR THE HURTING HEART

Tue 12   *Dorcas, who was always doing good and helping the poor. . . .
became sick and died. . . . When [Peter] arrived. . . . All the
widows stood around him, crying and showing him the robes
and other clothing that Dorcas had made while she was still
with them.* —ACTS 9:36–37, 39 (NIV)

AN UNDERSTANDING EAR

In the reception line at my mother's funeral, I privately prided myself
for remaining dry-eyed. I graciously greeted the guests and thanked
them for having come, so perfectly poised that people remarked, "My,
you're taking this well."

Yes, I remained poised . . . until the next day. Then, while I was going
through Mom's belongings, I came across a pincushion with a still-
threaded needle. Just a small, ordinary needle, but big enough to stab my
heart and trigger my tears. At that moment a friend walked in on me.
Janet patted my shoulder and said simply, "Tell me about your mother."

I began describing the frilly dresses Mom had made during my
growing-up days and the many costumes: a Jack-in-the-box outfit for
my school's dress-up day, angel wings for a church Christmas pageant. I
told Janet how throughout my married years Mom had mended seams
and sewed buttons on my entire family's clothes. "Mom quilted—even
darned socks—with needles just like this one."

Janet listened for an hour. When it came time for her to leave, I said,
"Thanks so much for coming and chatting with me." It wasn't until she
was gone that it dawned on me: *I was the one who did the chatting. Janet
had merely listened.*

*Thank You, Father, for those to whom You've given the special gift
of listening.* —ISABEL WOLSELEY

Wed 13

Every skilled woman spun with her hands and brought what she had spun. . . . —EXODUS 35:25 (NIV)

Grandma's spinning wheel had belonged to our family for generations. The wheel was as big as a wagon wheel, and the wood had been polished smooth by use and age. This colonial treasure proudly graced Mom and Dad's living room and later my sister Susan's home built on a hillside on Grandma's land. Then one day the heirloom was missing from Susan's house.

"Where's Grandma's spinning wheel?" I asked.

"I gave it to our second cousin," Susan said. "I prayed, and it seemed like the right thing to do because he's so crazy about family history."

I was stunned. I don't give away things very easily; I hang on, telling myself that I'll be ready to part with them sometime in the future.

A year later Susan's house burned to the ground in the middle of the night. Nothing was saved. "I'm so glad I gave away the spinning wheel before the fire," she told me.

"Me too," I replied gratefully. "Who would have thought that by giving away the spinning wheel you were really saving it?"

Sometimes the best thing I can do with things that seem well worth keeping is to give them away.

Dear Giver of All Good Things, help me to hear when You whisper
in my ear that it's time to pass on a treasure
that will add joy to another location in Your kingdom.
—KAREN BARBER

Thu 14

It is for this we labor and strive, because we have fixed our hope on the living God. . . . —I TIMOTHY 4:10 (NAS)

Stephen's big birthday present when he turned five this year was a subscription to the Young Scientist's Club. Yesterday Maggie joined us as we analyzed the color and hardness of the mineral samples in our first monthly package. Stephen happily wrote down our results in two-inch letters in his science notebook.

Inspired, this morning my two youngest immediately hauled out the "science box," our repository for all things experimental. Stephen donned goggles and set to work making a siphon. Maggie cleaned off some ancient lenses and peered at everything in sight. Seeing that the lamp of curiosity was lit, I volunteered a handful of experiments on air pressure.

Meanwhile, five e-mails about my freelance job had come in. I sighed, pried myself from the fun and returned to the computer. I like my work, but it's hard to balance with family life. The flow of freelance is erratic: One week it's manageable; the next it's an avalanche. I can be in the middle of teaching a homeschool lesson when a crisis hits, and the day's plans have to change entirely. There are very late nights and very early mornings.

And yet it works. Not smoothly, but I'm not sure anything goes smoothly when you've got five children. We make ends meet, we do what we have to do. There's no sin in struggling or in having to work harder than I used to. Sin only comes into the picture when I let the stress get to me and react poorly. I'm slowly beginning to understand that what will make this experiment of mixing freelance, homeschool and play a success is flexibility and plenty of deep breaths.

> *Lord, teach me to be less afraid of what's hard*
> *than of what's displeasing to You.*
> —JULIA ATTAWAY

Fri 15

Yet he has not left himself without a witness in doing good. . . . —ACTS 14:17 (NRSV)

My church offers a variety of different ways to help us express what we believe as a community. One of these is a statement that talks about God being found in art and music and writing and human interaction, and it concludes, "God has never been without a witness in the world."

To be honest, it sometimes makes me scratch my head: *Is that really true?* So recently when I heard it again, I decided I'd put it to the test in the most popular form of culture we have, television. I'd pick a night and watch: Would there be a witness for God on TV?

I found plenty of bad stuff. There was no mention of God or Jesus all night. And yet, far from simply seeing the godless culture I expected, I saw God at work in a whole host of ways.

I saw a promo for a new show about people giving away money to the needy and another about rebuilding houses; a car commercial where the father and son bring boxes of turkeys to a food pantry; and a news report about neighbors taking care of a family after a fire. I saw compassionate doctors and generous workers and, most of all, I saw real people struggling to solve real problems as best they could.

In some ways our culture is going downhill. But I learned that night that God is very much present in our world. And if I can't find God, it may be that I've been looking in all the wrong places.

> *Give me eyes to see You, God, ears to hear You, hands to offer You,*
> *feet to carry You,* in *the places and* to *the places I live my life.*
> —JEFF JAPINGA

Sat 16

Never be lacking in zeal, but keep your spiritual fervor, serving the Lord. —ROMANS 12:11 (NIV)

A friend of mine told me about an exercise she learned in an improvisation class. It's called "Yes . . . and," and it works something like this: A student calls out an idea for an improv, such as "We're kittens." Instead of dismissing the idea as dumb, another student must respond with an additional idea, saying, "Yes . . . and we're prehistoric!" Each student adds an idea to expand the skit and nobody knows where the whole thing is going.

I wondered if the same idea might work for me when facing God's challenges, especially the ones that I might be more inclined to avoid than enthusiastically embrace. So when our pastor announced that our church was planning a health fair for a low-income, inner-city neighborhood, my immediate reaction was *I'm not a doctor or nurse. What can I do?* But instead I said, "Yes . . . and I'll work wherever you need help." I was assigned to the registration table, and not only did I put my organizational skills to good use, I even used a little of my high school Spanish. I also had fun and finished the day knowing that I'd helped people get information and services that they really needed.

Now when God sends a challenge my way, I fight the urge to say "No" and instead say "Yes . . . and." I think of it as God's improvisation. His ideas may surprise me, but I can relax and follow His lead because He always knows where things are going.

> *Lord, open my mind to the many ways*
> *that You think I can serve You.*
> —GINA BRIDGEMAN

Sun 17

Bread gained by deceit is sweet to a man, But afterward his mouth will be filled with gravel.
—PROVERBS 20:17 (NKJV)

My minister-father was a storyteller, and the best part of Sunday was listening to his stories from the pulpit. One of my favorites was about an exceptional contractor who built beautiful homes. There was always a long waiting list of customers.

One day the contractor told his foreman, "I need to go East for a few months, and while I'm gone I want you to build this house for me." He showed the foreman the plans. "I want this to be the best house you've ever built for me. Spare no expense. I want it done right."

When his boss left, the foreman got to thinking, *This is a big project. I could make some extra money on it by substituting grade-B materials where they won't show. I could pocket the difference.*

When the boss returned, he was impressed. "The house is beautiful!" He put his arm around the foreman's shoulders. "The reason I wanted you to make this house special is that I want you to have it as an expression of my gratitude for your years of service to me."

The foreman's face fell, knowing that he had cheated only himself.

I cringed every time I heard that story. It made me determined to do good work when I grew up, knowing that I am the one who has to live in the house I build.

Lord, help me to do my best work so that I have no regrets.
—DANIEL SCHANTZ

Mon 18   *Give good gifts unto your children. . . .* —MATTHEW 7:11

"If only we had a car, we could go see Jimmie and her new baby," I complained to my mother when I was about six. After my father died, Jimmie came to our house and cared for me while my mother worked.

Mother beamed. "We *can* go, Mannie!" She polished my white sandals, dressed me in a pink sunsuit and sat me on the back of my new (secondhand) yellow bicycle. As Mother peddled, we bumped over the railroad tracks. I peeked around her to be sure our baby gift stayed in the basket. Suddenly we seemed to enter a brown world. Brown close-together houses, which needed painting. Brown dirt yards swept smooth. Brown children laughing. The brown mailman waved to us, as did the women hanging out sheets. We saw Jimmie's mother; she came running to meet us and hugged us.

Finally we saw Jimmie, lying in bed, holding her baby. Mother and Jimmie spoke in hushed tones while I marveled over the newborn. Jimmie opened the gift we'd brought, and I got to put the blue kimono on the baby.

Jimmie came back to care for me, bringing her sweet little son, and I pretended he was the little brother I longed for. When I got out my crayons, I reminded him to make the people in the coloring book brown and pink.

It was decades before I realized that my mother had also given me a remarkable gift that hot Southern summer day in 1942.

> *Father, help parents remember how simply*
> *children are taught life's lessons.*
> —MARION BOND WEST

Tue 19

*Jesus said to her, "Did I not tell you that if you believed, you would see the glory of God?" —*JOHN 11:40 (NRSV)

An old friend called the other day to ask how I was doing. We had been classmates in junior high more than thirty years before, and she had heard I was having a rough time.

"I know how tough this is, Jon," she said. "I went through the same thing a few years ago."

She asked if I was still praying, reading the Bible and going to church, despite my troubles. I was, I said, but I had to admit that it was only sometimes, that at other times my pain and the doubts it produced had gotten in the way.

"Stick with it, Jon," she said. "By doing just those little things, you show God that you're faithful even when you don't fully understand."

Some of God's truths are so simple that they escape my attention most of the time. The Swiss theologian Karl Barth once said that his decades of writing massive volumes of theology could be summed up in the words of a song: "Jesus loves me, this I know, for the Bible tells me so."

The Letter to the Hebrews (10:35, NRSV) says, "Do not, therefore, abandon that confidence of yours; it brings a great reward." By following my friend's advice, I've found that my confidence in God and God's promises need not ebb and flow with every question or doubt that enters my mind. I have plenty of questions these days; they come and they go. But I remain confident and full of hope that someday they will all be answered.

Dear Jesus, give me the faith of a child and the wisdom of an adult.
—JON SWEENEY

Wed 20   *"Oh that my words were written! Oh that they were inscribed in a book!"* —JOB 19:23 (RSV)

Early in the morning, making coffee for my lovely and mysterious bride, mixing the dough for what will be tonight's pizza, murmuring amiably to the sleepy parakeet, I get distracted by the incredible wealth of faces and voices on the refrigerator, and spend a few moments doing what we all do more than we think we do: reading the refrigerator.

Such subtle literature, aren't they, these enormous vertical pages in our kitchens? Festooned with cartoons and witticisms and comic strips and photos and essays and articles and letters and early homework misadventures of young residents of the home in which the refrigerator hums, the refrigerator is the fireplace of the twenty-first century, the warm glow around which everyone gathers until someone barks, "Close that door!"

We pin and post messages on them, and the lesser stories fall off or are removed by mortified children and hungry dogs, but the better ones stick—the nephew's wedding day, the first school photograph in which the child stuck his tongue in his nose, the shivering poems, the berry-pie recipe from Gramma, prayer cards and game tickets, school schedules and rules of the house.

If there's a place in every house that's devoted to stories of every shape and sort and size, that has oceans of prose and photographs, gobs of poetry and paintings, posters and prints, essays and articles, quotes and notes, yards of cards, and those stories are read and pondered by all ages and stages of readers every day, well, isn't a refrigerator a kind of large humming book? And if everyone stops there every day for a moment and contemplates the faces and voices he or she loves, isn't a refrigerator sort of a sweet, nutty chapel?

> *Dear Lord, so very many things are sacred spaces.*
> *Isn't that so? More than we ever see.*
> —BRIAN DOYLE

Thu 21

*Having gifts that differ according to the grace given
to us, let us use them. . . .* —ROMANS 12:6 (RSV)

Our friend Casey is the strongest person I know. Recently he carried our huge air conditioners to the attic, like sleeping babies in his arms. Casey has epilepsy, but surgery and medications have reduced his seizures. He is forty-two and self-employed; his business card reads: "I will do any work you need done. No job too big or too small, indoors or outside!"

Our Medford, Massachusetts, city ordinance requires homeowners to remove snow from sidewalks and driveways, and that can be difficult for senior citizens. So in the winter, a good part of Casey's business is snow removal. One February day a snowstorm roared into Medford. At noon Casey called to say his aunt had died and that her funeral was the next morning. When the storm finally ended at eleven o'clock that night, I wondered what I'd do about clearing the snow.

I was in the middle of a sound sleep when I was awakened by a scraping noise outside. I got up and peeked through the window, and there was Casey shoveling our snow at three o'clock in the morning. Casey took care of all his customers before dawn; then he hurried home, took a shower and went to his aunt's funeral where he sang her favorite hymn.

Yes, Casey is the strongest person I know—on the outside and within. We're blessed to have him in our community.

*Gracious Lord, may Casey's example teach me
still another way of serving You.*
—OSCAR GREENE

✿ TWELVE KEYS TO THE GIVING LIFE

Fri 22   *Give, and it shall be given unto you. . . .* —LUKE 6:38

GIVE FAITHFULLY

For forty years I suffered with head and mouth pain from tumors caused by an incurable disorder. I lived from moment to moment and went to great lengths to get my mind off the relentless pain. Then a curious thing happened: I began to notice that whenever I turned my thoughts to others instead of dwelling on myself, I experienced an incredible sense of well-being. Whether I was planning to give, anticipating the act of giving or doing the giving itself, I could feel my entire body change.

One of the most difficult aspects of living with intractable pain is getting started in the morning. So before turning in each night, I placed a gift for someone at work alongside my car keys. It might be as simple as an article clipped from a magazine or coupons for laundry detergent or a tea bag in a new herbal flavor. Or it might be a pair of earrings I really wanted for myself that God nudged me to give away.

I mentioned my newfound approach to my physician Dr. Brownfield. He told me that my discovery was supported by both the Bible and medical science. "Giving releases endorphins, the body's natural painkillers, Roberta. Studies have actually shown that volunteers, some of the most devoted givers of all, lead happier, healthier and longer lives." He closed our time together that day with a prayer that God would continue to bless me with the abundant life He promises in His Word, the giving life.

Since that day I've continued to give in the ways God directs. And I haven't needed a single dose of breakthrough pain medicine. I've come to understand that giving is a God-given tool—like exercise and a balanced diet—that helps us to live the full life He has in mind for us.

Thank You, Great Physician, for the healing power of giving that makes my burdens light and my joy unspeakable. —ROBERTA MESSNER

Sat 23

A man of understanding holds his tongue.
—PROVERBS 11:12 (NIV)

Mission Mississippi, our ministry, sponsored days of dialogue to encourage people to learn how to talk about major issues across racial lines. We held these events in ten different cities in the state.

In one of our sessions, a gentleman said, "From where I sit and from what I know about how the people around me feel, there are no racial problems."

The natural response from other people in the room would have been something like, "Where have you been all your life?" But the purpose of our dialogue was not to attack anyone or their views, but rather to listen and respond in a nonthreatening way. So the question we asked was, "Would you help us understand why you're saying that?"

We quickly learned that he had come to us because he wasn't used to talking in a racially diverse group; he was struggling to have an honest conversation about his own experience. When he discovered that he was in a safe environment, where no one was judging or criticizing him, he began to open up and talk more freely.

The hardest thing for most of us to do is to put aside our automatic reactions, to listen carefully and to hear the heart of the other person. If we can, not only will we build bridges across racial lines, but we'll strengthen all of our relationships.

Lord, may I learn to listen more and speak less.
—DOLPHUS WEARY

Sun 24   *"He was lost and is found."* —LUKE 15:32 (NIV)

My youngest son Kevin had moved into his own apartment. Although he lived just across town, I'd not seen him much.

Maybe I'm having empty-nest syndrome, I reasoned. After all, he was the last of my four children to leave home. I tried calling. I tried leaving messages. "Kev," I'd say, "how come you don't return my calls?" or "How come you don't stop by?" or "Don't you know we miss you?"

Finally I tried what I should have tried first: I sat down at my desk in the study, bowed my head and prayed. *I need Your words, Lord, because mine aren't working. Help me to say the right thing to my son. Amen.*

I looked up and noticed the church bulletin on my desk. I'd scrawled a few thoughts on it while listening to the sermon that morning. It was based on one of my favorite Bible stories, the prodigal son, who is welcomed back into the family fold after going off on his own. I read my notes: "No stern sermons, no lectures, no guilt trips. His father, instead, had thrown him a party."

"Of course, Lord!" I said out loud.

I called Kevin and left a simple message: "Hi, Kev. It's Mom. I'm cooking your favorites tonight: shrimp and sausage jambalaya, crawfish cornbread, and bread pudding. Come on by!"

That evening after dinner was over and the dishes were done and Kevin had gone back to his apartment, laden with leftovers, I prayed:

Father, thank You for the opportunity not just
to listen to my favorite story, but to live it.
—MELODY BONNETTE

Mon 25

"If you are willing and obedient, you will eat the best from the land." —ISAIAH 1:19 (NIV)

In *Daily Guideposts 2008*, Debbie Macomber wrote a devotional in which a friend decided to change her name in order to change her attitude. To overcome discouragement, she became "Sheila the Faithful." Debbie liked the idea so much that she decided to be "Debbie the Trusting."

That struck a chord with me and reminded me of something that happened when I was serving on the board of our church in California. To get an idea of how we elders saw our role in serving the congregation, our pastor asked each of us, "What is your passion?" I heard answers such as "Christian education" and "stewardship." When it came my turn to respond, all I could think of was simply "obedience."

How did that come to mind so quickly? I thought back over the years and remembered how well things had gone for my family and me when I simply did what God called me to do—and how I struggled when I failed to heed the call. Would I quit my job and move thousands of miles away to do whatever God showed me? I resisted that prompting for a year while my job became an albatross and our fellowship group slowly disintegrated. But when I finally obeyed, I found myself smuggling Bibles for Brother Andrew to persecuted Christians in Eastern Europe.

The lesson is clear: When I obey God's call, something wonderful happens.

Which leads me to think I'll change my name to "Harold the Obedient." It's a name I'd like to grow into.

> *Father, I desire to do Your will. It's my pleasure*
> *to obey when You call.*
> —HAROLD HOSTETLER

Tue 26 *Now some of the scribes were sitting there, questioning in their hearts, "Why does this man speak thus? It is blasphemy! Who can forgive sins, but God alone?"*
—MARK 2:6–7 (RSV)

When I was divorced some years ago, I needed the love and support of my old high school youth-group leaders. I hadn't seen them in years and was living in another state, but when I contacted them I was in for a rude awakening. Their harsh condemnation was crushing, and ever after I carried a deep sense of grief and loss.

Last year I returned to Arizona, where I went to high school, for the first time in thirty-eight years. When Gwen, one of the youth-group leaders, heard I was coming, she said that she wanted to see me. I was surprised—and I wasn't all that sure I wanted to see her.

Waiting for her at my friend Carol's house, I paced the floor. I'd determined I wasn't going to let the occasion pass without telling her about my feelings, but I wasn't sure how to handle it. I'd never stopped loving Gwen, and her condemnation was a badly healed scar.

To my surprise, when Gwen came up the walk, I saw her beautiful smile, a smile I've never forgotten and which has come back to me over the years in the most unexpected moments. She gave me a well-remembered hug, and before I could catch my breath, she gave me a warm and weepy apology. Her words to me had been bothering her for years, she said, and she was so grateful to God for giving her the opportunity to tell me how sorry she was. "I was young, I was brainless, I followed the script. Will you forgive me?" she asked.

Forgive Gwen? Refuse a gift I never expected? Sometimes forgiveness is so easy.

Thank You, God, for never forgetting our grief and loss, and for the healing power of forgiveness born of You.
—BRENDA WILBEE

Wed 27   *All . . . fall short of the glory of God.*
—Romans 3:23 (RSV)

When composing, Wolfgang Amadeus Mozart would sometimes whistle random phrases from the music he was working on.

One day in the spring of 1784, he visited his favorite Viennese pet shop to discover that the store owner had taught a young bird, a Vienna starling, to mimic snatches of a song popular at the time. Mozart tried whistling a phrase from his current work-in-progress. To the composer's delight the bird repeated the melody. Mozart immediately bought the young starling, recording the purchase in his Notebook of Expenses.

In time Mozart and the bird became fast friends, his pet often sitting on his shoulder while he worked and whistling along with him. There was one disappointment though: No matter how hard he tried, Mozart was never able to train the bird to get intervals exactly right. Always one or more of the notes was off pitch.

One day his pet flitted over and began to sing a phrase of a new concerto, singing a G-sharp instead of the G-natural Mozart had written and also missing other notes. I like to imagine that Mozart smiled. What we do know is that he took out new manuscript paper and simply rewrote the music, building the bird's imperfections into the Piano Concerto in G Major we've enjoyed ever since.

These days, when once again I fall short of an ideal I've aimed for, I remember Mozart's starling. Doesn't God do exactly what Mozart did? Rewrite our "music" so that in His hands even our shortcomings become part of His harmony?

> *Father, help me to appreciate more and more every day*
> *what a privilege it is to sing with You.*
> —John Sherrill

Thu 28

"As a mother comforts her child, so will I comfort you...." —ISAIAH 66:13 (NIV)

When I pressed the button on my answering machine, Angela's voice came on with a youthful "I'm trying to be casual, but I'm really in a panic" urgency. "Hi, Mary Ann. It's Angela. I don't want to bother you but ..."

Angela is the niece of a close friend. She's in her junior year at college. Now she was calling from her home in Massachusetts, and the gist of her message was this: She was scheduled to leave in two days for a semester abroad in Prague, and her visa hadn't arrived yet. Turned out it was still at the Czech Republic consulate in Manhattan; was there any way I could get it and express mail it to her so she could board the plane in forty-eight hours? She didn't want to put me out but ...

It took some maneuvering and feverish phone calls, including a fax from Angela authorizing me to do the pickup, but finally we figured it out. I arrived at the Czech consulate minutes before closing and announced my mission at the front desk. A woman in a business suit strode out with a packet. "You are her mother?" she asked. For a second I was startled, because there it was again, that unexpected lurch of my heart. I'd never had children, and although the deepest disappointment had passed years ago, there were still moments when I felt a stab of regret.

"You're her mother?" the woman repeated.

"I wish I was," I said. "I'm just a close friend." And then in an instant another thought surfaced. *For right here, right now, I am her mother.* In situations where a helping hand or a loving gesture is needed, I am someone's mother. The thought had a good feel to it—and the regret was gone.

Holy Spirit, please keep my mind open to being a mother to others.
—MARY ANN O'ROARK

Fri 29

For the eyes of the Lord run to and fro throughout the whole earth. . . . —II Chronicles 16:9

Okay, I know that it's a real pain to be able to be reached anywhere by cell phone or computer, but you know, it can also be a real blessing.

The other night I was at the office, working a little too late on a Friday and feeling a little too sorry for myself but determined to get a job done. I was filling out an online form. Flummoxed by the technology, I couldn't figure out how to put an X in a box without the box disappearing. *This is what I get for not doing this when someone was around to help me.*

In a fury I sent an e-mail off to my colleague Nancy, attaching the form and asking her how I was supposed to do it. Nancy, of course—exquisitely organized Nancy—had left the office at a reasonable hour. I wouldn't hear from her until Monday morning.

If I said a prayer, it was one of exasperation. *God, why can't I figure this out?* All at once my computer made that friendly *brrrring* sound that it does when I have a message, and expecting another irritating piece of spam, I was delighted to see that it was Nancy—devoted, hardworking Nancy—responding from home. "Double-click on the box," she wrote, adding the crucial details.

It worked, of course. I had to be grateful for an office with people who check on their colleagues long after they should.

Thank You, Lord, for the technology that links us
almost as fast as a prayer.
—Rick Hamlin

Sat 30   *"Do not be grieved, for the joy of the Lord is your strength."* —NEHEMIAH 8:10 (RSV)

Saturday morning services had become kind of routine: We sang the same songs; we said the same prayers. Some of the joy and mindfulness had gone out of the worship, and most of us hadn't actually noticed that we were only going through the motions.

Then one Saturday a woman we had never seen before came to a service with our social action chairwoman Clara. The new woman seemed nervous, despite the welcome we gave her. Clara explained that she had recently come over from the former Soviet Union, where she had not been allowed to attend a synagogue or even to admit openly that she had a religion.

Instead of having the Torah carried through the congregation before it was read, our rabbi had created a ritual of passing it from person to person. Each of us took the velvet-covered scroll from the person on one side of us and passed it to the person on the other. It all went as usual until Clara held out the Torah to the Russian woman.

For a moment she was just frozen, staring at it. Then she reached out, hands shaking, and let Clara put the scroll into them. She slowly lowered her head over the Torah, cradling it, and silently she began to cry. Several minutes went by before she could turn and let the person on her other side take the Torah from her.

We were stunned, and as the Torah made its way through the rest of us and up to the platform for reading, our surprise became excitement. The Russian woman had reminded us of how precious the freedom to worship together was and that we must never let it become routine.

Help us never to take the privilege of honoring You for granted,
our God, and God of our ancestors.
—RHODA BLECKER

Sun 31

May he give you the desire of your heart and make all your plans succeed. —PSALM 20:4 (NIV)

Several years ago I compiled a list of thirty people I wanted to meet. Since then I've met nineteen of them, including writers, musicians and actors. Inspired by my success, my son Dale decided to make a list of his own. Unfortunately, the person he most wanted to meet was Steve Prefontaine, the legendary runner who was killed in a car accident twenty-three days before Dale was born. Because Dale is a runner himself, he has read Steve's life story many times. Every term paper or school project he was assigned, from the time he was in grade school all the way through college, revolved around some aspect of Steve's life.

Because he knew it would be impossible to meet his hero, Dale and his best friend Andy, both runners themselves, decided to celebrate Steve's birthday in a unique way: They would visit all the key locations of his life on Steve's birthday, January 31. They started off by visiting Marshfield High in Coos Bay, Oregon, where Steve went to school, and ran around the track that's named after him. They toured the museum with Steve's memorabilia and then went to visit his gravesite. On the way out of town, they decided to take pictures of the house where Steve's parents lived. While they were there, a man came out and asked them what they were doing.

"Did you know this is the house where Steve Prefontaine's parents lived when he was born?" Dale asked enthusiastically.

"As a matter of fact, I do," the older man told them. "I'm Steve's father."

Mr. Prefontaine took Dale and Andy inside and showed them their hero's bedroom. They tried on Steve's letterman jacket and had their pictures taken in it. This proud father gave my son and his friend the thrill of their lives.

Dale and Andy came as close as it is possible on this side of heaven to meeting their hero.

Oh, we serve a mighty God, Who delights in giving us the desires of our hearts. —DEBBIE MACOMBER

THE GIFTS I'VE BEEN GIVEN

1 _____

2 _____

3 _____

4 _____

5 _____

6 _____

7 _____

8 _____

9 _____

10 _____

11 _____

12 _____

13 _____

14 _____

15 _____

January

16 _____

17 _____

18 _____

19 _____

20 _____

21 _____

22 _____

23 _____

24 _____

25 _____

26 _____

27 _____

28 _____

29 _____

30 _____

31 _____

February

By the breath of God frost is given. . . .

—JOB 37:10

🥁 GIFTS FROM ABOVE

Mon 1 *We glory in tribulations . . . knowing that tribulation worketh patience.* —ROMANS 5:3

A GIFT OF ADAPTABILITY

"To be effective, you have to be able to listen to a variety of points of view, to sy . . . syn . . . synnnnth . . ." I turned my eyes away from the article I'd been reading to my husband David as we drove home. "Synthesize viewpoints," I pronounced perfectly, once my eyes had left the paper.

I have a theory that might explain my tendency to stall on familiar words when I read out loud: According to my mother's count, I'm a veteran of twenty-eight schools. While our home remained in Chattanooga, Tennessee, throughout my school years, we often closed our house and went to live wherever my father's work took him. I suppose my reading-out-loud difficulty is one of the costs of having lived a few months here, a few months there. But I'm not complaining. My gains far outweigh my losses.

Imagine the pluck of a little girl with pigtails, the perennial "new kid," forced to find a place at the lunch table and to conform to yet one more educator's style of teaching—perfect training for my years as a minister's wife. I can walk into a room of strangers and not miss a beat; I'm comfortable in almost any setting. Not a bad trade-off, I think.

So although Dee Dee in Columbus, Ohio, probably doesn't remember how happy she made me when she invited me to ride her pony, and the fourth-grader in Port St. Joe, Florida, probably can't recall the day I gave her my alligator shoes, I carry the lessons I learned from them forward. Twenty-eight schools and memories of kindness, giving and getting along—even though I'm unable to pronounce a word every now and then, I wouldn't change a thing.

Father, thank You for unexpected gifts wrapped in challenges and bestowed in love. —PAM KIDD

Tue 2 As the deer pants for the water brooks, So pants my
soul for You, O God. —PSALM 42:1 (NKJV)

My favorite flowering plant is the hibiscus. Last summer I bought
a large potted red one and put it on our patio. Nurtured by rain
and our sprinkler system, the plant grew rapidly, and I enjoyed immensely
its rich green leaves and bright trumpet blossoms.

This winter, as the temperature dipped near freezing, I brought the
hibiscus into our sunny breakfast room to protect it from the cold. There
was one problem, however: I wasn't accustomed to watering the plant
and I soon forgot to. Last week I discovered the hibiscus wilted, its green
leaves now yellow, frail and falling to the floor.

I was disgusted with myself. I picked up the pot and slowly walked
toward the garbage can. But as I passed the kitchen sink, I decided to try
watering the hibiscus to give it one last chance. Today it's standing taller,
its stalk is greener and new growth is sprouting. The water has brought
the beautiful plant back to life.

This morning, as I sat at the breakfast table and looked at the hibiscus, it occurred to me that when I haven't attended to my spiritual life, it
begins to wilt and wither, and only prayer can bring back its vitality and
rekindle its hope. If, in the midst of winter, I've allowed the frost to touch
my soul, I cannot wait one more day to water it with prayer.

Father, in a dry and thirsty season, bend my knees,
bow my head and cause my lips to speak to You.
—SCOTT WALKER

Wed 3

"Surely God is my salvation; I will trust and not be afraid. . . ." —ISAIAH 12:2 (NIV)

I sat nervously in the waiting room of the hospital lab, reading a book to six-year-old Solomon and two-year-old Henry. When Henry's name was called for his blood test, my husband Tony picked him up and disappeared behind the door. In moments Henry's cries filled the room.

Solomon and I tried to read the next page of our book. From behind the door, Henry's screams escalated to panicked shrieks.

I reached for Solomon's hand. "It's okay," I said.

"I know," Solomon said. "Henry just doesn't understand."

I nodded. "You're right," I said. "He needs to have this done."

"Dad is with him, right?" Solomon asked.

"Yes."

Henry's cries went on for what seemed like hours. Finally my husband came out with a tear-streaked Henry, who looked down at the small trinket he held in his hands.

Tony nodded that all was fine and said, "He even got to pick a toy from the treasure chest."

In the car Solomon reached his hand over to Henry's and held it. "It's okay, Henry," he said. "We love you. We were right there, Dad with you and Mom with me right outside the door."

Henry smiled.

As I was going to bed, I thought about the day and my own struggles. So often I find myself crying over a situation that I just don't understand, an experience that will ultimately make me better, wiser, more understanding. Just like Henry, I'm not alone; I'm always embraced with love and, yes, I'm all right.

Father, thank You for always being there.
—SABRA CIANCANELLI

Thu 4 In the month of Ziv, the second month, he began to build
the temple of the Lord. —I Kings 6:1 (NIV)

The word *Ziv* in the Scripture above means "light." The month of Ziv (Iyar in modern Hebrew usage) was a time for healing. Even though the second months of the Jewish and Gregorian calendars don't correspond, the second month of the year has always been a time of light and healing for me. December and January are the cause of my seasonal affective disorder (SAD), the winter blues. February is the cure.

I once thought that the days (and my mood) would brighten after December 21, but because of the elliptical rotation of our planet, there is no significant change in day length or in the sun's angle from late November to late January. In the month following the winter solstice, the sun rises in the southeast, hangs low in the southern sky for nine hours and sets in the southwest. The days lengthen at an agonizingly slow rate.

By February the earth slips away from the end of its ellipse, and the resulting changes are dramatic. The shadows shorten on the north sides of our home and trees. The amount of daylight increases by more than fifteen minutes each week. At our latitude in Colorado, the sun climbs more than ten degrees above the south horizon by the end of the month. It rises just south of due east and sets just south of due west. The time of darkness is over, replaced by healing and light.

Thank You, God, for longer days and shorter shadows.
Thank You for February!
—Tim Williams

Fri 5   *Love . . . always perseveres.* —I Corinthians 13:6–7 (NIV)

Everything I'd read about labor and delivery promised ninety seconds of contractions maximum, with three to four minutes of relief in between. *I can handle that*, I thought. But the books lied, or else I missed the chapter about the labor-inducing drug that sent an army of torturers into my body every other minute for twenty hours! I was in shock from the intensity of the pain, and by the time I gave birth I was completely exhausted.

Perhaps I was still in a delivery-room fog, but the tiny baby now wrapped like a burrito and surrounded by family didn't quite feel like mine. "Do you feel like a parent yet," I asked my husband, hoping I wasn't the only one. Apparently I was.

Hours later, alone with the sleeping infant parked near my bed, everything still felt surreal. The baby was quiet and still like a doll, and had been asleep for hours. I needed sleep, too, but my body still hurt. I couldn't get comfortable, and every movement—no matter how small—was torture.

Finally I drifted off, but just as my dream began, the little burrito woke me up. His loud, urgent cry penetrated deep inside me to a place I'd never known. It made me sit up, gritting through the pain as I inched toward my son. I picked him up and cradled him close to my body, and to our mutual relief the crying stopped. And during that peaceful moment, as I fed my little boy, I finally felt like a mother.

Thank You, Lord, for the love that even in pain can find a gift of joy.
—Karen Valentin

Sat 6 *"The Lord gave and the Lord has taken away; may the name of the Lord be praised."* —JOB 1:21 (NIV)

I was skiing too fast. But I was only sixteen and I was a bit, well, reckless. As I came over a crest onto the steep section of the trail, I could see that my momentum was carrying me straight toward an unsuspecting skier about twenty feet below. I threw my foot sideways, sharply turning my ski—as an amputee, I use only one—so I skidded around him.

On my next turn, though, something felt wrong. I stopped by the side of the trail and looked down. My ski was cracked, on the verge of breaking in two. *What a disaster!* I thought. I didn't have the money for a new ski, so that crack spelled the end of my first season of ski racing. *How could You let this happen, God?*

But it wasn't more than a week later that my friend Justin showed up on my doorstep, holding a single orange ski. "I was skiing in some deep powder," he said. "One of my skis popped off and I couldn't find it in the snow. I remembered what happened to you and I wanted to give you the other one."

"Wow!" I said. "Thanks!"

As I inspected my new ski, I thought about how grateful I was that Justin hadn't just stuck it in the closet, feeling bitter about his loss. Instead, he'd allowed his mishap to be the solution to mine.

> *Lord, don't let bitterness about the past keep me from bringing*
> *a brighter future to someone else.*
> —JOSHUA SUNDQUIST

February

Sun 7

And he said unto me, My grace is sufficient for thee. . . .
—II CORINTHIANS 12:9

In Florida my wife Shirley and I attend a Sunday school class made up of mostly senior citizens—some *very* senior. There's Art from Pennsylvania, Paul from Michigan, Ralph from Iowa and Bill from New York, to name a few. All are about ninety, give or take a few months.

Each one has spent a lifetime in the church, and each brings a wealth of secular and spiritual experience to the class. Sometimes we stay on the Bible lesson for the day, but no one objects to a few detours. Their stories are full of faith principles that add to our discussions.

Bill, who taught the class for many years, said something one Sunday that I haven't forgotten. Someone brought up a particular horrendous deed and wondered if the sin could be forgiven. "Of course it can," Bill replied. "We serve a God of second chances. And remember, with Him, sin knows no size."

Sin knows no size. That's a tremendous truth. Whatever our offense, none exceeds God's grace.

> *As amazing and unlikely as it sounds,*
> *Our Father's grace knows no bounds.*
> —FRED BAUER

Mon 8

Wherefore comfort yourselves together. . . .
—I THESSALONIANS 5:11

During my first month working at the bookstore, a skinny man pushed his way through the line at the information desk and barked, "I need a book called *When God Wings!*"

The tiny woman at the front of the line kindly told him, "You may go ahead of me, sir." He looked at her blankly.

I smiled at the woman and told the man, "Oh, I know exactly where that book is." The author had been on a morning talk show, so we'd already received a few requests for it. "It's called *When God Winks.*" I began walking around the counter to lead him to the shelf.

He stopped in his tracks. "No, young lady, the book I want is called *When God Wings.* It's by . . . let's see . . ." He wrinkled his brow in thought. "Salmon Rushdell."

"You're close, sir," I said. "It's by Squire Rushnell."

"No, I know I'm right."

He seemed so sure of himself that I mumbled, "I'll check on the computer," while thinking, *Maybe there is something called* When God Wings *by Salmon Rushdell.*

Nothing came up. "Could you have heard the title wrong?" I asked.

"I'll buy it online!" he said and stormed off.

I was near tears as I turned to the tiny woman, who was still waiting patiently. "You were so nice," I told her, blinking hard to keep from crying. "You let him go ahead of you."

"And you were so nice to him too, dear." She laughed and patted my hand. "There are probably a hundred thousand stories in this bookstore," she said, gesturing toward the stacks around us. "And that sure was a funny one. 'Mr. Pompous at the Bookstore,' I'd call it if I were writing it."

Suddenly I was laughing too.

God, when times are tough, help me not to take them—or myself— too seriously. —LINDA NEUKRUG

TWELVE KEYS TO THE GIVING LIFE

Tue 9 *Neglect not the gift that is in thee. . . .* —I TIMOTHY 4:14

GIVE UNIQUELY

It was the worst snowstorm of the winter. All day long while I was at work, the white stuff poured from the sky. When it was time to head home, my car wouldn't budge from its parking spot. A team of strong men gave my vehicle a victorious push, but then my windshield wipers failed. Icy rain pelted the glass, obstructing my vision.

I pulled into a little grocery store, hoping to purchase some paper towels or a washcloth to wipe my windshield. Then, as if I needed anything else to go wrong, my direction light refused to work. Inside the store I heard myself wail, "Is anyone here good with windshield wipers? Make that direction lights too."

Enter an angel I later learned was named Rob. "That sounds like a bad fuse, ma'am," he said. "Let me check it out. I might have just the one you need in my minivan. I carry a little of everything around with me." Rob insisted I stay safe and warm inside my car while he investigated. As it turned out, a little green fuse was indeed the culprit. Rob not only replaced the faulty one, he also gave me a spare that fit inside the cutest clear plastic holder.

I tried to pay Rob, but he would have none of it. "I've worked on cars my whole life," he explained. "And I'm a truck driver. This is just what I do."

This is just what I do. The Bible says much the same thing about giving. "Neglect not the gift that is in thee," we read in I Timothy 4:14. Fixing a car doesn't come naturally to me. But Rob? It's his gift.

What is God asking you to give today? It may be large or small, but one thing is certain: It's something only *you* can give.

> *Show me, Lord Jesus, what You have created me alone to give.*
> —ROBERTA MESSNER

Wed 10 *"Which of you by being anxious can add one cubit to his span of life?"* —MATTHEW 6:27 (RSV)

My friend received bad news. Bad, bad, bad news; maybe the worst news she could have received.

Although I've been in this play before, there is no script. Someone says something awful, and we try to find words that will . . . what? They haven't discovered those words yet, and I'll bet they've called off the search.

I walked through the rest of the day sounding normal. I wasn't. People would say something, but I'd have to ask them to repeat it, sometimes twice. Parts of my brain were otherwise occupied, wondering about my friend's husband and their two small children, wondering about the future, wondering if *future* starts with *f* or *if*.

I realize I've lived my life in clichéd adjectives: *reliable, prepared, reasonable.* It's especially troubling to confront that last one; reason has left town without notice, and I've called off the search.

Now that the shock has worn off—okay, it hasn't worn off, but I've regained some footing—there's a certain newness to everything I do. Sometimes preparing for the future is a real luxury. What do I do with this day, this minute, this moment? What if I worshipped like Jesus did— in service, in kindness, in love? What if I eat the loaves and fishes, instead of focusing on the sponge filled with gall?

Lord, suffering came to my friend uninvited; why do I go looking for it?
Why not live this life the way You made it?
New, fluid, unreasonable, amazing, here, now.
—MARK COLLINS

Thu 11

Be devoted to one another in brotherly love. Honor one another above yourselves. —ROMANS 12:10 (NIV)

My sister Sally was calling me in Nashville, Tennessee, from Pittsburgh, upset at one of our relatives. "She hasn't returned my phone calls again," Sally said. "I don't know why she does that."

"You know she doesn't like talking on the phone," I said in my big-sister voice. "Don't take it personally. She'll call you in time."

Actually, her complaint took me by surprise because Sally is one of the most generous, forgiving people I know. She's always been able to let even the most irritating foibles of family and friends roll off her back, mine included.

There was silence on the other end. Then, in a small voice I had to strain to hear, she said, "But it makes me feel as if I don't matter."

Her words went 'round and 'round in my head. *How easy it is to take advantage of the Sallys of this world,* I thought. *How easy to let things slide because it won't bother them.*

The truth is, none of us is immune to the response of others. Deep down we all need to know we matter. And something as simple as a prompt phone call can make the difference.

> *Lord, help me never to take anyone for granted,*
> *no matter how generous they are.*
> —SHARI SMYTH

READER'S ROOM

My Bible study group decided to do a workbook on prayer. One week we studied "Being quiet before the Word." Driving home that day, I saw a car in front of me with the license plate B-STILL. Later that day I was looking through a catalog and came across a wooden sign that said, "Let us be silent that we may hear the whisper of God." God was telling me that day to be quiet and listen for His surprises.

—*Monna Perrenoud, Canton, Ohio*

Fri 12   *Therefore, if anyone is in Christ, he is a new creation;*
the old has gone, the new has come!
—II CORINTHIANS 5:17 (NIV)

R wanda is one of the jewels of Africa, a Maryland-sized place with
verdant peaks, crystalline lakes and one of the world's last popula-
tions of rare mountain gorillas. It's also desperately poor; most of
Rwanda's people survive on incomes of less than a dollar a day.

Recently I traveled to Rwanda for my job with a business magazine.
One afternoon I went out to the countryside, to a small town where
seventy-six women, all survivors of the nation's 1994 genocide, have
formed a cooperative to knit scarves. For some of these women, their
handiwork—which, by the time it reaches markets in the United States,
can go for eighty dollars apiece—is producing the first earned income
they've ever had.

They told me that their business opportunity had given them a new
sense of empowerment and hope for the future. They could pay their
children's school fees. They could buy extra food. One woman proudly
showed off the outfit she had bought—her first new skirt and top in ages.

Then the president of the cooperative shared a Rwandan proverb: "If
you don't know where you've come from, you won't know where to go."
They doubly appreciated what they had because they had not only been
through extreme poverty but also faced the prospect of imminent death.

As I listened, it struck me that it wouldn't be a bad idea if I looked at
my life with that proverb in mind. After all, Jesus has saved me from certain death. How can I forget where I've come from?

Lord, help me to remember where I've been, so I can better understand
how blessed is the path You've paved for me.
—JEFF CHU

Sat 13

Lo, the winter is past, the rain is over and gone.
—SONG OF SOLOMON 2:11

I spent most of this wintry day shivering in discontent. The mailman delivered nothing more personal than advertisements. My neighbor never knocked on the door. Under my breath I repeated a complaint I used to hear from my mother: "The phone hasn't rung all day." Her grievance referred to something bigger than the black box wired to the wall. She felt forgotten.

This evening, however, I discovered a long letter I'd tucked away in my journal. It was from Lois, a friend who had left town fifteen years ago. She'd come back to visit once or twice and sent me smiley wedding pictures, but then we'd lost touch. After several years of silence—on her end and mine—this past Christmas I'd sent her a card and letter. Tonight I reread her newsy January response to my holiday greeting, all the way to her closing: "Thanks for not forgetting me."

As I focused on that line, her warm gratitude melted my discontent. Energized, I made plans to connect with people who might have reason to feel they've been forgotten. Tomorrow morning I'll mail a note to the unacclaimed author of a book I'm enjoying, I'll e-mail a missionary friend in Europe, I'll call a local widow just to say hello.

> *Lord, when I start feeling sorry for myself,*
> *turn my attention outward, to others.*
> —EVELYN BENCE

Sun 14   *For this cause we also . . . do not cease to pray for you. . . .* —COLOSSIANS 1:9

W ill you marry me?"

After all that I'd been through (divorce, single parenting), I could hardly believe that I was saying those words—or that I was this nervous, trembling as I knelt on one knee.

"Of course!" Robin replied.

Looking back, I could see how I'd been set up: a lunch date arranged between my parents and hers, who had become friends over the past year. Robin was living in Los Angeles and thinking of moving back home to Nashville, Tennessee. She'd been away for more than ten years and didn't know anyone in town, so my mother offered me as her first new friend. To get my mom off my back, I agreed.

I pulled up to the restaurant and noticed a tall, graceful blonde striding up to the front door. As I stepped out of the car, she beat me to the punch. "Brock," she said, smiling confidently. "My mom sent me your picture."

Two hours later, we were still sitting in our booth, talking about her work in LA, my work in Nashville, our schooling, our childhoods and how my mother made goldenrod eggs on special mornings.

Robin moved back to Nashville, and we started dating. Over the next two years it became more obvious that I didn't want to live my life without her. My nine-year-old son Harrison sealed the deal when I overheard him saying, "Robin, I sure am ready for you to be my stepmom!"

When I look at Robin and anticipate our future together, I know it's the prayers of my family and friends that put Robin and me together and that will sustain our marriage in the years ahead.

> *Father, thank You for the gifts You give us in others.*
> —BROCK KIDD

Mon 15
*Sing unto him a new song: play skillfully
with a loud noise.* —PSALM 33:3

In January 1900, poet James Weldon Johnson, principal of Stanton
High School in Jacksonville, Florida, was pacing his office floor. He
was scheduled to address the school assembly on Abraham Lincoln's
birthday the following month. As an experienced orator, Johnson knew
how quickly speeches were forgotten. He needed something different,
something new, something that would engage the young people.

He thought of his father, a waiter, and his mother, a trained singer.
Johnson and his brother John Rosamond enjoyed standing at either end
of the piano as their mother played and the family sang. John Rosamond
had set poems to music; perhaps the brothers could compose something
to honor Lincoln.

Together they wrote a song and set it to music. On that anniversary
of Lincoln's birthday in 1900, it was sung by a youth choir of five hundred voices. Unexpectedly the students kept singing it at home, at play
and in their churches. In time, "Lift Every Voice and Sing" was being sung
at schools and churches throughout the South. The final words are:

> *"Shadowed beneath Thy hand,*
> *May we forever stand,*
> *True to our God,*
> *True to our native land."*

The next time we sing "Lift Every Voice and Sing" in our church, I
hope we all join hands—remembering we're family—and sing out from
our hearts.

Lord, music is the language of all nations. When we sing, let us give forth
with all You have given us and let our lives sing as loudly as our voices.
—OSCAR GREENE

Tue 16   *Enter his gates with thanksgiving, and his courts with praise! Give thanks to him, bless his name! For the Lord is good; his steadfast love endures for ever, and his faithfulness to all generations.* —PSALM 100:4–5 (RSV)

On a bleak windy morning I switch on my iPod to block out the noise of the city. It does, but increasingly I'm not sure that I can. Life drags with every footstep.

One of the things the iPod can do is "shuffle"—the little guy inside picks out song after song in random succession. I shuffle, and Mr. Shuffle lights on a track from Peter, Paul and Mary: "Take my hand, my son," they sing, "all will be well when the day is done." Their song speaks to daughters as well as to sons. The strong hand of God slips under my elbow, and my steps get a little faster and a little steadier.

We faithful readers of the Bible talk a lot about miracles, but do we notice the small miracles that happen to each of us when doing the dishes or walking home from work? I have 950 songs on my iPod. That in itself seems like a miracle. How does all that music tuck itself into a tiny plastic box that fits in the palm of my hand?

There are miracles wearing many different faces, making different sounds and offering different kinds of help. This one was just a song from a small piece of plastic, but it was one to treasure and for which to thank God.

May I watch for life's miracles, great and small, share them with others and always give You thanks, Lord.
—BRIGITTE WEEKS

Wed 17

He hath borne our griefs, and carried our sorrows. . . . He was wounded for our transgressions, he was bruised for our iniquities . . . and with his stripes we are healed.
—ISAIAH 53:4–5

An electrical storm crashed thunder and lightning into the predawn hours, shaking the heavens. *Appropriate*, I thought, *for this day when we reflect on our mortality*. It was Ash Wednesday, the first day of Lent, and at our church we have a special service. A small cross of ashes is placed on the forehead of each of those in attendance, with the admonition, "Remember that you are dust and to dust you shall return." This was a time for repentance, confession and forgiveness that for the next few weeks would focus us on the sacrifice of Christ.

As I knelt in my pew, I thanked God for Dr. Arlene, who had died not long before. Fired with a passion for the love and saving grace of Jesus, she and her doctor-husband had spent a lifetime as medical missionaries in Burundi, Africa. Her husband had been gone for several years, and for months Dr. Arlene had wrestled with a terminal illness that challenged the depth of her faith.

I spoke to her the week before the Lord took her home. Her voice, though weak, was radiant with conviction. "I have lived in the love of God and now I die in the love of God. There really is no difference. My heart is rejoicing as I come into the presence of my Lord!"

I open my heart, Lord, to the sacrifice of Your love that heals my sorrows, eases my pain and lifts me up from my defeats. Cleanse me and help me to live in Your triumphant love that gives me life everlasting.
—FAY ANGUS

Thu 18 "*Do not worry then, saying, 'What shall we eat?'. . .*"
—Matthew 6:31 (nas)

O n the plane headed to Iowa for a conference, I felt a little anxious.
Newly diagnosed with celiac disease, I had to think carefully about
my food—nothing containing wheat or gluten for me. This new way of
eating complicated life. *Will I have to endure questions and stares in restaurants?* I thought. *I have a few apples from home, but should I have brought
more?*

That first day at the conference I met Cynthia. "Hi," she said. "I heard
you have celiac disease. Me too. I brought some things to share."

"That is so kind," I said. I felt as I did on my first day of kindergarten
when my new friend shared cookies from her lunchbox.

Cynthia offered wheat-free granola, flourless brownies and peanuts.
"Take whatever you want. I have plenty."

Later in the cafeteria, I smiled at Cynthia as we filled our plates.
As the conference organizers had promised, there was gluten-free food
for us.

On the last night we joined a group at a restaurant. Someone had chosen a place with a gluten-free menu! I had a great time, but I had to leave
a little early. Later that night I heard a knock on my hotel room door. It
was Cynthia. "I brought you something. You missed dessert." Crème
brulée, three different flavors.

As I hugged Cynthia good-bye, my heart and tummy were both full.
God had provided, and He had sent a new friend who understood.

Lord, thank You for Cynthia, who's been there.
—Julie Garmon

Fri 19

Don't use bad language. Say only what is good and helpful to those you are talking to, and what will give them a blessing.
—Ephesians 4:29 (TLB)

When I was writing radio commercials at a big Milwaukee radio station, one thing I didn't like about the job was the bad language around the office. Each day I watched the stress level of the sales staff increase as they struggled to make their projected sales. As tensions rose, the entire sales staff got into the habit of using foul language to let off steam.

One day Tom, a radio salesman, mentioned a sermon he'd heard at church about the use of profanity. "You know," he said, "we really abuse it around here. Why don't we give up swearing for Lent? Each time one of us swears or curses, let's drop a quarter into a jar."

News of our Swear Jar quickly spread around the building of nearly three hundred employees, many of whom dropped in periodically to see how we were doing. Six weeks later a note appeared in our paycheck envelopes: "Congratulations to the AM Radio Sales Staff. Their Swear Jar full of 187 swears ($46.75) was delivered to the Rescue Mission this past Friday. AM Sales has decided to continue to watch their mouths and contribute to the jar when necessary."

> *Lord, if I'm ever tempted to let off steam with bad language,*
> *turn my words into a prayer instead.*
> —Patricia Lorenz

❃ THE GIFT OF SIGHT

Sat 20   As Jesus passed by, he saw a man which was
blind from his birth. —John 9:1

BLIND SAM

One day Mother dropped my brother Donal and me off at the movie theater to see a Shirley Temple film. She had just given us our allowances: a dime for me and a quarter for Donal, because he was older.

Sitting on the corner was a man with no eyes. It was the first time I'd seen a blind person and I was shocked. "That man doesn't have any eyes!" I said to Donal.

"*Shhh!* That's Blind Sam," whispered my brother. The man picked up a violin and began to play. I couldn't help staring at him.

"What happened to him?"

"Nothing *happened* to him, silly. He was born blind."

"You mean he's never been able to see?"

"That's right. People put money in that cigar box. He uses it to buy food and stuff. Come on, Slow Poke, or we'll miss the cartoons!"

"Wait a minute," I said and went back and dropped my dime in Sam's box.

"What'd ya do that for? Now you don't have money for the movie!"

"I don't care much about the movie anymore. My stomach hurts. I'm going home."

Donal gave me a disgusted look and said, "You can't walk home alone! You'll get lost!" He sighed and then dropped his quarter into Blind Sam's box, took my hand, and we started the twelve-block walk home. That night when we said our prayers, we added Blind Sam to our ever-growing list of "God blesses."

Thank You, Creator, for the glorious gift of sight. Bless all who are without it.
—Marilyn Morgan King

February

Sun 21

"Surely the Lord is in this place; and I did not know it." —GENESIS 28:16 (RSV)

Perhaps the hardest part of moving to New Hampshire nine years ago was transitioning to a new church after twenty-three years in the same Wyoming parish. All our babies had been baptized there; "our" pew still bore their teething marks. I had sung for countless services, dozens of baptisms, weddings and funerals. I had taught religious education, organized Christmas programs and cooked for church suppers. Now I had to start over.

At first my daughter Trina and I attended the parish we had visited when vacationing with my parents. After that church burned, we attended services in a tent until the winter, when our parish joined another one fifteen miles away.

Once Trina graduated and moved away, wintering on a lonesome lake lost its charm and I moved to Concord to be closer to work. Concord, a city of forty thousand, has several churches of my denomination, most of them ten times larger than the church I had left behind. I attended alone and introduced myself; I attended with friends who made introductions. Yet try as I might, I could not seem to find a church-home.

One Saturday I scanned the newspaper listing of churches and half-heartedly decided to try a new church each week. The blurb for one, St. Paul's, caught my attention: "A place to belong, whoever you are, just as you are." *Hmm, worth a try. I'll start there.*

And I'm still there. Not only did the parishioners greet me, they included me in conversations, asked my opinion, and invited me to potlucks and prayer groups. I'm becoming part of this vibrant body, and for the first time in my life I can walk to church.

Perhaps God wonders what took me so long. For two years I've been looking at St. Paul's steeple every time I look out my east windows!

Good Shepherd, thank You for enfolding me in Your flock at last.
—GAIL THORELL SCHILLING

Mon 22 *Immediately Jesus, perceiving in Himself that the power proceeding from Him had gone forth, turned around in the crowd and said, "Who touched My garments?"*
—MARK 5:30 (NAS)

When Jesus asked who had touched Him in the crowded street, a woman fell trembling at His feet and confessed. For twelve years she'd suffered a worsening health condition, going broke paying physicians. She had pretty much given up until she heard about Jesus. She thought if she could get close enough to touch just the fringe of His cloak, she would be made well.

Her plan was to sneak up behind Jesus in the press of people, reach out with a quick furtive touch and then disappear in the crowd. It almost worked. Only Jesus felt power go out from Him at the same instant the woman felt in her body that she was well. Her reach and Jesus' response met in a miraculous healing.

The Bible doesn't give her name, but I call her the *fringe* lady—*f*aith *r*eaching *in* God *e*xpectation. Jesus' parting words, "Go in peace and be healed of your affliction" (Mark 5:34, NAS), must have been a soothing salve for all of her remaining years.

I find real hope in this story. The fringe lady's faith was desperate, even frightened—the way my faith gets when my best efforts have failed and I think I'm out of options. Yet Jesus commended her, saying, "Daughter, your faith has made you well" (Mark 5:34, NAS).

Wherever I am—however alone or exhausted or distraught—when I sincerely reach for Jesus, I know that He will respond to the barest touch.

> *Holy Spirit, when I'm out of answers, help me*
> *to summon the faith to reach out for Jesus.*
> —CAROL KNAPP

Tue 23

"When He calls me to account, what will I answer Him?"
—Job 31:14 (NAS)

When our grandson Max was two years old, his parents began giving him "time-out" for unacceptable behavior. He was to sit quietly on the stairs leading up to his bedroom until such time as he was ready to obey.

The only problem was that Max wasn't willing to cooperate. Either he didn't understand their expectations or didn't want to—his parents couldn't quite distinguish between the two—and Max couldn't talk well enough to express himself.

And then one day while we were visiting, Max followed me into the bedroom just as Teddy the cat strolled by. Unable to resist the temptation, Max grabbed Teddy firmly by the tail and wouldn't let go. Forcibly peeling his fingers from around the cat's tail, I scolded him for being unkind to his pet. Without a word, Max headed for the stairs and sat down, guilt written all over his big brown eyes.

Seeing him sitting there, his dad asked, "What did you do?"

Max's response was one word: "Kitty."

That said it all. His dad knew it was not the first time Max had pulled the cat's tail, but more importantly, he now knew for certain that his son understood the consequences of his misbehavior.

> *Father God, when You call me to account for my sins,*
> *I can plead but one word:* guilty.
> *But being a loving Father, You also extend*
> *Your forgiveness with another word:* mercy.
> —Alma Barkman

Wed 24 Rest in the Lord, and wait patiently for him. . . .
—Psalm 37:7

Last winter, fourteen-year-old Elizabeth asked me to go with her to see a Metropolitan Opera simulcast on the Lehman College campus in the Bronx. After we'd settled into our seats, I was careful to turn off my cell phone lest it disrupt the performance. But not, apparently, careful in putting it back.

When the performance was over, we were greeted by an unexpected snow flurry. We hurried to our bus, and fifteen minutes later we were at the subway for our ride home. I patted my waist—no cell phone!

When we got home, I phoned the theater; no one had found my phone. I called again a few days later with the same result. Back at Lehman, two weeks later, to see another telecast, I visited the theater office, but again no cell phone.

With Julia and our five children constantly in motion around the city, a cell phone was more than a convenience. So I glumly made up my mind that, like it or not, I'd have to buy a new one. Julia was not convinced. "I've prayed about it," she said, "and I think you should wait."

And wait I did.

Then one warm spring Saturday morning, our phone rang. "Hello," a young voice said, "I'm calling from Lehman College. Did you lose a phone in the Studio Theater?"

"Yes, yes, I did!"

"We have it in the office."

So with twelve-year-old John and five-year-old Stephen in tow, I trekked up to the Bronx. A word to a student usher, a few minutes' wait and there was my phone, with some charge even left on the battery. I called Julia to tell her the good news. For some reason, she wasn't surprised.

Lord, when my patience seems to be running out with someone or something in my life, teach me to trust in You—and wait.
—Andrew Attaway

Thu 25

But hope that is seen is no hope at all. Who hopes for what he already has? —ROMANS 8:24 (NIV)

Yesterday I planted an indoor paperwhite narcissus garden. I'd never done this before, but my gardening guide assured me it was easy. I started with five bulbs, nut-brown spheres with lime green tufts. I found a glass bowl and filled it with clear marbles. Then I nested the bulbs, shoulder to shoulder, in their sparkling new bed. *Now for the water . . .*

The directions were very clear: The water must be below the bulbs; if it covers them, they'll rot. They "sniff" the water and grow their roots down to it. Without that effort, there will be no blooms.

Today, the project complete, I look past the bulb bowl to my real garden outside. The ground is frozen, covered with a dusting of snow. Stems and leaves are a sickly yellow. Branches are stark and bare. I'm not a big fan of winter, but I think it serves a purpose in my life. I read more. I try out recipes for hearty soups. I sit in my prayer chair a bit longer. And I *hope.*

Planting this winter garden has reminded me that good things are worth waiting for. Things like that first spring walk on the beach or running through the sprinkler with my grandkids. And, for now, things like the paperwhites soon to be blooming on my kitchen table.

> *Give me patience, Father, to wait for the blessings*
> *You're sending my way.*
> —MARY LOU CARNEY

Fri 26 *For this very reason, make every effort to add to your faith goodness; and to goodness, knowledge; and to knowledge, self-control; and to self-control, perseverance. . . .*
—II PETER 1:5–6 (NIV)

The nurse sitting across from me pricked my finger and squeezed out a drop of blood. It really didn't hurt. She showed me the meter. "Two-thirty-two," she said. "That's diabetic."

Tears popped into my eyes, I-cannot-believe-this-is-happening-to-me tears. I was angry—not at her, but at Sweetness.

Sweetness and I had been dating for a long, long time. He went with me everywhere, and I spent lots of money on him. I changed the way I dressed for him; he had a place in every room in my house. I think I loved Sweetness way more than he ever loved me.

When the doctor walked into the examining room, she could see that I was upset. "It's going to be all right," she told me.

"I'm just angry," I said, accepting the tissue she handed me. "I'm breaking up with Sweetness. I'm finished. I'm done. I'm toast. We're through."

"I can give you some pills that will help you," she said.

"No." I shook my head. "I needed to hear this. I've known I should break up with Sweetness for a long time. No more sugar."

So I cut Sweetness off. He tries to call me; he shows up everywhere I go; he tries to talk to me in my dreams; he even buys commercial time on television. He's trying hard; I give him credit for that. Whenever Sweetness calls, I walk or pray or both.

Eight weeks later, when I returned to the scene of the diagnosis, my doctor was ecstatic: My blood sugar was now normal. "I knew you were going to do it!" she said. She forgot that she was a professional and drew a happy face on my chart.

Dear Lord, I thank You that Sweetness and I are now through.
Give me the strength to keep it that way.
—SHARON FOSTER

Sat 27 When I was a child, I spoke like a child, I thought like a child,
I reasoned like a child; when I became a man, I gave up
childish ways. —I CORINTHIANS 13:11 (RSV)

W hen I was a child, there was something I really wanted. A strange
thing, it seems to me now, for a little girl to set her heart on: a
shorter number on our family's car's license plate.

I remember begging my father again and again to get us a clever one,
like others on our street. Maybe letters that spelled out a word or repeat
numbers like the ones on our next-door neighbor's car, D15F15. Or just
a plate with fewer than eleven digits.

Year after year, though, our license plate number would be not only
long but hopelessly scrambled, just as our car was always black, the most
common color then, and neither very new, nor very old. Our car, like its
plate, was totally undistinguished.

I understood that the answer to my brother's "Can we buy the latest
model?" my sister's ". . . choose a pretty color?" my ". . . get a snappy license
plate?" was "No." Why, I didn't know. I knew, of course, that my father was
a private detective. And I knew that the family car would sometimes be
gone for several days, replaced by an equally nondescript company car. The
intricacies of using and switching automobiles when staking out a location or trailing a suspect were not only unknown to me but unimaginable.

When I got a little older, of course, I understood why our father could
not give us what we asked for, why our car must not attract attention. It
gave me a new respect for his "No," a sense that there were good reasons
for things that for the present were beyond my comprehension. It helps
me now to accept the *No* of the Father whose reasons are good beyond
all imagining.

> *If my "license plate number" today is long and jumbled,*
> *Father, I trust You for the reason why.*
> —ELIZABETH SHERRILL

Sun 28   *"But go now to . . . your rest; for you will rise again and have your full share of those last days."* —DANIEL 12:13 (TLB)

My retirement celebration was on a Sunday afternoon, so the family gathered at our house on Saturday. My nephew Jeff provided a marvelous dinner of steak and garlic potatoes. Afterward adults and teens visited while the seven children under twelve played raucous games of hide-and-seek and climbed in and out of the window wells, shrieking with laughter.

Just before bedtime my great-nephew Dominick collapsed into his mother's lap and proclaimed with four-year-old earnestness, "This is my best day ever!"

"And tomorrow will be Aunt Penney's best day!" someone added. I smiled, but I wasn't so sure. The party would be fun, but what about the months afterward? I'd prayed about the decision and knew in my heart that retirement was the right choice. But I was leaving a job I'd enjoyed for twenty-two years. I'd miss the excitement of work and the daily conversations with colleagues who were also friends.

On Sunday morning our family worshiped together before heading to the celebration. What a joy to see friends from around Kansas! I received a precious memory book with cards, letters and pictures recalling my career; the directors surprised me with a check for a long-anticipated trip to Alaska; and an endowment fund was established in my name.

By the time I said my tearful good-byes, I realized it had truly been a "best day ever." Why? Because wonderful days don't require gifts, celebrations or even a job: They flow from the love of family and friends and the assurance that God walks with us through all the days in all the stages of our lives.

> *Jesus, guide and friend, help me make*
> *every day a "best day" with You.*
> —PENNEY SCHWAB

THE GIFTS I'VE BEEN GIVEN

1 _____

2 _____

3 _____

4 _____

5 _____

6 _____

7 _____

8 _____

9 _____

10 _____

11 _____

12 _____

13 _____

14 _____

15 _____

16 _____

17 _____

18 _____

19 _____

February

20 _____

21 _____

22 _____

23 _____

24 _____

25 _____

26 _____

27 _____

28 _____

March

He that spared not his own Son,
but delivered him up for us all,
how shall he not with him also
freely give us all things?

—Romans 8:32

❧ GIFTS FROM ABOVE

Mon 1 *Why are ye fearful, O ye of little faith? . . .*
—MATTHEW 8:26

A GIFT OF FAITH

We are on a bus driving through an off-road thicket, deep in a moonless landscape. There is no electricity for miles, and I can see nothing as I stare out the window into the darkness. The bus rumbles to a halt, and my husband David and I and our fellow passengers stumble toward a pontoon boat. Within minutes we're anchored in the middle of a forbidding bay. "This is the strangest tourist attraction I've ever seen," I whisper nervously to David.

Earlier, after we'd arrived on the Isle of Vieques for a special holiday, our taxi driver had said, "Put the Bioluminescent Bay at the top of your agenda." So here we are, listening to the pilot of the boat say, "To experience the miracle of the bay, you must jump into the water."

No one moves.

This is ridiculous. The water is as black as the night. We all wait.

Suddenly, David stands up and jumps into the unknown. In the pool of darkness, his body takes on a bright glow. His every movement radiates a flowing blue-green light. Mesmerized, I jump in, and others follow. I wave my arms and make angel wings, and then twirl and swirl in a trail of fairy dust. By now, everyone is laughing and splashing as our every move turns the night magical. The moment seems part fantasy, part science fiction as the energy of our bodies sets trillions of microorganisms aglow.

Later, back on the boat heading for shore, I think of the fear that wrapped around us. There in a dark bay, magic was waiting—waiting for someone who believed enough to take a chance and jump in.

*Father, take away my toe-first inclinations and fill me with
a leaping faith.* —PAM KIDD

Tue 2 Seek ye out of the book of the Lord, and
read. . . . —ISAIAH 34:16

For several years now I've been going on a walk as part of my exercise
routine. I head out after my younger son goes to bed, strolling
through our small-town New England streets to a small church about a
mile away. There I say a quick prayer in the parking lot and head back
home. The round trip takes about half an hour, and I always feel better
for it.

The trouble is I get bored on the walk. I've tried all sorts of ways to
pass the time. At first I listened to music, but my tastes run toward clas-
sical and it's frustrating to hear only a snippet of a symphony or an opera.
So I switched to recorded novels. That's worked better, and over the years
I've enjoyed the works of J. R. R. Tolkien, Homer, Charles Dickens and
dozens of other wonderful writers.

Recently, however, I've discovered something else to listen to that's
better than music or novels: the Bible. I prefer the King James Version
read by Alexander Scourby in his powerful baritone voice, but I've listened
to several other recorded versions and they all have their good points.
When I'm walking along familiar streets, listening to the words of Holy
Scripture, everything seems to be bathed in the light of God. Places I've
passed a thousand times before take on new beauty and meaning, my
worries sink to insignificance, and I always return home with a spring in
my step. Walking with the Bible is a simple investment that pays eternal
dividends.

May I always read the book of my life, Lord, with Holy Scripture
as my guide. —PHILIP ZALESKI

EDITOR'S NOTE: *We invite you to join us a month from today, on April 2,*
as we pray for all the needs of our Guideposts family at our fortieth annual
Guideposts Good Friday Day of Prayer. Send your prayer requests to Day
of Prayer, PO Box 5813, Harlan, Iowa 51593-1313, or visit us on the
Web at OurPrayerGoodFriday.org.

Wed 3

Abraham begat Isaac; and Isaac begat Jacob. . . .
—MATTHEW 1:2

In Hong Kong recently I visited a Chinese graveyard. The only other people there were an old woman and a little girl, who was carrying an orange. The two stopped before a crumbling, lichen-covered tombstone and bowed deeply. After perhaps two minutes, the little girl placed her orange on the grave and they left.

Back in the States, from a cobwebby corner of our attic I dug out a four-foot-long cardboard tube, which contained a gift from my great-uncle Will. As a boy I loved visiting Uncle Will in his one-room home. He collected old things: arrowheads, cattle skulls, petrified wood and family records. It was a copy of our genealogy, printed on blueprint paper, that he handed me one day. "This is where you come from, Johnny."

Uncle Will laid the genealogy on the floor and began unrolling it. Ruled lines connected entries in his fine penmanship. I read out a few names, English-sounding and unfamiliar to me, thanked him, rolled the record up and took it with me, where it ended up in the attic corner.

Now I carried the record down to the living room and rolled it out across the floor, thinking of a little girl placing an orange on an ancestral tomb. I have only the names and dates and a few scanty details, such as that my ancestors were farmers and tradesfolk and teachers. They labored and suffered and loved and grieved and kept their faith. They passed on a heritage to me that I'd taken for granted, with no appreciation for the lives that made my own possible.

Why, I'd always wondered, did the Bible allot so much space to those boring "begats"? Maybe, I thought, because the record of God's faithfulness to our ancestors is a portrait of the One Who is the same today, yesterday and forever.

> *Father, let me pass on the legacy of love, work and faith*
> *to generations to come.*
> —JOHN SHERRILL

Thu 4

For the invisible things of him from the creation of the world are clearly seen, being understood by the things that are made....
—ROMANS 1:20

I hadn't realized how tired I was until I pulled the quilt up over my shoulders. I turned out the lamp beside the bed, felt weariness wash over me and then groaned. "I forgot to get milk."

It was 10:30 PM. The wind howled over the Hudson River. It was twelve degrees outside. The impossibility of getting up and going out outweighed the near impossibility of preparing breakfast at 5:30 AM without milk. I shut my eyes.

"Do you want me to get it?" my husband Andrew asked.

"It's cold out there!" I replied.

"I'll go. We're out of coffee too."

"I can live for a day without it."

"Not without committing a crime. I'll get some . . . for the kids' sake." And without complaint my husband got up out of his reading chair, gave me a kiss on the forehead, donned his winter coat and headed out into the bitter night.

In the morning I blearily poured out milk to mix into batter for cranberry muffins. I sipped my coffee and stared at the familiar shape of the milk container. Then I peered into my cup at the coffee. It was a little weird, but somehow this was the shape of Andrew's love. Sometimes he tells me he loves me; other times he gives me a hug. And once in a while, when I remember to look for it, I discover the best evidence of his love in everyday, ordinary things like coffee and milk.

Lord, the outward and visible signs of Your love are all around me.
Help me to see them today and every day.
—JULIA ATTAWAY

Fri 5

Why, you do not even know what will happen tomorrow. . . . —JAMES 4:14 (NIV)

As I walked into the store, an elderly employee who was greeting shoppers gave me a big hello. "Why, I know you! You're that lady on television! I watch you all the time."

"Thanks. It's so nice to meet you," I said as I shook his hand. As an anchor on a local TV station, I enjoyed the opportunity to meet viewers.

Later, while putting my purchases into the car, I thought back to my chance meeting. *What a nice man,* I thought. I had two TV station baseball caps in the backseat of my car. *Maybe he'll be working the next time I'm here, and I can give him a baseball cap.*

I got into my car, started it, shifted into reverse and then stopped. The phrase "You can't go back to Moscow" floated into my mind. That phrase had become a mantra around the studio. John, an experienced cameraman at our station, shares it with all of our interns.

Years ago John traveled to Moscow with a news crew. "I knew that if I didn't have the footage I needed to produce the story when I got back to the studio in New Orleans," he said, "there was no going back to Moscow to get it. Make sure you make the best out of every moment. Who's to say you'll ever have that opportunity again?"

I put my car in park, turned off the ignition, grabbed a baseball cap and headed back into the store.

Lord, I want to make the most of all the moments that You give me.
—MELODY BONNETTE

Sat 6   *"Therefore I tell you, do not worry about your life, what you will eat or drink; or about your body, what you will wear. . . ."*
—MATTHEW 6:25 (NIV)

When my fiancé Brian and I began to plan our wedding, we anticipated finding a few speed bumps along the way. Maybe it would be the guest list or finding a wedding dress. As it turns out, we sailed through almost every element of the planning, from agreeing on flowers to selecting mixing bowls. We couldn't, however, find a minister to perform our ceremony.

The first one we asked had another obligation. The next, from Brian's home church, couldn't take time from his own congregation. The third and the fourth couldn't be out of town on the weekend we'd selected. The fifth—yes, fifth—the one whose church we were using, announced his retirement just before our wedding.

I called Brian, humbled and frustrated. "No one wants to do our wedding," I said. "I want it to be special."

He calmed me down and said, "It will be special because it will be you and me saying our vows. It's the vows that are important, not the person who prompts you to say them."

Brian was right—I'd been putting so much stock in having the right earthly person to administer our vows that I'd forgotten their real meaning came from our saying them to each other in front of our family, our friends and, of course, our God. We're still looking for a minister, but now I know that as long as I have God in my heart and Brian beside me at the altar, I have nothing to worry about.

Thank You, Lord, for gentle reminders that
You are the reason for all that I do.
—ASHLEY JOHNSON

Sun 7

*Whatever you do, work at it with all your heart, as working for the Lord.... —*Colossians 3:23 (NIV)

This year I'm serving as a deacon at my church. My first official act was to host the between-services breakfast of coffee, juice and doughnuts.

Normally I wouldn't mind getting breakfast ready and serving it, but that Sunday a new class was starting. Now, instead of sitting expectantly in the front row, I'd be in the kitchen cutting up doughnuts and trying to figure out how to wrangle the coffeemaker.

When breakfast was over, a fellow deacon and I washed coffeepots, wiped kitchen counters, and cleared and cleaned tables in the fellowship hall. By the time I finally reached the sanctuary, our pastor was well into his sermon.

I was just a tad annoyed. I mean, I'd missed a class I'd been eagerly waiting to begin. I'd spent more time than usual close to coffee grounds and dirty tabletops. And now I'd missed most of worship.

That's when I noticed it. Something was sticking to the side of my black boot. It was small and round and yellow, with a red heart in its center—a sticker. *How did that get there?* I bent down and pulled it off. *Jesus loves you.* The words were simple and clear, white lettering in a bright red heart.

I looked around at the gleaming wood of the communion table, at the loaf of freshly baked bread. I glanced at our pianist as she took her place for the next hymn. My eyes rested on the colorful banners on either side of the cross. *It takes lots of folks to make church happen*, I thought. In that moment I was genuinely grateful to every one of them. And grateful to *be* one of them too!

There are no small jobs in Your kingdom, Lord. Use me as You will.
—Mary Lou Carney

⧗ COMFORT FOR THE HURTING HEART

Mon 8

Each one should use whatever gift he has received to serve others. . . . —I Peter 4:10 (niv)

THE THINGS THAT CONSOLE

For months our son and his wife had awaited the birth of their first child, delighting in baby-shower gifts and in the excitement of the mother-to-be's bag packed for the day of delivery. The anticipation heightened when our son called to say, "This is it. We're heading for the hospital!"

My husband and I parked by the phone, eager for it to ring again. It did, but this time our son's stricken voice was barely discernible. "Our little girl was stillborn."

It's easy to *ooh* and *aah* over a warm, cuddly infant, but how were we to be with these grief-stricken parents who were painfully aware of an empty bassinet? Here's what we learned:

First, *do* recognize the mother's desire to cuddle, and give her a teddy bear, a pillow or simply offer your arm to hold. *Don't* interpret this as being clingy; it's natural.

Do simply say, "I'm sorry" or "I care," along with a hug or a hand squeeze. *Don't* say, "You'll get over it in time."

Do acts of thoughtfulness: notes, books, plants, flowers, food, calls, dinner out. *Don't* try to console by saying, "It's God's will" or "The baby's an angel now."

Do listen; the bereaved need to talk. *Don't* try to steer the conversation away from their loss.

Do help locate a support group. *Don't* ignore their need to share with those who have similar sorrows.

> *Oh, Lord, give us Your wisdom when we seek to console the ones who are left behind.* —ISABEL WOLSELEY

Tue 9

There is no fear in love; but perfect love casteth out fear. . . . —I JOHN 4:18

"G ene, getting older is downright scary," I told my husband as we sat in the living room one evening. "I'm more forgetful. My energy level isn't what it once was. I need naps, for heaven's sake!"

Gene gave a noncommittal *mmm-hmm* and continued to read the newspaper, so I fixed my attention on Gracie, the abandoned kitten we'd taken in almost two years ago. Her feral instincts haven't totally vanished; she's always on the alert for trouble and still doesn't trust us completely. She had never come to us to ask for affection. "Sweet-face Grace," I tell her over and over, "you're safe now. Relax, girl."

That night Gracie watched us from the doorway to a bedroom, where she could scoot under a bed if need be. But then she did the most amazing thing: She inched toward Gene, who was sitting in his easy chair with the paper in front of his face. Ever so slowly she climbed up on the chair and sat her little gray self down about two inches from his hand, staring straight ahead. As her sleepy eyes blinked, Gene stroked her head. Brave Gracie shut those yellow eyes, purred and relaxed totally against his hand.

Gracie overcame her fear that evening—and not just Gracie. I decided then and there that it's okay for me to slow down now, even if it means I won't accomplish as much. And it's even okay if, like Gracie, I want to enjoy a little nap now and then.

Father, I need Your help to curl up confidently, trusting Your hand.
—MARION BOND WEST

Wed 10   *"Seek the welfare of the city . . . and pray to the Lord on its behalf. . . ."* —JEREMIAH 29:7 (NAS)

O f all the racket a city dweller like me has to put up with, sirens are probably the worst. Sirens are designed to be impossible to ignore, and though I've become pretty good at pushing them into the background, there are still times when an ambulance or fire truck sounds like it's right in my living room.

That's what happened last night. Several police cars decided to stop outside our apartment building, sirens bleating, right under our windows. The sirens woke Millie, who went into a barking frenzy that woke up my wife Julee, who shook me awake to tell me to make Millie quiet down.

I lurched into the living room where Millie was barking at the window, her breath fogging up the glass. "*Shhh* . . . hush!" I said, dragging her away. She got loose and resumed her barking vigil. Finally I pulled the blinds, and she stopped. All the while the sirens continued. My head started pounding. How would I ever get back to sleep? I peered through the slats in the blind. Nothing seemed amiss on the block.

A memory of my mother came back to me: Whenever she heard a siren, even a distant one, she stopped what she was doing and said a quick prayer. We'd tease her sometimes, telling her it was probably just a couple of police officers hurrying back from their lunch break. But I came to admire Mom's Johnny-on-the-spot faith: Sirens mean people in distress, and people in distress need prayer.

The sirens had stopped by now, and Millie had unceremoniously taken my place in bed (she likes that nice warmed-up spot). I didn't have the heart to remove her. Besides, I wasn't going to get back to sleep now. I would sit for a while waiting to hear another inevitable siren come through the night. And I knew what I would do.

> *Lord, my mother taught me well. The world is*
> *full of opportunities to pray.*
> —EDWARD GRINNAN

Thu 11

*Yes, I will bless the Lord and not forget the glorious
things he does for me.* —PSALM 103:2 (TLB)

I drove past the shopping mall near my house today and noticed that
all of the big, beautiful pine trees were gone. Later I read in the newspaper that it's part of a "modernization" plan, a remodeling that's supposed
to update the mall's look—new lights, new signs and tall palm trees in
place of the pines.

I miss them already. We sometimes sat under those trees for an
impromptu family picnic after church. When our children were little,
they loved to roll down the grassy hills. The word *sometimes* makes me
sad; why didn't we enjoy this majestic gift from God more often? I guess
we figured those trees would be there forever and there was plenty of
time to enjoy them. Now, too late, we've discovered there wasn't.

That's true of all natural resources, but especially the most precious—
the people in my life. I think of my friends at a nearby retirement home
where I teach a class once a month. I'll think, *I should stop by in between
meetings and see how they're doing*, but then I get busy and don't do it. Like
those majestic trees, one day these wonderful friends will be gone and I'll
wonder why I didn't enjoy their company more often. Today, before I get
started on my to-do list, I think I'll call my friend Jane, just to say hello.
I know it will be time well spent.

*Lord, remind me that when I get too busy to spend a moment with
a friend, I'm busier than You want me to be.*
—GINA BRIDGEMAN

Fri 12   *"And do not seek what you should eat or what you should drink, nor have an anxious mind."* —LUKE 12:29 (NKJV)

My wife and I have reached that age where we often say to each other, "Now, if anything should happen to me . . ."

If anything happens to my wife, I'm likely to lose a hundred pounds. I don't cook and I don't want to cook. My philosophy is, "When I need to cook, then I will learn to cook." After all, Sharon couldn't boil water when we met, and if she learned to cook, so can I.

Just once, when she was bed-bound, I did try to make a meal for her. I warmed up some leftover roast beef and beans. I made some crunchy mashed potatoes, but then when I tried to make gravy, I stumbled. *Let's see, she mixes meat fat with milk and flour . . . I wonder how much flour?* I decided to start with just one cup of flour and I came up with the most wonderful beef-flavored play dough you've ever tasted. Now you know why I don't cook.

Sure, it would be nice to know how to cook, "just in case." And it would be nice to know how to deliver a baby, "just in case." And it would be nice to know how to do brain surgery, "just in case." But trying to prepare now for every eventuality would distract me from my present joys and responsibilities.

In the film *Out of Africa*, Meryl Streep's character says, "The earth was made round so that we would not see too far down the road." That's my philosophy exactly!

> *Lord, if anything happens to my wife,*
> *please have mercy on my soul.*
> —DANIEL SCHANTZ

Sat 13

He wakens me morning by morning, wakens my ear to listen. . . . —Isaiah 50:4 (NIV)

I woke up wanting scrambled eggs and bacon. As I pulled on my boots, I envisioned ordering breakfast in a neighborhood coffee shop and settling in to read and to write in my journal. I scooped my notebook and book into a grocery bag for easy carrying and bundled up.

I walked two blocks to Broadway. Even this early the restaurant was crowded, but I got a table in the corner and ordered breakfast special number 2 with rye toast and grapefruit juice. Now for my reading and journaling. Sipping a steaming cup of coffee, I reached for the grocery bag and thrust my hand inside. And hit metal.

I was carrying cans of cat food and some sponges to scrub the sink, items I'd bought on the way home the night before. I'd brought the wrong bag! My good mood was ruined along with my morning. Now what would I do?

Instead of reading and writing, you can look at what's going on around you, a voice spoke gently inside me. I took a deep breath and looked around. The woman at the table next to me was rustling through an immense mound of mail; a nearby toddler was burbling in his oatmeal. Outside there was an abrupt downpour; a jovial couple rushed in shaking off raindrops and announced to no one in particular that they were from New Zealand. An acquaintance from my building looked up from an adjoining booth, and when our eyes met brought over his son so he could introduce us. The New Zealand couple were served their food and—was I imagining this?—bent their heads for a moment. Were they saying grace? Now instead of being mad at myself for bringing the wrong bag, I wanted to say grace too. So I did.

Thank You, God, for nourishing not only my body but my soul.
—Mary Ann O'Roark

Sun 14　*So he went down and dipped himself seven times in the Jordan, according to the word of the man of God; and his flesh was restored like the flesh of a little child and he was clean.* —II KINGS 5:14 (NAS)

"What will you do if someone wants to wash your feet?" my wife Elba asked.

The conversation on the drive to church focused on the foot-washing service. I had never participated in one and I wasn't sure about doing it now. "I don't think I'd let them," I said.

"If you choose not to be part of the ceremony, what message will you be sending?" In my heart I knew she was right because I am a minister.

At the service the pastor told us, "Jesus showed His servant spirit by washing the feet of the disciples. He was teaching them how they should serve others." Then Todd, six feet and four inches tall and an executive with a major corporation, walked forward and slowly took off his shoes. He was followed by Betsy, a young mother in her thirties.

I could sense the power of the ritual, but I kept hoping that no one would ask me. Then I heard a familiar voice: "Pablo, I'd like to wash your feet." It was Terry, a new member of our congregation whose life had been totally transformed by Christ. How could I say no?

I walked to the front of the church, sat on a chair, took off my shoes and socks, and put my feet in the washbowl. Terry began to wash my feet and prayed, "Lord, thank You for Pastor Diaz. He has been a mentor to me. Bless his ministry and his family."

I was deeply humbled by the love that Terry poured over me as he poured the water over my feet. And I was thankful that through this simple action, God was teaching me not to let my feelings get in the way of following Him.

> *Lord, help me to surrender to Your ways and*
> *to step outside of my spiritual comfort zone.*
> —PABLO DIAZ

Mon 15

"In his hand is the life of every living thing and the breath of all mankind." —JOB 12:10 (RSV)

I was visiting a grade school, as is my wont, on the general theory that these are the beings who are going to own the world pretty soon and I want to stay on their good side. And as a salty, testy, thankful older man, it's my duty and joy to try to connect to as many kids as possible and remind them that we are inundated by the profligate generosity of the Maker. Maybe we all don't celebrate that quite enough, being also inundated by worries and bills and car troubles and back pain.

In this classroom I was blathering on and on about the sea of miracles, and a girl—it's always girls who ask the piercing questions—raised her hand and said, "Yes, sir, but have you personally experienced miracles? Or is this just a lecture?"

There was a long pause, and I said with dawning wonder, "Oh, child, yes, oh, dear Lord, yes, yes, yes. I have seen bears the size of cars. I have heard whales moaning in dark oceans. I have had a child say, 'I love you more than I could ever figure out words for my love, Dad.' I have been graced by burly brothers. I have had sicknesses that looked to be the cause of gravestone engravings but here I am, cheerfully mumbling in your classroom. Here I am and that is a miracle beyond accounting, and here you are and that is an even cooler miracle, because you are young and strong and possible in ways that I am not anymore. Yes, my young friend, I have seen miracles. Every moment of every day. Every breath. Yes. Any other questions?"

Dear Lord, it's an utterly confusing gift You have given us, crammed with pain and joy; but what a gift! The greatest that ever was! We are alive!
—BRIAN DOYLE

✹ TWELVE KEYS TO THE GIVING LIFE

Tue 16   *Be hospitable to one another. . . .* —1 PETER 4:9 (NAS)

GIVE HOSPITABLY

One cold winter day Charlie and Carman Lee Miller, a couple in the church where I grew up, invited all the young people over to their home. They promised good food and a good time, and about twenty of us showed up. But the main reason for the event was to celebrate the safe return of one of our parishioners from his tour of duty in Vietnam. Wendell was now on his way to Europe to serve our country there, and the Millers wanted us to pray for his continued safety.

Charlie and Carman Lee were well known in our little church for their warm hospitality. On this evening we gathered in the living room of their snug red brick home and feasted on finger sandwiches, veggies and dip, homemade baked beans and potato salad.

At the end of the party, all of us gathered in a circle and joined hands. Charlie began the prayer: "Thank You, dear Lord, for keeping Wendell out of harm's way while he was in Vietnam. We thank You for bringing him back to us and ask You to continue to keep him safe and ever close to You."

Wendell was the first real soldier I had ever known. His service in Vietnam was one of the things that led to my thirty-one-year career as a registered nurse caring for our nation's veterans.

Charlie and Carman Lee's gift of hospitality also taught me something profound about prayer. If our pastor had simply challenged the youth "to remember Wendell in your prayers," a few of us would have likely done so. But get a group of hungry teens together and feed them some great homemade fixin's, and you've set the stage for some real praying.

Thank You, Lord Jesus, for open hearts and open homes.
—ROBERTA MESSNER

Wed 17

Some take pride in chariots, and some in horses, but our pride is in the name of the Lord our God.
—PSALM 20:7 (NRSV)

St. Patrick is one of the handful of saints that everyone seems to know by name. We all know about the parades, concerts and parties that are held today to commemorate him and celebrate the Irish heritage, and most of us know that, according to legend, he drove the snakes out of Ireland. But the stories that have come down to us about him are much richer than that.

His life was full of contests with the Druids, the Celtic magician-priests who opposed his attempts to spread Christianity in Ireland. In one story Patrick resolved to celebrate Easter on the hill of Slane in what is today County Meath. He climbed to the top of the hill and lit the paschal fire. The king of Ireland was holding a festival in his palace across the way, and it was the custom that no fire should be lit unless one was first seen lit at the royal house. So when the king's Druids saw Patrick's fire, they said to the king, "Unless this fire is quenched tonight, it will never be quenched. And the one who kindled it will seduce all the people of your realm." So the king took nine chariots and drove to the hill of Slane.

When Patrick saw the chariots, he quoted Psalm 20:7. The Druids challenged Patrick, but Patrick was up to the task and he converted at least one of them on the spot. Then, at Patrick's prayer, darkness fell and the earth quaked and the Druids and the chariots fled.

What stands out for me in this story is Patrick's confidence, his assurance that no matter what the challenge, he would prevail. It was a confidence that rested not on any abilities of his own, but on his faith in God, Who is always able to do the unexpected.

Gracious God, be with me today and let me do Your work.
—JON SWEENEY

Thu 18 *Perseverance must finish its work so that you may be mature and complete, not lacking anything.* —JAMES 1:4 (NIV)

I don't want to do this anymore," my six-year-old granddaughter Gabriella announced, climbing off the stool at our kitchen counter. She'd been cutting out shamrocks to decorate the table for a family dinner.

I smiled, wanting to warn her that she was at the beginning of one of life's steepest learning curves: to keep doing what we don't want to do anymore. She went off to play, and while I continued cutting up vegetables for fajitas, I thought of some recent examples in my own life: finishing all twenty push-ups in an aerobics class when I was only on ten and my arms hurt; staying at the computer to complete a project when I'd rather have eaten cookies in the kitchen; sticking to a diet (because I ate too many of those cookies) rather than giving up; cleaning out a closet when I wanted to quit because I was tired of making decisions about what to keep and what to toss or give away.

Soon Gabi's daddy came into the kitchen, sweating from a training run for an upcoming marathon. I asked him how he keeps going when he feels like stopping. "It's hard," he admitted, pouring himself a glass of water, "but when I push through that painful temptation to stop, I usually get a second wind."

Lord, if I practice pushing through hard places, I learn perseverance.
I guess that's what You told me in the first place.
—CAROL KUYKENDALL

March

Fri 19   *"O Israel, I will not forget you."* —ISAIAH 44:21 (NIV)

For many years my wife Shirley has jotted down the birthdays and anniversaries of new friends and sent them cards every year when their special days roll around. Over time her list has grown into the hundreds, and she's on a first-name basis with most of the card sellers for miles around. I joke that I need to buy stock in the companies that print the greetings.

Shirley includes annotations with her cards and keeps track of all kinds of vital statistics. All of her notes are recorded in a tattered address book that has served her for ages. I've suggested that she could file the information on our computer, but "it's not personal enough for me," she responds. She finds something satisfying about making handwritten notes. I call it her ministry, and when I hear the gratitude of her recipients, I know it's indeed a labor of love.

I remember once talking to someone who asked if I believed in a personal God. "I certainly do," I responded. "One Who hears and answers prayers."

"That must be very satisfying," she returned.

Ah, yes, something like receiving a personal greeting from a friend who never forgets.

> *We feel Your love, Lord, in answered prayer,*
> *Blessed assurance that You really care.*
> —FRED BAUER

Sat 20   *"You're blessed when you feel you've lost what is most dear to you. Only then can you be embraced by the One most dear to you."* —MATTHEW 5:4 (MSG)

During my senior year in high school, our basketball team had never lost. Everyone thought we were headed to the Oklahoma State Championship.

During the district tournament we were to play a team from a little town. The first time we played them, only one of their players had even scored, so we weren't worried. But the month before the districts, that team had seen Arizona play using a two-handed jump shot. They practiced it for weeks and beat us by one point in overtime.

Muskogee High School, another team in our district, went to the finals. We had beaten them twice. I hitchhiked with a buddy to see the championship game in Oklahoma City.

During the game I kept explaining to my friend in a too-loud voice that we'd beaten that team twice during the regular season and I was just sick that we weren't there. A man sitting behind me finally got tired of my whining and said, "Then why aren't you out there playing instead of those guys if you're better than they are?"

I turned around and said, "Mister, don't you know what somebody sounds like when their heart's broken?" Then I turned around and watched Norman beat Muskogee about as bad as we did.

I try to be a little more sensitive now when I hear somebody bragging or showing off, because inside that obnoxious person there may be a broken heart.

Lord, thank You for the lessons You teach me through the pain and disappointments that I try so hard to avoid.
—KEITH MILLER

Sun 21

*Abraham planted a tamarisk tree in Beersheba, and
there he called upon the name of the Lord. . . .*
—GENESIS 21:33 (NIV)

Several weeks before my second mission trip to Honduras, I was wondering how to overcome the problem of fitting in personal prayer time, which I'd had on my previous trip. When you're staying in a room with six other women, there's always something interesting to talk about!

My Bible was open to Genesis, and I came to the verse above. Back in the days of communal living when there weren't any private rooms or quiet chapels, Abraham found a tree. I could too.

On our first morning at the ranch in Honduras, I saw two incredibly large trees. Long grassy moss hung down from limbs covered with bromeliads. What an amazing personal prayer chapel, built by the Creator's own hands, complete with hanging gardens!

On the last morning I snapped a photo of the trees. Back home I downloaded the photo onto my computer as a screen saver. After all, even at a computer desk, all of us need our own prayer chapel where we can go to cry out to the Lord in the middle of a crowded life.

*Dear Creator, help me plant and plan places all over my world where
I can slip away and meet You in prayer.* —KAREN BARBER

READER'S ROOM

I needed to drop off a prescription at the drugstore. As we pulled into the parking lot, a brown van had to go around—with much aggravation—to get to the front door of the store. As I exited the car with my prescription, the wind pulled the paper right out of my hand. I took off across the parking lot, chasing it, but each time I got near it, it blew away again. I walked back to the front of the store, and as I stood there looking around, the brown van pulled up in front of me and one of the people inside rolled down a window and, much to my surprise, handed me my prescription!

—*Rebecca McAlindon, Parma, Ohio*

❈ THE GIFT OF SIGHT

Mon 22   *The eyes of the Lord are in every place. . . .*
—PROVERBS 15:3

AGING EYES

During a routine eye exam three years ago, Dr. Bode noted that my right eye had the beginnings of macular degeneration. Two of my aunts and my mother-in-law had lost their sight from macular degeneration. Edna, who had been an avid reader, could no longer see print on the page, nor could she do the needlework she loved or even watch TV. Aunt Connie was both deaf and blind during her last illness, isolated from those around her. Then there was Aunt Alta, who said, as she was dying, "Oh! He is so beautiful!" Aunt Alta was totally blind at the time.

Now I have the beginnings of this incurable disease. My left eye was still clear, but the doctor said macular degeneration usually starts in one eye and then moves to the other. The diagnosis meant that, if I lived long enough, I would eventually lose the sight of both eyes. *I will be blind!* I could hardly let the thought in.

Then one evening an idea came to me during my silent prayer time: I couldn't know how much time I had left to see, but with God's grace I could use my eyes to gather and savor as much beauty as I could while I could. I couldn't take a camera with me into blindness, but I could "breathe in" images of beauty and light to carry with me, if the path should become dark before I reached home.

> *O Holy One, lead me into paths of beauty while I see, and*
> *I will trust Your perfect vision to lead me safely home.*
> —MARILYN MORGAN KING

Tue 23   O Lord my God, I cried to thee for help, and thou
hast healed me. —Psalm 30:2 (RSV)

It was around 6:00 PM when our phone rang. "Is this Mrs. Harrah?" a man's voice asked. When I said *yes*, he said, "I work at Defined Fitness Gym. Your husband is on his way to Presbyterian Hospital. He collapsed a while ago and asked me to call an ambulance and then to call you. His right leg has turned numb and he thinks a blood clot is cutting off the circulation."

My heart froze. Larry had recently had abdominal surgery, and the surgeon had warned him to get to the hospital as soon as possible if either leg turned numb. I phoned our daughter, who came at once to drive me to the hospital. When we got there, Larry was already being wheeled into surgery. Soon our son arrived too. The three of us prayed for God to guide the surgeon's hands.

Larry came out of the surgery okay, and I felt grateful that our family has medical coverage and access to good doctors. But the next day I got to wondering: *What about the homeless here in New Mexico who have no health care, no insurance, no medicine, no access to trained doctors or nurses?* I felt the need to help, but what could I do?

I made several phone calls and learned there is an organization here in Albuquerque called Health Care for the Homeless. They have doctors, nurses, dentists and psychiatrists who offer care to people with little or no money. The clinic has several sources of funding, but it also accepts donations of money and supplies. Since then I've sent a donation every month, and I pray for that clinic each day.

*Dear Lord, thank You for all health-care workers who tend to the
homeless. Hold them and their patients in Your healing care.*
—Madge Harrah

Wed 24   *I have called daily upon thee, I have stretched out my hands unto thee.* —PSALM 88:9

There's always some know-it-all at the gym who will be a spoilsport no matter what. Just the other day I was on the floor, going through a series of stretches, working out the kinks in my back, thighs, calves and hamstrings, and, of course, Mr. Know-It-All walked by and said, "You know, I read a study that showed stretching doesn't prevent injuries when you work out."

"I hadn't heard that," I said, grunting as I reached for my toes.

When I got to the office, I logged on to the Internet and couldn't find the study that showed the uselessness of stretching; on the contrary I found plenty of articles that talked about its value. I could add to them. Stretching just makes me feel better: My body is more relaxed; my back doesn't ache; I feel more limber.

All day his comment irritated me; it was as though someone had told me, "Don't bother to pray. It doesn't do anything for you." I could point to countless studies that argued that point vociferously, but I don't pray because researchers tell me it's beneficial or effective. I pray because it's part of my life—my mind stretching to reach God, my heart bending toward Him. I can even do it while I'm stretching at the gym.

"Still at it?" Mr. Know-It-All asked me a couple days later at the gym.

"You should try it," I said with my arms over my head. "Stretching makes you feel good."

I reach out for You, Lord, as You reach out for me.
—RICK HAMLIN

Thu 25

*So, as those who have been chosen of God, holy and
beloved, put on a heart of compassion. . . .*
—COLOSSIANS 3:12 (NAS)

I drive a fifteen-year-old car I named Gubby because its license plate has the letters *GUB*. One day Gubby and I got in a minor scrape with a semitrailer at a stoplight. My car ended up with a crunched driver's door and a disabled side-view mirror.

My helpful husband pounded out the door so that it opened and closed—somewhat arthritically, but then Gubby isn't exactly hot off the assembly line. I didn't mind driving with a creased door minus a little paint; I did mind the replacement mirror my husband installed.

Attached to a metal rod and mounted in blaring chrome high up on my bent doorframe, the new mirror looked like a menacing alien insect. On the road, I thought I was so conspicuous that everyone gawked at the lady with the weird mirror. My fears were confirmed when my neighbor, honking and waving on the Interstate, shouted, "I knew it was you because I saw the mirror!"

To my great relief my husband eventually found an undamaged door with an intact mirror at a salvage yard. Gubby, however, had proved to be an apt teacher. My experience with being conspicuous made me more sensitive to the ways people see themselves as undesirably noticeable—from a physical feature or limitation, to a personality quirk, to the behavior of family members. The list is long and painful.

Thanks to God and Gubby, when I look in my side-view mirror these days, I see a more merciful me.

Lord, no one wants to be singled out in an awkward way.
Today, show me how I can ease the discomfort of others.
—CAROL KNAPP

Fri 26 *For with God nothing shall be impossible.* —LUKE 1:37

I was thrilled when the University of Kansas team made it to the 2008 NCAA basketball championship game. But with 2:12 left in the fourth quarter, the Jayhawks trailed the Memphis Tigers 60–51. I gave up hope, but the Jayhawks continued to battle. With 2.1 seconds left in regulation, Mario Chalmers hit a three-point shot to tie the score. Inspired, the Jayhawks won, 75–68, in overtime. For fans like me, it was a miracle.

A little more than a month later, my husband Don and I were attending our church's worldwide quadrennial meeting in Fort Worth, Texas. When someone held up a basketball to make a point, Kansas Bishop Scott Jones got an idea. He collected $420 in pledges from our delegation members and publically challenged delegations from Memphis, North Carolina and California-Pacific (teams the Jayhawks had defeated on their way to the championship) to make higher bids. Funds raised would go to "Nothing But Nets," a project that raises money for mosquito nets to protect children in Africa from malaria.

Those conferences raised the bidding, and others joined the action. Bill Gates Sr. announced that the Bill and Melinda Gates Foundation would match the highest bid. After six days of spirited bidding, the West Ohio Conference won the auction with a bid of $80,000. The losers all paid too! The final total was $428,030, more than a thousand times the original pledge and enough to save the lives of nearly fifty thousand children.

Lord, You fed the multitudes, healed the sick and rose from the dead that we might know the awesome power of possibility.
—PENNEY SCHWAB

📖 ENCOUNTERING JESUS

Sat 27

Mary then took a pound of very costly perfume of pure nard, and anointed the feet of Jesus and wiped His feet with her hair; and the house was filled with the fragrance of the perfume. —JOHN 12:3 (NAS)

SATURDAY BEFORE PALM SUNDAY:
MARY OF BETHANY

This is the Mary who sat and listened to Jesus while her sister Martha got things ready for dinner; the Mary who cried in anguish when Jesus arrived too late to save her brother Lazarus. But the power of what Jesus did next—bring Lazarus back to life—changed Mary of Bethany forever.

For several days Jesus has been talking about His coming death, and no one seems to be listening or understanding. But Mary understands, and so she anoints him for burial while everyone else expects Him to set up an earthly kingdom. Yet—and here is the magnificent thing—she does the anointing while Jesus is alive, the first to believe that the grave would never hold Him.

All of us need a Mary of Bethany in our lives, someone who believes our darkest hour is not our last. My Mary's name is Joy—friend, wife and mother of our sons. She didn't believe the doctors who said that I'd never survive the injuries I'd suffered in an accident. Day after day she sat at my bedside, bringing me the healing presence of Jesus through her unshakable faith. One wedding, thirty-five years, three sons and one granddaughter later, her believing for the impossible continues to amaze me.

> *Lord, thank You for the people in my life who believe*
> *even when I can't.* —ERIC FELLMAN

❧ ENCOUNTERING JESUS

Sun 28

But when the chief priests and the scribes saw the wonderful things that He had done, and the children who were shouting in the temple, "Hosanna to the Son of David," they became indignant and said to Him, "Do You hear what these children are saying?"... —MATTHEW 21:15–16 (NAS)

PALM SUNDAY: THE CHEERING CHILDREN

After years of walking the dusty roads of Palestine, Jesus decides to take a donkey ride. The crowd opens, coats are spread on the ground to make a carpet, the children chant and the religious leaders rant. Quoting a verse from Psalm 8, Jesus tells the leaders that the children are doing exactly what God planned for them.

These are likely the same children whom the disciples tried to turn away on the road a few days earlier. But Jesus gathered them to Himself, and now they have come with their parents to the festival in Jerusalem and, seeing Jesus again, they can't contain their joy.

My nephew Richard is a master sergeant in the US Army. When he was assigned to a war zone, where bombs could fall or bullets fly at any moment, he noticed that every time there was a lull in the action, children popped out of their hiding places and began kicking around a soccer ball or chasing one another in a game of tag. All the military might of a great power and a cruel despot could not extinguish the children's joy.

It was the same with the children of Jesus' day. The angry religious bureaucrats were just leg-filled robes whom they had to dash around on the way to see Jesus. Why? Because they trusted Him, believed in Him, and not even the Cross the authorities were planning could keep them from proclaiming His kingdom.

> *Lord, give me the childlike faith to look to You even when all those around me are fearful and angry.* —ERIC FELLMAN

❊ ENCOUNTERING JESUS

Mon 29

Now there were some Greeks among those who were going up to worship at the feast; these then came to Philip, who was from Bethsaida of Galilee, and began to ask him, saying, "Sir, we wish to see Jesus."
—JOHN 12:20–21 (NAS)

MONDAY OF HOLY WEEK: THE GREEKS

The feast of the Passover was the biggest event in the Jewish calendar of Jesus' day. Even non-Jewish "God Fearers" who followed the teachings of Moses traveled to Jerusalem for the celebrations. So these Greeks, in town for a holiday, have heard rumors about the Messiah and come to see for themselves. The ministry executives (Philip and Andrew) huddle to consider the request and take the usual executive action: They bump it up the organizational chart to the Master. Jesus' response is almost a series of riddles: seeds dying, losing your life to find it, serving by following. But, because they are truly seeking Him, He promises them, "My father will honor the one who serves me" (John 12:26, NIV).

Years ago I visited a famous church in Scotland where John Wesley and Charles Spurgeon had preached. I climbed into the pulpit so that I could look out and imagine speaking, like those towering figures, to a full and attentive congregation held spellbound by my oratory. Then my eye was caught by a small brass plate set into the pulpit desk. On it were these words: "Sir, we wish to see Jesus." More than two thousand years after these Greeks made their first request to the disciples, people are still looking for the same thing from those claiming to have something to say about faith.

> *Lord, let my life show You to someone today.*
> —ERIC FELLMAN

✺ ENCOUNTERING JESUS

Tue 30

And when Jesus saw that he answered wisely, he said to him, "You are not far from the kingdom of God"....
—MARK 12:34 (RSV)

TUESDAY OF HOLY WEEK: THE SEEKING PHARISEE

Today a group of Pharisees come to Jesus with a series of trick questions, and Jesus amazes them with His answers. But one question seems to come from the heart of a seeker. Seeing how wise Jesus is, a Pharisee asks Him, "Teacher, which is the greatest commandment in the Law?" (Matthew 22:36, NIV).

Jesus answers, "Love the Lord your God with all your heart and with all your soul and with all your mind.... Love your neighbor as yourself" (Matthew 22:37, 39, NIV).

We will never know for sure, but I believe this man was among those who Acts 6:7 tells us "believed and obeyed" Jesus' teaching after the Resurrection.

When traveling in India recently, I met a man from a remote region closed to influence from the outside world. He had been a passionate follower of Jesus since his teens. I asked him how that could have happened.

"My father was a fisherman," he told me, "and often we would go out on the water and come back with empty nets. Then he would tell me, 'We will look elsewhere. The fish are there. We just need to find them.' When I told my father I wanted to find God, instead of telling me what tradition to follow, he gave me the same instruction: 'Keep seeking.' One day an older friend who had gone to the city gave me a copy of the Gospel of John, and when I read Jesus' statement, 'I am the way, the truth, and the life' [John 14:6], I had the answer I needed. I have been following Him ever since."

Lord, let me find You in the confusion of my life today. —ERIC FELLMAN

✦ ENCOUNTERING JESUS

Wed 31   *And he called his disciples to him and said to them, "Truly, I say to you, this poor widow has put in more than all those who are contributing to the offering box. For they all contributed out of their abundance, but she out of her poverty has put in everything she had, all she had to live on."*
—MARK 12:43–44 (RSV)

WEDNESDAY OF HOLY WEEK: THE GIVING WIDOW

In the middle of one of the grandest, most expensive structures of the day, surrounded by wealthy people who move by without seeing her, an unnamed woman expresses her devotion to God in the most practical way: She gives all she has to honor Him. Her gift is for the support of the temple, and it's likely her few pennies won't even pay for a worker to polish one of the temple's sets of gold candlesticks. But that doesn't matter; she is giving to God.

A friend of mine named George worked for many years to build up a large real estate practice with many branch offices. One day a group of investors came to him with a proposal to buy his business. They offered an incredible amount of money, and George accepted it. On the day he received the funds, he rushed to his bank to open a new checking account. He wanted the name on the account to be "God's Account," and the banker balked at the idea. "Who'll sign the checks?" he asked. "Oh," George replied, "it's all God's money, but He's let me be the custodian, so I'll write the checks on His behalf to whomever He tells me."

George, now in his eighties, is one of the happiest people I know, despite a bout with cancer. His joy doesn't come from earthly things, but from the commitment he made long ago to dedicate his life and his possessions to the Lord.

Lord, let me give to You out of my substance—be it much or little—with an eye for the needs all around me. —ERIC FELLMAN

THE GIFTS I'VE BEEN GIVEN

1 _____

2 _____

3 _____

4 _____

5 _____

6 _____

7 _____

8 _____

9 _____

10 _____

11 _____

12 _____

13 _____

14 _____

15 _____

March

16 _____

17 _____

18 _____

19 _____

20 _____

21 _____

22 _____

23 _____

24 _____

25 _____

26 _____

27 _____

28 _____

29 _____

30 _____

31 _____

April

*For God so loved the
world, that he gave his
only begotten Son, that
whosoever believeth in
him should not perish, but
have everlasting life.*

—John 3:16

❧ ENCOUNTERING JESUS

Thu 1   *"If I then, the Lord and the Teacher, washed your feet, you also ought to wash one another's feet." —*JOHN 13:14 (NAS)

MAUNDY THURSDAY: JESUS THE SERVANT

The night of Jesus' arrest and trial looms large in the Gospel record. It begins with the Last Supper, goes through His agony and arrest in the Garden of Gethsemane, to the religious court, and then to the civil courts and sentence of death. The event that moves me most, however, is when, right after the Last Supper, with an argument among the disciples about who would be greatest still ringing in the air, Jesus takes off His outer garment, assumes a servant's role and washes their feet. Then He gently rebukes them, telling them that they should do for one another what He has done for them.

Shortly after the end of the first Gulf War, Gen. Colin Powell was at a large gathering where he was to be honored for teaching his troops the values that had produced a successful military campaign. Also on the program was Dr. Norman Vincent Peale, then in his nineties, with whom I was traveling. With his keen eye for detail, General Powell noticed that one of Dr. Peale's shoes had become untied. Without a word, he stepped forward, knelt down and tied the errant lace. Dr. Peale was flustered for a moment, but General Powell eased his embarrassment with a joke. One of the general's aides leaned over to me and whispered, "Now you know why he wins battles. We'd all go through the fire for a man like that."

Lord, help me to follow Your example and serve someone today.
*—*ERIC FELLMAN

❧ ENCOUNTERING JESUS

Fri 2   *When Jesus then saw His mother, and the disciple whom He loved standing nearby, He said to His mother, "Woman, behold, your son!"* —JOHN 19:26 (NAS)

GOOD FRIDAY: MARY THE MOTHER OF JESUS

We can hardly imagine what Mary is thinking and feeling today when her son—naked, beaten, bleeding and crowned with thorns—looks down from the Cross and tells His best friend to take care of her. Perhaps Jesus knows that after His Resurrection He will return to His Father, and He wants these two to have each other's comfort and support.

A US Army officer friend of mine was stationed for a while in Pakistan. While he was there, he met a believer in Jesus, who risked his life daily to share the good news. They became friends, and one day the officer solemnly promised to care for his friend's family should anything happen to him.

Not long after, there was a wedding at which the Pakistani's grandfather presided. During the ceremony the elders of each family signed the marriage contract. My friend was stunned to be asked to be one of the signers. Later he discovered that by Pakistani tradition, his promise to care for his friend's family had given him the status of an elder brother.

Through the blood Jesus sheds today on the Cross, He makes us all children of God, brothers and sisters in the family of faith, responsible for each other.

Lord Jesus, even on this day of suffering You give me an example of how I should love and care for my brothers and sisters. —ERIC FELLMAN

EDITOR'S NOTE: *We invite you to join us today as we observe our annual Good Friday Day of Prayer. Guideposts Prayer Ministry prays daily for each of the prayer requests we receive by name and need. Join us at OurPrayer.org and learn how you can request prayer, volunteer to pray for others or contribute to support our ministry.*

❧ ENCOUNTERING JESUS

Sat 3   *Nicodemus also, who had at first come to [Jesus] by night, came bringing a mixture of myrrh and aloes, about a hundred pounds' weight.* —JOHN 19:39 (RSV)

HOLY SATURDAY: NICODEMUS

On the evening of the day Jesus died, just before sundown turns Friday into the Sabbath, two members of the Sanhedrin come boldly before Pilate and ask for Jesus' body. One of them is Nicodemus, the thoughtful scholar who came to Jesus secretly and asked about His teachings. Later, Nicodemus spoke up in defense of Jesus but backed down before the determination of his fellow Pharisees.

But now, after he has witnessed the Crucifixion, Nicodemus comes forward, not questioning but worshipping, intending to give Jesus the honor and respect he has previously withheld. This is a newborn Nicodemus, not perfectly understanding, but completely committed.

Not long ago I met a modern-day Nicodemus, a high official in the Indian Bureau of Investigation who came to talk to me about helping to make the Scriptures available in a region of India where Bibles are often burned. When I asked him why he had come, he handed me a DVD and motioned for me to play it on my computer.

The images were shocking: mobs of angry people beating others and burning Bibles in the street and even in some nearby houses. Pointing to one badly bleeding man on the screen, my guest said, "Later that day he died, not cursing, but praying for the forgiveness of his tormentors. If that is what the Bible teaches, we need it."

> *Lord, let Your new life be born in me today so that Your light*
> *can shine through me and illuminate the path for others.*
> —ERIC FELLMAN

✸ ENCOUNTERING JESUS

Sun 4   She said to Him, "Sir, if you have carried Him away, tell me where you have laid Him, and I will take Him away." Jesus said to her, "Mary!" . . . —JOHN 20:15–16 (NAS)

EASTER: MARY MAGDALENE

According to John's account, Mary Magdalene comes to Jesus' tomb early on Sunday morning and finds the stone that had covered its entrance rolled aside. She runs to tell the disciples that the body has been taken away.

Peter and John examine the empty tomb and go away to digest what has happened, but Mary lingers, weeping. She loves Jesus so much, her heart is so broken, that even when she goes into the tomb and sees the angels, she can only imagine that someone has stolen the body.

When Jesus appears before her, she mistakes Him for the gardener. Then He speaks one word—"Mary"—and she knows.

Not long ago I attended a choral performance by a group of Ugandan orphans, victims of the Lord's Resistance Army that kidnaps children and forces them to become soldiers. One brainwashing technique these men use is to tell them over and over that they are forgotten and no longer have a name. Once the children are rescued by brave volunteers, houseparents begin teaching them about the love of Jesus. The first song they learn and the first song they sing at every concert is "He Knows My Name." Leaping and dancing, the children sing that line repeatedly, their joy spreading through the entire crowd.

Christ is risen—and He knows our names!

> *Thank You, Lord Jesus, for speaking my name clearly*
> *in the deepest places of my heart.*
> —ERIC FELLMAN

April

Mon 5

"I am with you and will watch over you wherever you go. . . ."
—Genesis 28:15 (NIV)

Lively cafes in Barcelona, savory *tapas* of spicy meat and roasted vegetables, pounding flamenco music, quiet chapels flickering with candlelight—I was on my first trip to Spain with a group of friends, and the new sights and sounds were mesmerizing. And the highlight of our trip was yet to come. At the little town of Santo Domingo de la Calzada, our bus would stop in the countryside and our group would walk on the *Camino de Santiago de Compostela,* a route across northern Spain used by pilgrims since the Middle Ages.

The entire pilgrimage route is nearly five hundred miles long and would take three to four weeks, but our group would spend only an afternoon on the legendary path. My traveling companions talked eagerly about what a spiritual experience this would be. I was still feeling jet-lagged and tired from our previous days of sightseeing and exploring. "How far will we walk?" I asked uneasily.

"Oh, about four miles," our leader said cheerfully.

The day was blustery and cold. Our bus pulled to the side of the road, and my friends pulled on sweaters and rain parkas and began to disembark. I did a quick spiritual reality check. Yes, I'd often prayed for strength to do things I didn't feel like doing. Often what I'd dreaded ended up being enjoyable. But then there were other times . . .

"I don't think I'll join you," I told our leader. I waved at my comrades as they strode away, took the bus back to town, had lunch and visited a church. Several hours later my friends wandered into the hotel, damp and footsore and ecstatic that they'd done it. When I began to say, "Maybe I should have gone," my friend Lalor waved her hand. "It's all good," she said. "Whatever you decided to do, it's all good."

And the true peace of pilgrimage settled on my heart.

Help me to remember, God, that when I travel with You in my heart,
I'm always on pilgrimage. —Mary Ann O'Roark

Tue 6

Moses did not know that the skin of his face shone. . . .
—EXODUS 34:29 (NKJV)

I've had a bad case of the humbles recently, wondering if my life has really mattered to anyone. It seems rather beige to me.

One day I was reading about Moses and I pondered, *Did Moses know that he was Moses? Or did he see himself as the chump who got stuck taking care of two million former slaves in the desert?*

Did he know that from that horde of slaves would come Solomon, David, Isaiah, Paul and Jesus?

Did he know that three thousand years later mothers the world over would be reading to their children the story of baby Moses in the basket on the river?

Did he know that today you can buy Moses and Zipporah dolls in Bible bookstores or that you can rent one of several versions of *The Ten Commandments*, from DeMille's classic to the animated *Prince of Egypt?*

Probably not. He was too busy settling disputes and looking for freshwater to have time for thoughts of his legacy.

I'm no Moses, and no one is going to make a movie of my life. But if someday my grandson says, "See all these big oak trees? My grandpa planted them and he let me help him. I loved my grandpa." Well, that's all it would take to make my face glow!

Father, help me to forget about my legacy and to concentrate on loving the family and friends You have given me.
—DANIEL SCHANTZ

April

Wed 7

When times are good, be happy; but when times are bad, consider: God has made the one as well as the other . . . .
—ECCLESIASTES 7:14 (NIV)

"What helps you most when you feel sad?" I asked a friend as we sat outside a coffee shop, enjoying the first nice day of spring and catching up with each other. Like me, she'd faced some challenges in the last year.

She fiddled with her napkin for a moment and then answered, "A friend who listens and doesn't try to rush me into 'happy.'"

I smiled at her choice of words.

"Sometimes I just need to talk about my feelings," she continued, "so I want someone to listen without trying to resolve my problem or fix me—someone who will simply sit with me in my sadness for a little while."

We fell silent for a moment and then she asked me the same question.

"What helps me most is remembering that I don't have to be afraid of feeling sad," I said. "I think of sadness as a place I go through on my way to somewhere else. It's like a dark hallway I'm passing through. And I know that God has something for me to discover in that place, so I try to explore the possibilities, like greater trust or quiet rest or the surprising way I can feel both glad and sad at the same time."

"Or that being in that place makes you a better friend to someone else who's passing through it," she added.

Lord, maybe our sadness is a gift from You, because as we pass through the darkness, we seek to see and know You better— and learn to walk alongside others going the same way.
—CAROL KUYKENDALL

❦ TWELVE KEYS TO THE GIVING LIFE

Thu 8 *Bear with each other and forgive whatever grievances you may have against one another. Forgive as the Lord forgave you.*
—COLOSSIANS 3:13 (NIV)

GIVE FORGIVINGLY

Some years ago a friend gave me the most gorgeous umbrella I had ever seen. It was made from a plastic-laminated floral chintz fabric, and it gave me such a feeling of being loved and protected that I felt the Lord nudging me to give away umbrellas myself.

Anytime I found umbrellas on sale, I snapped them up. Before long I had quite a supply in the trunk of my car and my hall closet. I designed calling cards with the words "Jesus is your shelter in the time of storm" and attached them to the umbrellas. Whenever I spotted someone running for cover or struggling with an umbrella, I gave them one of mine.

One April day our neighbor Jerry came over to see my husband on business. Jerry had treated a close relative of mine poorly, and I still harbored a grudge.

Suddenly there was a terrible downpour. Jerry stood in the shelter of the porch, waiting for it to pass. Just then, God spoke to my heart: *Give him one of your umbrellas, Roberta.*

I argued with the inner voice: *Then he'll think what he did was okay.*

Simply offer him the umbrella, Roberta, God seemed to say. *Trust Me to take care of the rest.*

With considerable hesitation I gave Jerry one of my umbrellas and learned a powerful lesson about giving: If you can't feel forgiveness in your heart for someone, find some way to give to them anyway, and as sure as April showers bring May flowers, the feeling will follow the act.

Teach my hesitant heart to forgive, Lord Jesus.
—ROBERTA MESSNER

April

Fri 9

And the earth brought forth grass, and herb yielding seed after his kind, and the tree yielding fruit, whose seed was in itself, after his kind: and God saw that it was good.
—GENESIS 1:12

This week my wife Shirley and I arrived back in Pennsylvania. I tell people in Florida that we go North early to see the daffodils—and see them I do, out our kitchen window. Their bright yellow heads dance in the cool wind, just as William Wordsworth described them in his oft-quoted poem:

> *A host, of golden daffodils;*
> *Beside the lake, beneath the trees,*
> *Fluttering and dancing in the breeze.*

Also in spring bloom is a saffron field of forsythia that we brought with us when we moved here from Princeton, New Jersey. Our former neighbor, Mrs. Vaughn, then in her eighties, loved forsythia. (She called it "for-sigh-thia.") Up and ready to open their eyes, too, is another transplant, our Virginia bluebells. What makes them special is that they were a gift from another neighbor, Mrs. Braden, who majored in botany and could call everything in her yard by its Latin name. The plants she gave us have multiplied, and we have passed some of them along.

A rain-dampened Shirley, who's been weeding around some beautiful magenta tulips, just came inside, singing, "Though April showers may come your way, they bring the flowers that bloom in May." I answer with a riff from that old hymn "Showers of Blessings." I'm still thinking of Mrs. Braden and the blessing she was. I remember her for her kindness and generosity. Those aren't bad traits to be remembered by at this time of year when nature everywhere speaks of God's bountiful handiwork.

> *Dear Lord, in all things bright and beautiful I see*
> *Your great love and creativity.*
> —FRED BAUER

Sat 10   *"When all was ready, he sent his servant around to notify the guests that it was time for them to arrive. But they all began making excuses . . . ." —*LUKE 14:17–18 (TLB)

I'm not a huge baseball fan. My friend Jack took me to a Tampa Bay Rays game shortly after I moved to Florida, but I was more interested in the live stingrays in the big tank behind center field. A few years later I agreed to go to another Rays game but only if Jack would buy me anything I wanted to eat. He agreed, poor guy.

In 2007 the Rays had more losses than any other professional team in the country. But 2008 was another matter. That year the Rays went from worst to first. They not only won first place in their division, but they beat the Boston Red Sox for the American League pennant and played in the World Series against the Philadelphia Phillies. They became the first team to reach the World Series while having the lowest payroll in the American League.

The Rays inspired me to stop making financial excuses to myself. I can't take that watercolor class because it costs too much? Well then, I'll ask about scholarships. I can't afford a bigger car? I'll just smile more when I step into my little old red car, thankful that it's still getting me where I need to go. I can't take that expensive vacation like some of my friends? I'll treasure the opportunities to travel with family and friends who have access to "friend passes." I can't afford to eat out as much as I'd like? I'll cut more coupons and pay attention to the buy-one-get-one-free meals that my friends and I can enjoy together.

You don't need lots of money to be a winner. The Rays proved it.

Lord, help me to find the many creative ways there are to enjoy all of the blessings and gifts You've provided.
—PATRICIA LORENZ

☀ MEETING SUNRISE

Sun 11   *"But the Lord will be a refuge for his people . . . ."*
—JOEL 3:16 (NIV)

THE COURAGE TO HOPE

Saturday, 1:30 AM: I fumbled my key into the back door lock and lugged my suitcase inside. Heartbroken, I'd just flown in from a weeklong trip; Tessa, my seven-year-old German shepherd, had died unexpectedly while I was gone. I hadn't even had a chance to say good-bye. Tears streamed down my face as I walked through the house, past the empty dog bed, the bone in the living room and the dog bowls in the kitchen.

I threw myself into bed and slept. I woke at first daylight, rolled over and reached down to pet Tessa. Nothing. *Lord, it's too empty around here.*

The dawn light streaming in the window shone on my prayer chair, an antique oak-and-leather rocker. I snuggled into it and forced myself to sing along with a praise-and-worship album. Watching the sun rise over the mountains, I knew the best thing I could do would be to get a new dog. I wanted a golden retriever, and it might take six months to find a pup.

My thoughts drifted to Jim, a long-distance friend I hadn't seen in years. He had a male golden retriever. I had a strange feeling that I ought to call him, just to see if he knew of any kennels. Jim was surprised to hear from me. When I asked about kennels, he burst out laughing. "Rebecca, I've got puppies that'll be ready to go in ten days."

Maybe, just maybe, Lord, one of those puppies is mine.

> *Lord, thank You for a sunrise of hope in my darkest hours.*
> —REBECCA ONDOV

Mon 12 For by grace are ye saved through faith; and that not
of yourselves: it is the gift of God: Not of works, lest
any man should boast. —EPHESIANS 2:8–9

On one particularly brutal day I fell desperately behind at work and
found myself swimming in a sea of paper. I sat back and thought,
I can't do this. I. Cannot. Do. This.

Just then I received an e-mail from Maggie, my coauthor on several
articles about Fred Rogers of *Mister Rogers' Neighborhood*. It said: "I ran
across this quote from one of Fred's speeches and I thought of you—

"It's important to give up—maybe daily—the old longing to be
perfect.... Of course, I think we want it so strongly because we
reason that if we *are* perfect, if we do a perfect job, we will be perfectly lovable.... What a heavy burden. Thank God we don't have
to earn every bit of love that comes our way."

I have too much machismo to admit I wept. I don't know what touched
me more, the quote itself or Maggie's kindness in sending it to me just
when I needed to hear it. I thought about how I've struggled to be the
perfect worker, the perfect husband, the perfect father.... How arrogant
of me, thinking such things were possible, then feeling sorry for myself
for falling short of the unreachable. What a heavy burden. Thank God I
don't have to earn every bit of love that comes my way.

Thank You, Lord, for Your grace, freely given.
Now please help me get this stuff off of my desk.
—MARK COLLINS

Tue 13

"I have refined you, though not as silver; I have tested you in the furnace of affliction." —ISAIAH 48:10 (NIV)

My cat had a hacking cough; I thought it was a hairball. Two hundred and thirty-eight dollars later, I learned it was a respiratory infection. "You'll want liquid antibiotics, right?" my veterinarian asked me. "Even though they cost more."

My empty checking account leered at me. "No, I'll give Prince a pill."

He lifted one eyebrow. "Twice a day for two weeks? You can't miss a day."

"I can do it," I said.

I switched from praying nightly for my cat to recover to praying that I would live through the two weeks. I put a tablet in with his food; he ate around it. I crushed one and mixed it with liver (his favorite); he left the liver so long it developed a crust. I wrapped a towel around him; he clawed it to shreds and poked me with his tooth.

When I finally got the medicine down his throat, I cried, "Yes!" and let him go—only to find the tiny white pill lying in the corner of the room. He knocked over the TV table, he pulled down a blue curtain; I was so covered with scratches that I looked like I'd fallen on a cactus. And I was late for work again.

"You're part of a team," my manager scolded as she wrote me up—again. "I know that you're a good employee, so getting a reprimand must be a hard pill to swallow."

"What did you just say?" I asked. That's when it all clicked. I'd just received something that would make me better.

"I'll be on time from now on," I promised.

And I was.

God, is there a change I need to make that's a "hard pill to swallow"? Let me see it as an opportunity to make myself what You think I can be.
—LINDA NEUKRUG

Wed 14 *And understand with their heart.* . . . —ACTS 28:27

I don't use a computer; my husband Gene and I don't even own one. I'm frequently subjected to the well-meaning advice of savvy friends and strangers who think I'm off my rocker. No one seems to understand that I simply prefer handwritten notes, typed letters, waiting for the mailman, the satisfying hum of my twenty-seven-year-old IBM Selectric (my cats adore it too), and doing research at the local library.

Then one glorious day I received a letter from someone named Yvonne in North Carolina. She'd read that I wasn't computer literate; she understood and wanted to encourage me. Her handwritten letter looked like the Declaration of Independence, magnificently written on Clairefontaine paper. Yvonne was about to attend a calligraphy camp in Winston-Salem, where she'd study in a Spenserian writing class.

Yvonne and I have been corresponding for years now. I had to get past comparing her masterpiece letters to mine scrawled in my terrible penmanship or hurriedly typed with misspelled words and uneven margins. She even created a framed calligraphy copy of Habakkuk 3:17–19, my favorite Scripture. It now hangs in our entrance hall, encouraging me in my stubborn determination to stick with my pen and typewriter.

Father, bless Yvonne and others who quietly encourage.
—MARION BOND WEST

READER'S ROOM

While driving to town one early March day, I focused on the rocky, barren hills that loomed on each side of the road. *Those hills sure are ugly!* I thought. A few weeks later those barren old hills were clothed from top to bottom in a magnificent array of brilliant orange poppies, purple lupine, and blue and yellow wildflowers. Now it is mid-May, and those old hills are again drab and scraggly. But I see them now as just waiting for their time of glory to arrive. —*Phoebe Barber, Canyon Lake, California*

April

Thu 15

May your unfailing love come to me, O Lord, your salvation according to your promise . . . for I trust in your word.
—PSALM 119:41–42 (NIV)

When I was a boy getting ready for school each morning, I often found my mother sitting at the kitchen table, reading her Bible. After seeing my father off to work in a Pennsylvania coal mine, she turned to the Good Book before making breakfast for her three children. I can still visualize her bowing her head over her well-worn King James Bible, eyes closed, chin resting on a half-clenched hand, probably praying for each of us.

It took twenty years from the time I left home before I gave my heart to Jesus, but when I did, the first thing I wanted to do was read the Bible. In nearly four decades since that eye-opening moment I've read God's Word from cover to cover almost every year, in more than a dozen different translations. My favorite is the New International Version, maybe because I spent a year working for the International Bible Society during the time it was producing the NIV Study Bible and I was able to contribute some thoughts for its footnotes.

And today, as I finish yet another reading of Psalm 119, I can't help but remember one of the reasons I feel so drawn to the Good Book.

Thanks, Mom.

Father, thank You for the light You give me in Your Word.
—HAROLD HOSTETLER

Fri 16 *This is the fruit of my labour. . . .* —PHILIPPIANS 1:22

During the winter I'm satisfied with tending my windowsills full of African violets and Christmas cacti that bloom their heads off in my sun-drenched apartment. In March I'm content to poke seeds into tiny plastic six-packs of earth and watch them sprout indoors. By April, however, I'm restless to dig in the earth, to plant a real garden of huge flowers and maybe a few tomatoes. Suddenly pots, even those too heavy for me to lift, just aren't enough. I need land to work—a real challenge for someone who lives in a second-story apartment.

So this spring as I strolled around our neighborhood, I felt particularly envious of a patch of tulips and daffodils here, emerging lavender there. Even the nearby Adopt-a-Spot, one of many miniature city gardens nurtured by volunteers, seemed to have been raked and weeded. A call to the Adopt-a-Spot coordinator confirmed my suspicions: All the spots had been taken. Try again next year.

As I drove my scenic route to work one bright, chilly morning, I stopped at a three-way intersection near the nursing home. I saw a woman kneeling over yet another minuscule Adopt-a-Spot. An elderly man lay on the ground next to her, propping up his head with his left hand while he weeded with his right. His walker stood a few feet away. I turned my corner and watched them in my rearview mirror as long as I could. As their figures receded, my shame grew. *He found a way to garden. Why can't you?*

Over the next few weeks I observed the diligent couple setting out bedding plants and weeding. Thanks to their example, I stopped fuming and joined the garden ministry at my church, where I now dig, plant, rake and trim on the spectacularly beautiful grounds until I work up blisters. I don't need to possess the land to enjoy tending it.

Lord, keep me mindful that caring for Your creation keeps me close to You.
—GAIL THORELL SCHILLING

April

Sat 17

The blessing of the Lord was upon all that he had in the house, and in the field. —GENESIS 39:5

Not long ago my wife Carol and I were visiting twenty-one-year-old William at his college for Parents Weekend. "Have you seen Guitar Hero?" he said. No, we hadn't . . . and I wasn't sure whether it was a movie, TV show or computer game.

"It's a computer game, Dad," Will said. "Here, try it." He logged on to his laptop and handed me a fake plastic guitar.

"What am I supposed to do with this?"

"You play it," he said. "Just follow the directions on the computer."

I slung the guitar over my shoulder and, staring at the screen, attempted to follow an obstacle course of signals as I played "Sunshine of My Love"—an easy one, my son assured me. It took all my concentration to change chords and strum at the right times, bouncing on the balls of my feet.

A couple of weeks later, Timothy, our younger son, exclaimed, "Dad, did you know you're on Will's Facebook page?" There I was, a skinny, gray-haired wannabe rock star, biting his lip and bouncing out of his sneakers.

"My dad, Guitar Hero," Will had written.

To honor your father and mother can take many different forms these days. Being called a hero—even teasingly—on Facebook is fine by me.

Lord, give me the courage to try the unfamiliar.
—RICK HAMLIN

🌿 GIFTS FROM ABOVE

Sun 18

And Jesus, moved with compassion, put forth his hand, and touched him, and saith unto him, I will; be thou clean. —MARK 1:41

A GIFT OF TOUCH

Dot, in her early nineties, was famous around our church for speaking her mind. I could tell she had news as she dashed up to greet me at the coffee table after church one Sunday.

"I was in the bank this week, Pam, and your son Brock left his office and came out to see me. He was so tall and handsome. And he put his arms around me and hugged me! You have no idea how good it feels to be hugged by a man in a starched white shirt when you've lived alone for thirty years."

Dot's words reminded me how encouraging and comforting touch can be. I've always found it to be a great antidote to weariness or feeling alone. Once, when I was a girl, I lay semiconscious with a 106-degree fever. All these years later, I can still feel the cool touch of my mother's hand on my face.

As my awareness of touch grew, I found myself extending my hand to others. "Hope something good happens to you today," I said as I touched the hand of the harried employee at the department store returns counter. Visiting a sick friend in the hospital, I leaned close and stroked her cheek. I touched the shoulder of a man cleaning up litter in the park and thanked him for his fine work. I patted the back of the woman who asked me for a dollar in the restaurant parking lot. And every time I did, I sensed a connection that ran from my hand to the other person's heart.

Touch me with Your hand, Father, and use me to pass on Your touch to others. —PAM KIDD

Mon 19   *Your ears will hear a voice . . . saying, "This is the way; walk in it."* —ISAIAH 30:21 (NIV)

My granddaughter Isabelle Grace is learning to walk. She's done the usual things to prepare: pulled herself up, tiptoed her way around furniture, walked with her tiny hands secure in adult ones. But the other night she *did* it. She walked from her dad to her mom. Then from me to her PaPa. Again and again. We clapped and cheered every time she successfully covered the territory between us. But when we enlarged the space and tried for longer distances, she sat down and began to scoot.

When it comes to walking, Isabelle is still a bit tentative. If someone she loves is waiting with open arms, she toddles across the floor with sure-footed confidence. She feels safe heading for a familiar harbor. But if you try to launch her out into the deep water of the living room, scoot alert!

I can understand how Isabelle feels. Sometimes it's hard for me, too, to keep walking. Life's path is filled with pebbles, stones that either trip me up or find their way into my shoe. The hills are steep. And way too much of the trek has to be done in the dark. The urge to stop—to sit, hunker down, scoot—is strong. But something else is stronger: the pull of God's loving arms reaching for me, the confident voice that says, "This is the way. Walk in it!"

So like Isabelle Grace, I dust myself off and, balancing briefly to get my footing, I step out in faith. Someone Who loves me is waiting with open arms for my safe arrival. All I have to do is keep walking.

> *Thank You, Father, for setting me on my feet . . .*
> *again and again and again.*
> —MARY LOU CARNEY

Tue 20   Show me thy ways, O Lord; teach me
thy paths. —P SALM 2 5:4

O ur telephone rang early that Wednesday morning. "Oscar, you'd
better get down here quickly." It was Fred, the library custodian.
"We just put out a ton of books, and the trash men will be here shortly."
I have a ministry recycling books to a supermarket bookstall, and this was
an opportunity I couldn't miss.

I got into my car and rushed to the library. There were green trash containers, bags and boxes, overflowing with books. I filled the trunk and
jammed books into the backseat and into the passenger seat in front. For
a moment, I felt like Midas. Then worry swept over me.

Some years before, when I was conducting a book sale at the library, I
injured my back, lifting boxes of encyclopedias. I was in the hospital for
thirteen days, followed by five months of physical therapy. The therapist
warned me not to lift anything heavy again.

As I headed to the supermarket, my concern increased. My wife Ruby
wasn't well, and I was her caregiver. In addition, our son and his wife
were about to leave on a long-delayed vacation. Reinjuring my back would
be a burden for them and saddle me with an additional burden of guilt.

At the supermarket I loaded two shopping carts and headed to the
bookstall. "Lord," I whispered, "please help me."

Almost at once a tall woman, heading in the other direction, stopped
and asked, "Would you like me to help you?" I knelt as she handed me
the books one by one until the stall was filled and overflowing.

I stood up, shook her hand and noticed that she had selected an arm-
ful of books. I thought back to my prayer; perhaps an invisible hand had
brought us together to fill both of our needs.

> *Heavenly Father, there is always a way—*
> *Your way—if I listen and follow.*
> —O SCAR G REENE

April

Wed 21

But each of us was given grace according to the measure of Christ's gift. . . . for building up the body of Christ.
—EPHESIANS 4:7, 12 (NRSV)

A friend was telling me about two boys in his son's high school class a few years back who shared the exact same name but seemingly little else. One was an all-state swimmer on his way to being class valedictorian and about to choose one of the six elite universities that had offered him scholarships. The other often skipped class, refused to play sports (although he was built like a linebacker, my friend said), and likely wasn't even thinking about college. Two very different kids headed in two very different directions.

"That just doesn't seem fair to me," I said.

My friend smiled. It turns out that both ended up going to college and both are doing very well. Do you know why? Because the talented kid decided to invest some of his talents in another kid with the same name—and it all added up to two successful young men. "You're right, of course," he concluded. "Life isn't fair. But God is. That's why God gave me what I have, not just for my own use but to benefit the lives of the world around me."

That day a friend shared his wisdom with me. Today I'm passing it along to you. After all, it's only fair.

Show me, generous God, where I can use what
You've given me to benefit someone else.
—JEFF JAPINGA

❈ THE GIFT OF SIGHT

Thu 22   He will make her wilderness like Eden. . . . —ISAIAH 51:3

THE EDEN PROJECT

Shortly after deciding to collect images of beauty to memorize and savor in case I lost my sight to macular degeneration, an opportunity arose for us to take a garden tour of Cornwall in southwest England. First we visited the Eden Project, the creative idea of a young man named Tim Smith. Here is his recipe for Eden: "Take a deep, steep-sided pit, stripped of its china clay and abandoned as being 'used up.' Add 83,000 tons of soil made from recycled waste. Colonize with plants from all over the world, housed in huge geodesic domes called *biomes*." So far Tim and his group have created a rainforest biome, a Mediterranean biome and an outdoor biome.

I came away from Eden with many stunning images. As we arrived, we looked down upon a huge expanse of land dotted with gigantic glass domes. It was as though we were looking into the future!

From the rainforest I carried away mental pictures of monkeys leaping from tree to tree; a mother monkey grooming her baby; several birds with brilliant red, gold and green plumage; and a plethora of green foliage and exotic flowers. With the images also came sounds: exotic bird calls, monkey squeals, and the sudden hushing of human voices as they entered the biomes with reverence and awe.

I've been to Eden, and I'm taking home some mental photos of a very old but always new creation, a creation steeped in hope.

> *Creator God, my heart is filled with gratitude for the gift of sight.*
> *I see Your hands still at work through human hands*
> *creating and recreating our world.*
> —MARILYN MORGAN KING

Fri 23

When thou passest through the waters, I will be with thee; and through the rivers, they shall not overflow thee. . . .
—ISAIAH 43:2

I was driving through a rainstorm in upstate New York one Friday last spring, headed east on Route 23 toward my house in Great Barrington, Massachusetts. Millie, barely a year old, was curled up in the back of the Jeep in her dog bed.

There was a crack of thunder, and lightning slashed at the Berkshire Hills ahead. Then negotiating a curve beside a nearly overflowing swamp, I felt the wheels slip from under me. Foolishly, I must have hit the brakes instead of steering with the skid. We veered off the road toward the swamp, and all of a sudden we were airborne.

The Jeep rolled once, twice, bouncing crazily down an embankment, so fast and so violently that there was no time for my mind to register it. We landed wheels down in the swamp a good twenty feet from shore and in about three feet of water. Mud and ooze caked the windshield. The passenger's side roof was crushed; water sloshed over the floorboards.

Millie! I undid my seatbelt, pushed the door open and waded to the back of the Jeep. She was trembling with fear but otherwise unharmed. I popped the hatch. "Honey, you're going to have to learn to swim," I muttered, easing her out into the water and steering her toward shore, one arm under her belly. She struggled to keep her chin above the muck and paddled heroically. "Good girl!"

Cars had pulled over and people met us with blankets and looks of amazement. One woman, a total stranger, hugged me and said, "It's a miracle you survived. I saw the whole thing. There was an angel watching over you and your dog."

I was aware of very little when the Jeep flipped over. But Someone was in control.

> *I have no doubt now, God, that in my greatest need*
> *You are closer than ever.*
> —EDWARD GRINNAN

Sat 24

*All the days ordained for me were written in your book.... —*PSALM 139:16 (NIV)

Stephen bounded into my lap, grinning despite the early hour. "My, you're in a good mood this morning!" I exclaimed.

"That's because it's Annoy Elizabeth Day!" my imp replied gleefully.

With a nine-year gap between them, you wouldn't think a special day was needed. Five-year-old Stephen is as uninterested in fourteen-year-old Elizabeth's French books as Elizabeth is in action figures. Yet there are a few things that unite the two: They both like Charlie Chaplin, the Marx Brothers and Fred Astaire. And almost every night this week, Stephen has run to the girls' bedroom to listen to Elizabeth's silly stories.

Elizabeth has a remarkable gift for weaving intricate, ridiculous tales. She combines characters from books and movies, mixes up plots, and transforms them all into a hilarious story. Darth Vader might end up tap dancing with Ginger Rogers; Gollum might fall in love with the principal at Elizabeth's school; Superman might swoop in to the rescue only to find Robin Hood barring the way. The other children chip in ideas and dialogue for the characters, but mostly they howl with laughter.

Stephen enjoys the silliness and loves being part of the group. It warms my heart that my little guy and big girl are joined in this way, through a story. Stephen now understands that stories can be fluid and changing, made up of unexpected characters, sudden plot twists, and an ongoing battle between good and evil. I hope this will help him grow into his role in the bigger story of which all of us are a part. And even if it doesn't, it's allowed him to expand Annoy Elizabeth Day into Annoy Elizabeth Week. My eldest doesn't seem to mind.

Author of Life, even when the plot twists in ways I don't understand,
I love being part of Your story.
—JULIA ATTAWAY

April

Sun 25

*When the people of Israel saw it, they said to one another, "What is it?" For they did not know what it was. And Moses said to them, "It is the bread which the Lord has given you to eat." —*Exodus 16:15 (RSV)

One April I froze a little blossom, snipped from my yard, in each of the ice cubes I later slipped into water glasses as Sunday guests arrived. At dinner my friend Tatiana took a sip and then smiled quizzically. "What's this—purple?"

"A violet," I said.

English is Tatiana's third language, which might explain why she didn't remember the name of the delicate edible flower that soon floated to the bottom of her tumbler. When she tried to replicate my frozen garnish, I was the one who smiled quizzically. "I went to a florist," she reported, "and asked to buy those tiny flowers. They just didn't understand what I was looking for."

"A florist wouldn't have violets," I gently explained. "They're wildflowers. Some people say weeds. I'll give you some." I dug up a few of the shiny-leafed plants and sent them to Tatiana, clear across the city.

A few days later she called to say thank you. "I didn't know," she said. "I already have this flower in my own yard."

This morning I awoke convinced that I'm lacking a God-given "I don't know what"—a talent or mystique—that would be the perfect complement to my workaday, plod-along life. This afternoon, when I plunked a few ice cubes in a glass of tea—made with mint snipped from my yard—the Spirit reminded me of Tatiana and the delight of her unexpected discovery.

> *Lord, You have given me all I need to live an abundant life.*
> *Help me to find any unidentified resources*
> *that are right under my nose.*
> —Evelyn Bence

Mon 26

"My God, my rock, in whom I take refuge. . . ."
—II SAMUEL 22:3 (RSV)

Our cat Chi weighed only fifteen ounces and was barely six weeks old when we brought her into our home in Los Angeles. No sooner had we done so than we started getting the house ready for an eventual sale. For the first two years of Chi's life, we packed several boxes of "clutter" a week and moved them out to the garage. Books and bookcases vanished. Furniture changed location. Chi would hesitate in the doorway of a room as if she thought the floor might have changed too. We hoped she would realize we were the constant presence, even as the background shifted, but she was very nervous.

When we began showing the house, and strangers were coming in singly or in groups, Chi would have to be crated until they left. Repeated confinement was not to her liking. After a week the house sold and she was given her uninterrupted freedom again, but the packing accelerated. The moving van showed up, and the house was suddenly empty. Chi was completely flummoxed.

On the two nights we spent in motels on our drive north, she wouldn't come out of her crate. And when we reached our new home, the entire upstairs was being remodeled, so we had to move into the basement for three months. She was just getting used to that when the upstairs was done, and we moved up there. Three years after that final move, Chi finally relaxed.

I, too, am hesitant when the landscape of my life keeps changing. And just as I hoped Chi would understand that we were still there, I tell myself that there's a constant for me. I just have to recognize God's presence.

Help me not to forget that You're there, Lord,
no matter what else isn't.
—RHODA BLECKER

Tue 27   *"Having eyes, do you not see? . . ."* —MARK 8:18 (NAS)

O ne of my colleagues was getting blinding headaches. Each morning she'd be fine, but by the end of the workday she could barely tolerate the sight of her computer screen. Finally we cajoled her into going to see an eye doctor.

It turned out that her vision was horrible: Everything was blurry. "I thought," she told the ophthalmologist, "that was just the way the world looked."

The day after she got her first-ever pair of glasses, I asked her how things were looking. Her face lit up, and the words rushed out. Everything seemed magical, from the leaves on the trees ("So many!") to the words on her computer screen ("So sharp!"). Even our concrete office floor had had its dullness wiped away: The boring, old slab suddenly had, in her rejuvenated eyes, dozens of shades of gray.

In my mind that's a little like what the Bible can do for me. To see life through a biblical lens is to put on new glasses, which can refresh how I see the world around me as well as give me perspective that I didn't have before.

Lord, You're the one optometrist Who
can connect my eyes to my soul.
—JEFF CHU

Wed 28   *"So in everything, do to others what you would have them do to you. . . ."* —MATTHEW 7:12 (NIV)

I'd been on the phone with a representative of the cell phone company, trying to figure out our family's plan. He put me on hold several times but always returned with thorough answers to my questions.

"Thanks, you've been really helpful," I said as the conversation was ending.

"That's because you're nice," he said.

"You mean people aren't nice when they're asking you for help?"

"You'd be surprised," he said, and I admit I was.

A similar thing happened when I was shopping the following week for a coffeemaker. When I asked the store manager if a discount that had been advertised the week before was still available, she said, "It is for you because you've asked so nicely."

I had to wonder, *Is it such a big deal to be nice?* It reminded me of a card my mom gave me years ago, when I was entering my teens. The simple message has stuck with me: "Be kind; everyone you meet is fighting a hard battle."

Maybe the guy on the other end of the phone fought with his wife that morning, or the cashier just learned that she's being laid off. Maybe they have some of the same aches or worries that I have. By being nice to each other, we can help our days run a little more smoothly. Jesus had another way of saying it: "Do to others what you would have them do to you."

> *Heavenly Father, help me to think before I speak*
> *and then to speak with kindness.*
> —GINA BRIDGEMAN

April

Thu 29

*So teach us to number our days that we may get
a heart of wisdom.* —PSALM 90:12 (RSV)

When I was in my twenties and studying adult development in graduate school, I remember hearing someone say, "The secret to growing older is learning to make wise adjustments within the inevitability of decline." As a young man I tucked away this maxim as sage advice. But now that I'm fifty-eight, I'm discovering its truth.

I've always been a runner. I run because I enjoy it, but I've also learned to use running as a spiritual discipline and an effective way to reduce stress. Over the last few years, however, I've had to deal with chronic Achilles tendonitis. Experienced runners know how painful this is and how difficult it is to heal. In fact, when the inflammation is chronic, the only thing to do is stop running.

The thought of drastically reducing my running didn't make me happy, but I bought a bicycle designed for riding long distances on highways and country roads. At first I griped about the tight riding pants and the necessity of wearing a helmet. And I discovered that riding a bike is not as easy as stepping out of the front door and running a quick mile or two. But I've made the adjustment, and in doing so I've discovered that I love biking down country roads, drinking in the scenery and getting to know the quaint little Texas towns. And if I behave myself, I can still run at least once a week without pain.

*Father, give me the patience, flexibility and perseverance
to accept change with graciousness and courage.*
—SCOTT WALKER

Fri 30 The fruit of the Spirit is love, joy, peace, patience, kindness,
goodness, faithfulness, gentleness and self-control.
Against such things there is no law.
—GALATIANS 5:22–23 (NIV)

My husband and I both grew up in small towns. Colville,
Washington, Wayne's hometown, had the only stoplight in the
entire county when we married. Twenty-four years ago, when we moved
to Port Orchard, there was only one stoplight in town. Even now neither
of us is accustomed to dealing with a lot of traffic. We know we're spoiled,
and that's the way we like it.

When Jazmine, our oldest granddaughter, was around three years old,
I picked her up in Seattle and drove her to Port Orchard. As luck would
have it, I hit heavy traffic. For what seemed like hours we crawled at a
snail's pace toward the Tacoma Narrows Bridge. In order to keep Jazmine
entertained, I sang songs to her and made up silly stories. She chatted
away happily in her car seat, utterly content. Not so with me. My nerves
were fried.

Finally I couldn't stand it any longer. "Jazmine, just look at all these
cars," I muttered as I pressed on the horn. *What's the matter with these
people anyway? Obviously, they don't realize I have places to go and people to
see.* Normally the drive took forty minutes, and I'd already been on the
road an hour.

"Grandma," Jazmine asked from the backseat, "are we in a hurry?"

*Oh, Father, thank You for my sweet granddaughter and the reminder
of what is really important: spending time with her.*
—DEBBIE MACOMBER

THE GIFTS I'VE BEEN GIVEN

1 _____

2 _____

3 _____

4 _____

5 _____

6 _____

7 _____

8 _____

9 _____

10 _____

11 _____

12 _____

13 _____

14 _____

15 _____

16 _____

17 _____

18 _____

19 _____

20 _____

21 _____

April

22 _____

23 _____

24 _____

25 _____

26 _____

27 _____

28 _____

29 _____

30 _____

May

And I will pray the Father, and he shall give you another Comforter, that he may abide with you for ever.

—JOHN 14:16

ᚦ GIFTS FROM ABOVE

Sat 1   *Behold, now is the accepted time; behold, now is the*
day of salvation. —II CORINTHIANS 6:2

A GIFT OF READINESS

To my way of thinking, there was never a more glorious chocolate bunny than the one I received on my seventh Easter. It had long ears, a silk bowtie and toes perfect for nibbling ... but not yet!

That bunny was just too good to eat right off the bat, so I ceremoniously placed it, box and all, atop the chest in my bedroom. "When are you going to eat your bunny?" my brother would ask, having polished off his before its first sundown.

"Not yet."

"Better eat that bunny before it gets stale," my mother reminded me.

"I'm saving it."

"Old Peter's getting pretty old," Daddy said with a laugh.

"I'm waiting for the perfect time."

And then one midsummer afternoon, my mother came through the living room, holding my bunny at arm's length. "Ugh," she said, "this thing is full of worms!"

Years later, I met a lady who had a huge pantry stacked with lavish china. Yet she never invited a guest to her dining room table or drank a single cup of tea out of one of her beautiful cups.

I've saved a new dress for the "right" occasion and then found it tucked away and out of style, or put off that walk through the woods until the green of spring had faded.

Like manna from heaven, our gifts come ready to be enjoyed, to be shared, but never to be hoarded.

> *Lord, show me how You wish me to use the gifts*
> *You are giving me today.* —PAM KIDD

Sun 2

*He read from the book of the law of God daily, from the first day to the last day.... —*NEHEMIAH 8:18 (NAS)

At one point in my life, wanting to do great things for God, I decided to read through the whole Bible, from Genesis 1:1 to Revelation 22:21. Realizing I had bitten off more than I could chew, I quit. A few months later I tried again, but this time I dived in with such determination that any blessings I might have derived from my reading were consumed in my haste to keep up with the schedule. And so I went back to my old habit of reading the Bible in bits and pieces.

And then I heard a minister say, "If someone is in medical school, training to be a doctor, he or she reads the *whole* book on anatomy, not just bits and parts. If an apprentice is taking a course in mechanics, that person reads the *whole* manual, not just paragraphs here and there. The Bible is our manual for life, so we ought to read it from cover to cover, again and again."

His words challenged me, so I decided to try again. This time I read through the Bible systematically, but at my own speed, day by day, month by month, year by year, a little at a time. I've been able to note the context of the passages and jot down a daily verse on my desk calendar. Best of all, reading through the Bible over and over again has given me ample opportunity to learn more about the Author.

God, I may never do great things for You, but through Your Word,
You certainly do great things for me.
—ALMA BARKMAN

EDITOR'S NOTE: *Take a look back at "The Gifts I've Been Given" journal pages, and let us know what gifts you're grateful for this year. Send your letter to* Daily Guideposts *Reader's Room, Guideposts Books, 16 E. 34th St., New York, New York 10016. We'll share some of what you tell us in a future edition of* Daily Guideposts.

☀ MEETING SUNRISE

Mon 3   *"Serve Him with a loyal heart and with a willing mind. . . ."* —I CHRONICLES 28:9 (NKJV)

A WILLING HEART

The six-week-old golden retriever puppies wiggled at my feet, chewing on my shoelaces and tackling one another on the lawn. They were so cute, I wanted them all. *Lord,* I prayed, *help me choose the right one.*

A week before I had paid a deposit, but I couldn't decide which adorable butterball I wanted. Then I discovered a book, *The Art of Raising a Puppy,* that had a puppy test to help in making a choice. It said to separate each puppy from its siblings and mother, put it through a series of simple exercises, and match its responses to the ones listed in the book. Each response earned points, and the point total indicated a particular canine personality. To keep track of each puppy, I stuck a colored star on its head.

I scooped up Red-star, set her down a hundred yards away and called her. She ran to me with her tail up, and I checked response number three. Systematically I scored each pup. One wasn't even interested in the test, but the others had the same score, except Green-star.

When I crouched down beside her and waved a puppy-size cloth dummy in front of her face and then tossed it, she chased it and pounced. She lay down and chewed on the end, then suddenly lifted her head and looked at me as if to say, "Oh, I forgot something." She stood up, grabbed the dummy and brought it to me, setting it down in my hand. I reached down and ruffled her fur.

I didn't have to total up Green-star's score; I knew I was in love.

Lord, like the puppy You chose for me, let me have a willing heart.
—REBECCA ONDOV

Tue 4   We should make plans—counting on God to
direct us. —PROVERBS 16:9 (TLB)

I have a blue mug filled with pencils on my desk, at least two dozen of all lengths and colors. It really amazes me that when I reach for a pencil I always seem to reach for one that needs sharpening. More often than not, they all need sharpening.

Sometimes I feel like those pencils—dull-pointed sticks with a bit of lead in them. I watch too much TV, make excuses not to exercise and waste time checking my e-mail a dozen times a day. I could be—should be—experiencing more of life: visiting museums and art shows, attending plays, musicals or the ballet, making new friends, volunteering, taking a walk, meeting new people, taking a class. Doing things!

One day I decided to use my pencil holder as a reminder to get out more and enjoy the bigger things life has to offer. I taped the words "Get Out There" to the side of my pencil mug. Every time I look at the mug or reach for a pencil, it reminds me to make plans to do something outside my home.

"Get Out There" has nudged me to invite more people out for breakfast or lunch, visit the local historical village, take a walk in the botanical garden with a friend, visit the library, walk around the neighborhood more often, enjoy a festival at a church that's not my own and organize a group of people in my community who like to write.

Lord, help me to get the lead out and
sharpen my skills and interests
and to be a doer, not a sitter.
—PATRICIA LORENZ

Wed 5 But without faith it is impossible to please him: for he that
cometh to God must believe that he is, and that he is a
rewarder of them that diligently seek him.
—HEBREWS 11:6

It's been more than ten years since I was last treated for cancer—the
non-Hodgkin's lymphoma variety—third grade, fourth stage, they told
me. The third regimen of chemo, in combination with stem cells drawn
from my own good bone marrow, achieved a remission. Though many
succumb to the disease, the Lord apparently had more work for me to do.
The chemo scarred my lungs and made it more difficult to breathe, but
I thank God daily for my recovery.

At one stage I considered throwing in the towel, but my oncologist
challenged me with a maxim I'll never forget. "You can stop here, if you
choose, but to catch the brass ring you'll need to get on the merry-go-
round."

For a moment I was puzzled. Then I remembered riding on the
carousel: To get a free ride, you had to catch the brass ring as you whirled
around. I prayed about the decision and was led to go on.

When trouble like thunder shatters our soul,
We know that You, Lord, can make the broken whole.
—FRED BAUER

Thu 6

*He named it Ebenezer, saying, "Thus far has the Lord helped us." —*I SAMUEL 7:12 (NIV)

I was helping conduct a service at our church for the National Day of Prayer. I prayed out loud about different issues facing our nation and then paused for short periods of silence. During one of the silences, I heard a very faint but distinct tune, which I recognized as the hymn "Come Thou Fount of Every Blessing."

I opened my eyes to see where the melody was coming from. The pianist was sitting still in a front pew with her eyes closed. A single verse of the tune played and then stopped.

After the service I asked others if they'd heard the mysterious tune. Many said *yes*. Wondering if it had been a message from God, I opened a hymnbook and read the words. Verse 2 says, "Here I raise mine Ebenezer; Hither by thy help I'm come." It alludes to I Samuel 7:12. *Ebenezer* means "stone of help," or as Samuel said, "We've gotten this far through God's help."

Ebenezer is the perfect message for our National Day of Prayer. Despite all our problems, we've come this far by God's help, powered by the unseen legions of faithful praying folks who lift up our land to God day and night.

> *Father, we're grateful You've given us a small part in the healing,*
> *unifying work of praying for our nation and our world.*
> *Continue to bring us toward You.*
> —KAREN BARBER

Fri 7   *Now be ye not stiffnecked, as your fathers were....*
—II Chronicles 30:8

I have a shocking confession to make: I don't own a cell phone.

It's not that I'm against technology. I've been using computers for decades; I have a long-standing addiction to e-mail, love the Internet and probably spend too much time on it. I consume a lot of information digitally, and I'm convinced that I'm one small reason newspapers are in decline (I used to buy three a day). But a cell phone? No way.

This resistance to telephonic bondage drives some people crazy, including my wife Julee, who was probably the first person in North America to own a cell. Julee conducts a good deal of her life on the phone, but I prefer face-to-face or written communication. Most of all, I need a certain amount of solitude in order to think, meditate or to just turn off my brain for a while.

Okay, so I have lots of excuses. Yet perhaps the real problem is that, stubborn as I am, it's hard to reverse my stand. I've held out for so long that to capitulate now would be a humiliating surrender. Plus everyone would be calling to congratulate me on joining the twenty-first century. I keep hoping there will be some kind of backlash against cell phones, but almost everyone agrees that pretty soon you won't be able to function without one. Even now, with pay phones disappearing faster than newspapers, it's getting harder to check my landline voice mail.

Maybe it's time for me to wriggle out of the straitjacket my stubbornness has put me in and just get a cell. Yes, there will be the inevitable chorus of "It's about time, Edward!" Yes, it will probably make things more convenient in the long run. And people who care about me and depend on me will be relieved to know that I'm reachable—and can reach out—in an emergency.

As you can see, I'm thinking about it.

Lord, help me to know the difference between
taking a stand and just digging in my heels.
—Edward Grinnan

Sat 8   *"I will not leave you orphaned. . . ."* —JOHN 14:18 (MSG)

My brother Earle was killed in a plane crash when I was a boy. After my dad died, I said to my aunt, "All my life I've had this delusion that my father loved Earle more than me."

Without missing a beat, she said, "That wasn't a delusion. He really did like him a lot more. We all felt so sad for you."

I was stunned. Then I remembered Dad going off to Earle's baseball games. Earle, five years older than I, already played very well. I was too little to go, but I practiced all the time, hoping Dad would want to be with me.

One Saturday, with two mitts and a baseball, I finally got up the courage to ask, "Daddy, will you please go out and play catch with me?" Frowning, he nodded and took the mitt I offered him.

In the next five minutes I discovered a horrible thing: Dad couldn't catch a ball! He'd run track at Oklahoma University, so I assumed he was an all-around athlete. Dad was very embarrassed; I was heartbroken. I saw that Dad's interest was in Earle, not in baseball.

My dad was a fine man and taught me a lot about integrity and determination in coming back from his own failures. My need to get Dad's attention motivated me to become a tenacious competitor in sports and in life. And it left me in a place where I was able to hear God whisper, *"Keith, you have a Father now Who will never be too busy to hang out with you, teach you, encourage you when you win, console you when you lose—and love you forever. And you'll never have to be alone again."*

> *Lord, I'm very grateful for the way my loss and pain*
> *led me to a miraculous life in You.*
> —KEITH MILLER

❀ TWELVE KEYS TO THE GIVING LIFE

Sun 9   *He that hath a bountiful eye shall be blessed. . . .*
—PROVERBS 22:9

GIVE HAPPILY

It was Mother's Day, and though it had been nine years since my mother's death, it seemed like only yesterday that I'd said good-bye. I drove to a local restaurant for what I hoped would be a quick breakfast away from all the holiday hoopla. I was disappointed to find the place filled with mothers and their children.

While I waited for an open booth, I filled my mug at the self-serve coffee station. As I sipped my coffee, a small woman and a little boy entered the restaurant. "Money, Mama," the boy begged, his eye on the jukebox.

"No money for music, Jules," the woman said. "Settle down. Mama worked all night, and she's tired."

Tired didn't begin to describe her—try worn out by life. One thing was certain: No one was taking her out for Mother's Day.

The woman collapsed into the chair next to me in the waiting area. "Coffee!" she said.

An idea hit me: *Ask her how she takes her coffee and serve it to her with a smile.* I was arguing with the inner voice as I stirred two sweeteners and a creamer into the dark liquid. *What good could this possibly do? This woman's problems go way beyond a cup of coffee.*

As I served her the coffee, I gave her knuckles a little squeeze. Her face stretched into a weary smile. "I wanted some coffee all night long," she said. "Never did get around to it though."

Later, as I left the restaurant, I caught sight of the woman and her son. She was still smiling. The boy sat perched on the edge of the booth. His long slender arms reached across the table until his hands found hers.

Help me to reach out to strangers, Lord, with a happy heart.
—ROBERTA MESSNER

Mon 10

Take therefore no thought for the morrow: for the morrow shall take thought for the things of itself. . . .
—MATTHEW 6:34

On a day when I was worrying too much about money—the immensity of college tuitions occupying too much of my brain—I stepped away from the computer and picked up an old family photo album.

There was a picture of William's pirate birthday party when he was five, his classmates dressed in eye patches and bandannas, brandishing plastic swords and searching for buried treasure. There was a shot of Timothy in white with a silver halo circling his blond head, the perfect angel dressed for the Christmas pageant. There were photos of the boys in their baseball uniforms and snapshots of us at picnics in friends' backyards—that was me pushing Tim in a swing, both of us laughing so hard you could see our tonsils. My eye lingered at the one of Carol and me sitting in beach chairs, the boys splashing in the bay, neither of us with a care in the world. . . .

Until I remembered all the things I worried about that day at the beach, like how would we ever afford nursery school and would Timothy ever learn his colors and would William please get a base hit at least once. In fact, if I looked closely at the photos, I could recall worries that had plagued me at every moment—all the way back to the proud moment I first held William in my arms.

I closed the album and went back to the computer. *See,* I told myself, *you got through that just fine. You'll get through this too.*

> *Lord, I promise not to let worries for tomorrow*
> *rob me of the pleasures of this day.*
> —RICK HAMLIN

May

Tue 11 _"And God will wipe away every tear from
their eyes."_ —REVELATION 7:17 (NIV)

I've always been ashamed to cry in front of my children. Take one morning last week, for instance. I'd been accumulating a bunch of stuff worth crying about for quite a while. Then early that morning, I got up to let our dog out and stepped right into a squishy pile of poop—barefooted. A couple of hours later, my daughter Kendall stopped by and I pinched my finger in the hallway closet door. That did it—I started crying.

"What's wrong, Mom?" Kendall asked.

I quickly turned away, trying to hide my tears and avoid answering her. We both knew that I was crying about more than a pinched finger.

"It's okay to cry," she told me gently.

That's what I used to tell her when she was growing up, but somehow the message didn't fit me. Parents don't cry, especially in front of their children. I wanted to appear strong and capable; I didn't want our children to worry or feel responsible for me.

Later, when I recovered from my meltdown, Kendall and I had an adult-to-adult conversation about crying.

"I didn't see you cry very often when we were growing up," she remembered.

"So what did my lack of crying mean to you?" I asked.

She hesitated. "I guess I didn't know what made you sad."

I've been thinking about her answer for a whole week now, and her words are changing my perspective. Although I don't need to start sobbing every time I feel a little sad, I also don't need to hide my tears. Sometimes it's okay to cry.

> _Lord, You give us tears for a purpose._
> _May mine make me more honest._
> —CAROL KUYKENDALL

Wed 12   *Therefore, strengthen your feeble arms and weak knees.*
"Make level paths for your feet," so that the lame
may not be disabled, but rather healed.
—HEBREWS 12:12–13 (NIV)

Uncle Jay, my mom's older brother, does what he can to strengthen his knees, even if he can no longer straighten them. His arms are strong though—I know, because I join his predawn workouts when we visit him and his wife in Phoenix each year.

Uncle Jay invited my wife and me to a Rotary Club luncheon a couple of years ago. One of the club's projects was supplying people in Mexico with special wheelchairs, rugged vehicles made for uneven, unpaved paths. My uncle volunteered to get the signatures of the club members who were donating money for the chairs during the meeting. Uncle Jay is a big man, so to avoid disrupting the guest speaker's presentation, he knelt at each table as he collected the signatures.

My uncle knelt by placing his hands on the table, putting all his weight on his arms and lowering himself to the floor. He got up by holding on to the edge of the table and lifting himself. As he painfully went from table to table, it occurred to me that some of those wheelchairs would go to people who had knees like my uncle's.

I hope that thirty years from now, I have half the determination my uncle has. And I hope that thirty years from now, God will use me the way He continues to use Uncle Jay.

Dear God, please give me the strength of will always to do Yours.
—TIM WILLIAMS

Thu 13

For if I go not away, the Comforter will not come unto you; but if I depart, I will send him unto you.
—JOHN 16:7

My seven-year-old granddaughter Hannah gave me a big squeeze as I was about to end my visit. "It's hard to say good-bye," she said. My throat tightened. My home in the Midwest was a long way from hers on Alaska's Kenai Peninsula.

"I know about good-byes," Hannah continued. "I had a friend named Flora when we lived in Kaktovik [an Arctic island Eskimo village]. I didn't want her to leave, but she had to go away to college. After Flora left, I found out we were moving too. So then it was a fair good-bye because we both had to go."

A fair good-bye—I had never linked those words before. So many farewells seem wrenchingly unjust. Whether it's death or divorce or a move or a visit that ends, farewells create a gap that someone didn't want, and the heart cries, "Unfair!"

Jesus knew that pain of farewell, and so at His Ascension, He promised His followers, "I go to prepare a place for you. . . . I will come again, and receive you unto myself; that where I am, there ye may be also" (John 14:2–3). He emphasized, "I will not leave you comfortless" (John 14:18), speaking of the Comforter—the Holy Spirit—Who He said will "abide with you for ever" (John 14:16).

No matter where the partings are in my life, Jesus shares those empty spaces with me. His comfort is totally there . . . and totally fair.

> *Jesus, faithful Friend, through all my good-byes*
> *You are the One Who never leaves.*
> —CAROL KNAPP

Fri 14

Worship the Lord in the beauty of holiness.
—I CHRONICLES 16:29

I stepped out of our hotel early that morning, hoping for better air than we'd breathed since touching down at Bangkok's Suvarnabhumi Airport the evening before. But again the city's stench assaulted me. A swarm of three-wheeled Tuk Tuk taxis roared by, leaving blue smoke clouds behind them; a beggar's face was masked against the foul smog; a dog with runny eyes sniffed at an orange peel in the gutter.

My walk took me to the refuse-clogged Chao Phraya River. And it was there that I saw her, a tiny woman with pitted skin and shaking hands. She wore a threadbare ankle-length green dress and she was as bony as the dogs scrounging for food in every alleyway. Around her neck was a rope of tiny purple orchids so fresh and perfect that they must have been in the orchid market ten minutes earlier. As I watched, she took the lovely flowers from her neck, placed them on a small quayside altar, arranged them with great care, stepped back to judge the effect, made a few small adjustments and left.

This lady's religion was not my own, but her gift was also a gift to me. She was bringing an offering of beauty, creating an oasis of order and harmony in one corner of a chaotic city.

From that moment on I began to see Bangkok differently. I noticed a woman scrubbing the sidewalk in front of the closet-sized store where she sold spools of thread; a man cleaning his ancient but gleaming car with a feather duster; a teenager helping a blind man onto the bouncing ferryboat that crosses the river.

All works of beauty are manifestations of God, and by the time I left Bangkok, I was seeing Him everywhere. It's a beautiful, beautiful city!

Help me bring some of Your beauty, Lord,
to my corner of the world today.
—JOHN SHERRILL

May

Sat 15

Oh, praise the Lord . . . ! He is my strength, my shield from every danger. . . . —PSALM 28:6–7 (TLB)

During the heat of the California summer, we invite our neighbors to come over anytime for a dip in our pool. Van is a favorite; he loves to cycle up and down our hills, his forehead dripping under his protective helmet, and it's great to see him park his bike by the pool and plunge in, staying under so long that it's a relief when he eventually surfaces.

This particular weekend his son was with him. On leave from his base in San Diego, he was tall, with the upright, straight-as-an-arrow deportment typical of the military, a firm handshake and steady eyes that locked into those of the person talking to him. I liked him. I liked him even more when he peeled off his T-shirt to take a swim, for across his upper torso, under his collarbone, was a tattoo: *Carpe Diem*, Latin for "seize the day." I was fascinated. "Tell me about this," I asked.

"I want to make every moment of my life count," he said, giving me his father's wide smile. "My service to God, to my country and to making the world a better place. This is a daily reminder of my commitment."

He sprang from the diving board and swam the length of the pool in one swoop, like a torpedo. On the return lap, his arms were turbojets churning the water. *Wow*, I thought, *if he represents the caliber of our military, we're in good hands!*

Merciful God, hear our anxious prayer
For those who serve, both far and near,
Be their shield and keep them safe,
In Your loving care.
—FAY ANGUS

Sun 16

His divine power has given us everything we need for life and godliness through our knowledge of him who called us by his own glory and goodness. —II PETER 1:3 (NIV)

Our grandson Little Reggie stays with us every weekend. When he was three, he said to Rosie, "Grandma, I don't want to wear these clothes. I want to wear the kind of clothes Pops wears." (*Pops* is Little Reggie's pet name for me.)

Rosie looked at him and asked, "Why do you want to dress like Pops?"

"I want to be like Pops," he said.

Little Reggie repeated his request over the next few weekends. Finally Rosie bought him a suit and tie. After he put on the suit, he said, "I want to dress like Pops because I want to be a preacher like Pops."

We've heard Little Reggie share that wish many, many times since, and Rosie and I like to think of him letting that seed of faith grow and allowing God to use him to be a blessing for many. Tomorrow or ten years from now, his mind may change and he may have another goal for his life, but whatever Little Reggie grows up to be, we know that God will give him everything he needs to do whatever work He has in store for him.

*Lord, help me to encourage the children in my life
to be the people God wants them to be.*
—DOLPHUS WEARY

READER'S ROOM

Thanks to the mothers, like mine, who give *Daily Guideposts* as a gift. We are so encouraged. Sometimes I read the story and it's just what I need that moment, that day. —*Judith Harmon, Potosi, Missouri*

Mon 17

"The little you had . . . has increased greatly, and the Lord has blessed you. . . ." —GENESIS 30:30 (NIV)

I just spent $43.87 at the dollar store. How could I spend so much money at a place where things cost only a dollar? I went in to buy paper cups and craft sticks for a church project and Spanish moss if they had it. Maybe I'd stroll through the aisles and see if they had any pretty gift bags.

Turns out the store had all these things—and much more. Like this cool nail file that has green sparkly flowers on one side. Paper towels, sunglasses, a magazine that's only slightly out-of-date. Chewing gum. I even found a darling yellow straw hat for my granddaughter. And this purple plastic pill organizer that lets me put all my supplements for the week in one place.

Wait. I'm beginning to see how I could spend $43.87 at the dollar store. I did it one dollar at a time.

Little things tend to add up. A cookie here, some ice cream there—a pair of jeans that won't zip. A week too busy for devotional reading, a day so crowded that there's no time for exercise, an evening when one TV show turns into hours spent staring at the tube—then I wonder why I'm feeling sluggish, physically and spiritually.

But it works in a positive way too. One little act of kindness, one smile at a hassled clerk, one card sent to brighten someone's day—and the world doesn't seem as hostile, as hopeless. So here's to little things. Well managed, they can have big results.

Remind me, God, of the power of little things done in Your name.
—MARY LOU CARNEY

Tue 18   *Hear my prayer, O Lord; listen to my cry for mercy.*
In the day of my trouble I will call to you, for you
will answer me. —Psalm 86:6–7 (niv)

"Dad, how does prayer work?"
This morning I finished my breakfast and was on my way up the stairs for a shower when my daughter Christine came out of her bedroom and asked me this question. The look on her face told me it was serious and more than a theological question.

At first I wasn't sure how to respond. I stumbled along and then slowly began to say, "Sometimes we pray . . . and God gives us what we ask for. Other times the response takes longer or never seems to come. I'm not sure why . . ." While I was trying to say something that made sense, I could see that Christine was very upset.

She followed me into my room and said, "Dad, I keep praying for something, but nothing happens." Tears were streaming down her cheeks.

Once again I tried to find the right thing to say so that my daughter wouldn't lose her faith in prayer and, more importantly, in God. What I wanted to say but didn't was something I heard once from a Guideposts prayer volunteer: "I don't know *how* God is going to answer these prayers. But I do know that God answers them."

In spite of Christine's seemingly unanswered prayer, she hasn't stopped praying or believing—and neither have I.

Lord, may Your love sustain me when my faith is weak.
—Pablo Diaz

❁ THE GIFT OF SIGHT

<u>*Wed 19*</u> *And God said, Let the earth bring forth grass, the herb yielding seed, and the fruit tree yielding fruit. . . .*
—GENESIS 1:11

INNER EYES

On our tour of Cornwall in southwest England, my husband Robert and I were eager to visit the Lost Gardens of Heligan, a thousand-acre estate that belonged to the Tremayne family for more than four hundred years. At the end of the nineteenth century, its seemingly endless acres were at their zenith; yet only a few years later bramble and ivy were beginning to bury the gardens. In the late 1990s Tim Smith, the young man who started the Eden Project by planting gardens in abandoned clay pits, bought the old house and the long-neglected gardens hidden beneath layers of tangled vines. Tim and a friend began to rescue and restore the gardens, a labor of love that is still in progress.

As we walked through Heligan, I recognized a familiar scent: wisteria. These many-petaled lavender blossoms took me back to my childhood, when I spent many pleasant hours swinging in the wisteria arbor in our backyard. I breathed in the subtle perfume and the visual beauty of Heligan's wisteria and carried it away in my heart.

The rhododendrons were in full and magnificent bloom, ranging in color from light pink to deep rose. I took a picture of Robert standing in front of a twenty-foot-high rose-colored rhododendron bush that matched his shirt. It made a lovely memento of this beautiful trip we took together.

Holy One, You found me in fear of losing my sight and You gave me the gift of beautiful memories and the inner eyes with which to see them.
—MARILYN MORGAN KING

Thu 20   *Then he opened their minds to understand at last these
many Scriptures!* —LUKE 24:45 (TLB)

One of my favorite activities is working the newspaper's daily cross-word puzzle. A friend has done crosswords for years and always uses a pen. "I never make a mistake," she says. But my first attempt was nearly my last. I spent the seven-hour trip home from Colorado to Kansas try-ing to complete a puzzle with an average solution time of twenty-eight minutes. (Fortunately my husband Don was driving.) I knew a few of the answers: *Yakima* was a Washington city, and *bookkeeper* was a CPA. Don knew that *sera* was the same as *antitoxins*. But *leading lady?*

I bought a crossword dictionary and kept trying. I learned that puzzle writers use the same clues over and over, and knowing their lingo helps. Two years later I still use a pencil and I can't finish the *New York Times* Sunday crossword. But I nearly always beat the average time for easier puzzles.

Solving crosswords gives my mind a workout. It also has had an unanticipated benefit: making me a better Bible student. The process of understanding Scripture, I discovered, is a lot like working a puzzle. Often a passage is clear. Other times I get help from Bible commentaries and chronologies. I know to be alert to common clues. When Jesus says, "The kingdom of heaven is like . . ." He's about to tell a story! My Sunday school classmates provide answers and insights too. Best of all, I have the wonderful privilege of seeking understanding from the "author and fin-isher of our faith" (Hebrews 12:2), Jesus.

P.S. *Leading lady* is almost always *Eve.*

> *Lord Jesus, open my mind and heart that
> I might understand and live Your Word.*
> —PENNEY SCHWAB

⧗ COMFORT FOR THE HURTING HEART

Fri 21 *Now we know that if the earthly tent we live in is destroyed,*
we have a building from God, an eternal house in heaven, not
built by human hands. . . . For while we are in this tent, we
groan . . . to be clothed with our heavenly dwelling. . . . it is
God who has made us for this very purpose. . . .
—II Corinthians 5:1, 4–5 (NIV)

A CONSOLING WORD

Incredibly, years after our younger son and his wife lost their first child at birth, our older son lost his wife and their first child too. Kristen, due to deliver in two weeks, suddenly collapsed and died of an aneurysm. Their boy lived only ten days.

During Kristen's memorial service we learned how she'd affected others positively. These accolades were consoling; her life had been productive. But during the second memorial service we wondered, *What about their baby's life?* Had he made it through nine months in his mother's womb, plus ten days outside it, for nothing?

When a wise friend pointed out the verse above, the oppressive burden that had staggered us was partially eased. While God makes each of us for the very purpose of spending eternity with Him, this baby boy simply had made it to his very purpose sooner than the rest of us.

> *Sometimes death seems purposeless, Lord, yet we are aware that in*
> *Your great plan nothing happens that takes You by surprise.*
> *Help us to understand that You, Who knows the end*
> *from the beginning, are always in charge.*
> —Isabel Wolseley

Sat 22

A man who has friends must himself be friendly. . . .
—PROVERBS 18:24 (NKJV)

In my high school days I lived to fish. I chummed around with Keith, a farm boy who lived near Grabill, Indiana, where the St. Joe River flows like molten bronze through the cornfields and clover.

Early Saturday morning we would pack a lunch and begin the long trek through the dew-drenched alfalfa fields, where our trousers made a musical *swish–swish* and grasshoppers sprang away in fright. When at last I saw the river, my heart felt a frisson of anticipation as we slid down the steep bank to our favorite fishing spot.

"Last one to catch a fish has to clean them!" Keith called out. Amazingly, we always caught our limit and threw back the small ones. It wasn't until much later that I discovered why we always caught fish. A day or two before we went fishing, Keith would hike to the river and sink a gunnysack filled with ears of field corn, a practice known as "chumming." Attracted to the odor of the corn, the fish would gather in that spot, waiting for us to catch them.

The principle of chumming was a good one, I think. If I want to have friends, I need to do something to attract them. I need to smile more, for one thing. I'm too serious. And I have a bad habit of staring at my computer when someone is trying to talk to me. It wouldn't hurt me to slow down a bit when I walk through the halls of our college to take time to chat with some of the staff and students.

If I want to have chums, I need to be chummy.

Lord, I really need friends, but sometimes I put them at the bottom of my list of things to do. Help me to be more available.
—DANIEL SCHANTZ

May

Sun 23

To set the mind on the flesh is death, but to set the mind on the Spirit is life and peace. —ROMANS 8:6 (RSV)

Years ago our family celebrated Pentecost Sunday in a Russian Orthodox church in Wiesbaden, Germany. The service concluded with lengthy "kneeling prayers" for renewal in the Holy Spirit. As we knelt, I tried to pray—but mostly I struggled to hold my squirming ten-month-old son Mark and inwardly complained about my sore back. I also looked forward to the delicious brunch we would eat afterward with some new friends from America. Finally the service ended, and we drove to the restaurant.

After the meal we lingered in the hot, humid banquet room. I began to be irritated by my children's interruptions and annoyed with the other family's grandpa's long-winded tales. Soon our foreheads glistened with sweat, and we fanned ourselves with menus. I looked longingly out the window at the blue sky, the sunshine shimmering on the lawn and the leaves quivering in the breeze.

Then our friend Ted said, "Maybe I can get this window open." He tried a crank, but the window didn't budge. "*Hmm*, it seems to be locked." He felt along the window, released a lever and then pushed the window open. A cool draft wafted over us.

"How wonderful that feels!" "What a relief!" we exclaimed. I finally relaxed and enjoyed the sweet fellowship, speaking English and sharing what we missed about home. Grandpa's stories now seemed charming!

Sometimes my life feels like that stifling banquet room. I see glimpses of blue sky and green trees glistening in God's kingdom—a glorious Spirit-filled life—yet I seem trapped by problems, challenging relationships or my not-so-glorious life. Pentecost is a special opportunity to open my heart to let in God's light and fresh breeze of love.

> *Come, Holy Spirit. Fill my life anew that I may enter*
> *into deeper union with You and others.*
> —MARY BROWN

Mon 24   *"Choose my instruction instead of silver, knowledge rather than choice gold, for wisdom is more precious than rubies, and nothing you desire can compare with her."*
—PROVERBS 8:10–11 (NIV)

A few years ago I received an e-mail saying that the White House was considering me for a presidential appointment as a national advocate for volunteerism. *Wow,* I thought, *this is so exciting!* I figured the interview would be a breeze because I had been volunteering and encouraging others to do so for many years.

But during the interview, such simple questions as "Can you please list the volunteer positions you've held?" and "Why do you care about volunteerism?" left me struggling for words. Needless to say, I wasn't selected for the position.

Soon after, I asked my dad what he thought went wrong.

"Did you prepare?" he asked.

"A little," I said.

"Well, when I have a job interview, I try to prepare as much as possible. In fact, I try to overprepare."

I took his words to heart. Last year I applied for a position cohosting an Internet TV show in Los Angeles. I was going to be given an on-camera audition that would test my knowledge of current events. This time I went in prepared—overprepared, in fact. I spent so long providing commentary on my first question that the producer actually cut me off, saying, "That's enough for that topic, you're obviously very knowledgeable." I got the job. More importantly, I'd learned the lesson Dad had taught me.

Lord, when I'm facing an important decision, speak to me through the counsel of those who are wiser than I am.
—JOSHUA SUNDQUIST

Tue 25 *Have mercy upon me, O God, according to thy lovingkindness. . . .* —PSALM 51:1

After years of aching and wincing and acting huffy when people asked why I was limping, I finally gave in: I decided to have replacement surgery for my right hip. The prospect did not appeal to me. I'd had my tonsils and adenoids out when I was six and my appendix removed when I was in my thirties, and I didn't remember the experiences as being much fun.

I tried to bluff it out, but my friends Jeanne and Mona insisted on coming to the hospital with me for check-in and even appeared in the recovery room, and my friend Nancy was close by to field phone calls and relay messages. Nonetheless I was by myself when an orderly wheeled me out of recovery to my room and shifted me into bed. I heard the rails on the bed go up with a click, felt the IV in my arm being adjusted. I was vulnerable, weak, sore. And very much alone.

I opened my eyes to see a smiling woman beside my bed. "Hello," she said quietly. "My name is Mercy. I'm the head nurse on the ward." She showed me the button to push if I needed help. "We'll take good care of you," she said. "Now rest."

Mercy. She wrote her name on the blackboard that hung on the wall at the foot of my bed. I stared at the name. *Mercy.* I'd never thought much about mercy before. And yet now with my defenses down and my body compromised, mercy was exactly what I needed. Throughout the evening, all night and the next day, as I drifted in and out of sleep, every time I opened my eyes I saw the name, the word, before me on the blackboard.

> *Mercy. My name is Mercy. I will take care of you. Now rest.*
> —MARY ANN O'ROARK

Wed 26   *"No one can receive anything except what is given him from heaven." —*JOHN 3:27 (RSV)

Did you ever think about the many gifts you've been given that you didn't really want and would have refused if you could? Maybe they've been glorious and crucial and necessary gifts in ways that you will never understand, even if you had a million years to ponder it all.

I've been thinking about dark gifts this morning, here at the breakfast table, head in my hands, after my beloved son stomped out of the house, snarling and slamming the door, "You're not the boss of me!" and "I'll do whatever I want!" trailing behind him and scaring the rippling crows on the fence. Amid the sadness at the tension, and the way I miss the warm, sweet, friendly kid who's inside that testy teenager flopping down the street, I wonder if maybe his thrashing around is a kind of mysterious good thing. Maybe he has to tear chunks off his dad to build himself up. Maybe the best way for me to love him is to find a patient island on which to wait while his hurricane subsides.

I think of all the dark threads in my life over these five decades— minor physical ills, the eyesight of an ancient turtle, a confusing and sometimes tempestuous marriage, a wild flurry of infant children who are now a teeming horde of hormones, the constant worries about cash, and I think, *What if these are all sweet, quiet gifts that I just don't see from the right angle? What if all the worries made me a harder worker and a gentler, humbler soul? What if everything I thought was a pain was actually a present?*

It would be just exactly the thing He would do, the way He would operate, don't you think?

> *Dear Lord, would You help me see the grace of the gift a little more?*
> *Because here I am, sighing at the breakfast table again.*
> —BRIAN DOYLE

May

Thu 27

Pride goeth before destruction, and an haughty spirit before a fall. —PROVERBS 16:18

On the subway en route to a play, my daughter Elizabeth turned to me and grinned. "I was immature all afternoon, playing with Mary and her friends," she said. "Now I'm going to be mature with you!"

I love this about my fourteen-year-old: She's secure enough in herself to play with ten-year-olds, yet she enjoys adult plays and concerts.

That evening we were headed to see Henrik Ibsen's *The Master Builder*. I hadn't read the play in decades but vaguely remembered it as one of those there's-not-enough-sunlight-in-Norway pieces. The plot summary in the program confirmed my hunch: An intense, aging architect feels threatened that his assistant will surpass him. A young woman comes into the architect's life, bringing tension and confusion. She encourages his desire to remain the master builder, building up his self-centeredness until, in a burst of ego, he plunges to an unfortunate death. A classic case of "pride goeth before a fall."

After the final curtain I said something about the acting; Elizabeth pointed out a bit of symbolism. Then, laughing at myself, I said, "I can't believe it took me until the end of the second act to realize that the real master builder is God!"

My teenager looked at me in disbelief. "You're kidding! When you told me the title of the play, I thought it was *only* going to be about God!"

Huh? I'd assumed I was the more God-centered one, the mature Christian, the one who would catch that kind of stuff. What was it I'd just been saying about pride? Maybe teenagers really do know it all!

Lord, save me from my assumptions.
—JULIA ATTAWAY

Fri 28

Then the king, with the queen sitting beside him, asked me, "How long will your journey take, and when will you get back?" . . . —NEHEMIAH 2:6 (NIV)

When I was in elementary school in Illinois, we were allowed to walk home for lunch. Some of us used the time for gastronomical adventures.

There was a place called Bob and Jerry's not far from our school, where children, a thundering grimy herd of us, would shove a quarter through a one-foot-by-one-foot window. In return, a small bag of deliciously greasy French fries, an even greasier burger and a cherry cola in a paper cup were shoved back out. After smothering the grease in ketchup and mustard, we made our way back to school, our white socks slipping off our ankles while the oily fries slid down our throats.

But my greatest adventures I had alone. Separating from the pack, I was a secret solo diner at a restaurant whose name I can't remember. To get to it, I had to cross State Street, a road we were only supposed to cross when the crossing guard was on duty. I'm not certain how I found the place, nor am I certain why they served me. There were no other children there, not even with their parents. And though it didn't occur to me then, I probably unintentionally integrated the establishment.

I would wiggle my way onto a stool at the counter. Sometimes I ordered their cheeseburger; it was very flat and very dry, but what it lacked in grease, it made up for in "grownupness." At other times I ordered the chili; it was different from my mother's—very thick, beanless and surrounded by packages of round oyster crackers. When I finished my meal, I paid the check—imagine, a check!—but unfortunately for the waitress, I'd never heard of a tip. Then I'd return to the playground and smile for the rest of the day, thinking of the new world I'd just seen.

> *Lord, thank You for the journeys on which You send me.*
> *Help me to enjoy them like a little child.*
> —SHARON FOSTER

Sat 29

*When Lamech had lived a hundred and eighty-two years, he became the father of a son, and called his name Noah, saying, "Out of the ground which the Lord has cursed this one shall bring us relief. . . ." —*GENESIS 5:28 (RSV)

I turned fifty-six on May 29. On January 10 and May 31, my two grandsons Rome and Nathan, respectively, turned six—fifty years younger than I. On the evening of May 30, my son Blake and I were at Rome's house, sitting with him on the floor while he hunched over a breastplate he was making for his cousin's birthday party the next day. The theme was Star Wars, and Rome intended to go to Nathan's all decked out.

"How was your birthday?" he asked me.

"I decided I don't like turning fifty-six, Rome."

He switched green for red in the crayon box. "Why?"

"I don't know. Maybe because it means I'm sliding right into old age. I don't like that."

When he's concentrating, Rome sticks out his tongue a bit and rests it in the corner of his mouth. He went on coloring, tongue twitching. Suddenly he said, "Excuse me a moment, please," jumped up and headed for his room.

Blake looked at me with eyebrows raised as if to say, *What's he doing?* I had no clue.

Rome came back with a race car he'd built for the youth club at his church, a race car reminiscent of the ones his Uncle Blake and Uncle Phil had built years ago in their own youth clubs. "Here," said Rome. "Maybe this will make turning fifty-six more fun. See?" He pointed out the number he'd painted on his car: fifty-six.

Blake and I laughed out loud. "Yes, Rome," I said, "this will indeed make being fifty-six more fun."

God, it was the best birthday present ever.
—BRENDA WILBEE

Sun 30

The Lord is with you, while ye be with him. . . .
—II CHRONICLES 15:2

Seven-year-old Maggie was craving "special time"—the not-so-easy-to-attain exclusive attention of a parent. So she was eager to join me for my Sunday afternoon walk.

We headed into Fort Tryon Park, stopping to watch the butterflies, and took in the view up the Hudson to where the river widened into the Tappan Zee. Behind the Cloisters museum, the path descended to Riverside Drive and Dyckman Street, where balloons and boom boxes marked birthday parties in the playgrounds and people crowded around vendors selling shaved ice topped with sweet tropical-fruit syrups.

Then we were on our way up the trail in Inwood Hill Park and into Manhattan's largest forest, where the urban noises quieted to a faint buzz amid the rustling of squirrels and chipmunks and the calls of birds in the branches of the trees. We climbed to the crest of the hill and found the trail headed down and out of the woods to where a plaque marked the site where once stood the great tree under which, so legend has it, Peter Minuit bought Manhattan for twenty-four dollars from a wandering band of Native Americans.

A few herons and egrets waded amid the ducks in the salt marsh as we made our way east and out of the park to the little café on Indian Road where we shared a pastry and a cold drink. When Maggie had rested her legs, we headed back home, this time taking a shorter route over the sidewalks that skirted the parks.

Two hours after leaving, we were home. We'd enjoyed the quiet and the birds and the flowers and the snack, and we'd talked a bit about what we were seeing and about what Maggie's week had been like. But what really made it special was that it was just the two of us, taking the time to be together.

Lord, even if it's only for ten minutes, let me crown every day
with a special time with You.
—ANDREW ATTAWAY

Mon 31

Thy kingdom is an everlasting kingdom, and thy dominion endureth throughout all generations. —PSALM 145:13

It had been five months since my sister Maria died in her sleep, and now I was in the cemetery, sitting at her grave and remembering.

Living in the same town, Maria and I were more than sisters; we were best friends. I always thought we'd have so much time together. I used to picture us grown old, sitting in lawn chairs at the neighborhood pool, talking about our grandchildren. Then, without warning, the future I'd looked forward to was gone. All that seemed to remain was this little plot of land.

My mother and I had done our best to make it joyful. We'd planted flowers and decorated the grave with a garden gnome, an angel statue, cut flowers, seashells and sand from our family vacation spot on Cape Cod.

The cosmos had grown tall and burst with blooms in shades of pink and white. As I sat, thinking about Maria, I began to pluck the spent flowers from the stems. Maria had often laughed at my lack of knowledge about them. Was it only a year ago that I'd held up an iris bulb and asked her which way it went into the ground?

Collecting the cosmos' dead heads, I became filled with loss. *What if there is nothing?* I thought. *What if my sister is just gone?* Without thinking, I began to twist the dead blossoms in my hand, gripping them as I cried. Finally, I pulled myself together and opened my hands to see my palms covered with seeds.

I smiled at the much-needed message: Death is not the end. Like flowers, it holds the seeds of a new beginning.

*Father, Your love is always there. Help me to feel Your comfort,
especially during times of sorrow.*
—SABRA CIANCANELLI

THE GIFTS I'VE BEEN GIVEN

1 _____

2 _____

3 _____

4 _____

5 _____

6 _____

7 _____

8 _____

9 _____

10 _____

11 _____

12 _____

13 _____

14 _____

15 _____

May

16 _____

17 _____

18 _____

19 _____

20 _____

21 _____

22 _____

23 _____

24 _____

25 _____

26 _____

27 _____

28 _____

29 _____

30 _____

31 _____

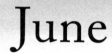

June

*And I will give them an
heart to know me, that
I am the Lord. . . .*

—JEREMIAH 24:7

❦ GIFTS FROM ABOVE

Tue 1 *Freely ye have received, freely give.* —Matthew 10:8

A GIFT OF GENEROSITY

P am, would you consider sharing your cobbler recipe with me?" my friend Becky asks. Funny, how a simple request can snowball into an avalanche of memories.

In a flash, I'm in another kitchen, one that exists now only in my head. I'm at the sink, rinsing blue-flowered dessert plates as I talk to Carolyn. I am very young, just starting life as a minister's wife and a new mother. Carolyn is a mentor to me. She's lovely both in appearance and in spirit. Everything she does is done with flair. I admire her grace, her style.

"Oh, Carolyn," I say with a long sigh, "everything you do is perfect." I've just helped her host one of those old-time Southern parties where ladies gather to discuss Robert Browning or listen to a pianist playing Elizabethan melodies. "I don't know how many times I've heard, 'Carolyn makes the best coffee I've ever tasted' or 'Carolyn's caramel pie is the envy of Nashville.' Really, I could never hope to entertain as flawlessly as you do."

Carolyn surprises me by laughing, and then a mischievous look crosses her face and she whispers, "I have secrets."

"If you have secrets," I answer, "I sure would like to know what they are."

"All you have to do is ask," she says, as her image fades back into the past.

"It's not a secret recipe, is it?" Becky is asking.

"No, Becky," I say. "All you have to do is ask."

> *Father, let me give freely, naturally, as You give to me.*
> —Pam Kidd

Wed 2   Ye have heard that it hath been said, Thou shalt love thy
neighbour, and hate thine enemy. But I say unto you,
Love your enemies, bless them that curse you, do good to
them that hate you, and pray for them which despitefully
use you, and persecute you. —MATTHEW 5:43–44

According to anthropologists, ancient tribes often practiced unlimited retaliation for offenses committed against them. And if one tribe responded more harshly than another, they raised the ante until all-out war resulted. Then, according to our Judeo-Christian heritage, the Law of Moses was given. These laws, which contain far more than the Ten Commandments, number more than six hundred and include such teachings as "eye for eye, tooth for tooth" (Exodus 21:24). These laws were less harsh than previous practices, limiting retaliation. But forgiveness was still on the back burner.

Then Jesus came along and espoused something that was revolutionary: unconditional forgiveness. Check your Bible concordance and note how many times Jesus spoke about it. He told His followers to practice unlimited forgiveness (seven times seventy, or without end), which is spelled out in Matthew 5:44: "But I say unto you, Love your enemies, bless them that curse you, do good to them that hate you, and pray for them which despitefully use you, and persecute you."

Once I interviewed the renowned missionary E. Stanley Jones. While working in India, he told me, he became a friend of Mahatma Gandhi, who, though a Hindu, was a great admirer of Christ. According to Jones, Gandhi considered Christ's statement about forgiving one's enemies Jesus' most memorable commandment and the most difficult to keep. Difficult? Yes. Impossible? Not with God's grace.

Teach us, Lord, when we would hold grudges,
We all must stand before Him Who judges.
—FRED BAUER

Thu 3

God hath made me to laugh, so that all that hear will laugh with me. —GENESIS 21:6

I'm a teacher, not a trained psychologist, but early in my career I learned this simple truth: Help students to laugh and they will perform better. Plenty of research supports my observations. So when I teach adults, whether at my community college or in a corporate setting, I depend on humor to defuse taut nerves. Enter my assistant: Henry, the rubber chicken.

With goose-bumpy skin, a waggling neck and legs that flop like noodles, Henry made his debut in a business-writing class. Most of the students had been out of school for years—decades, even—and didn't want to look silly. Not a problem. Henry looked so ridiculous demonstrating prepositions ("Henry is wiggling *over* the basket, *in* the basket, *under* the basket") that one very staid manager collapsed into giggling fits that left her gasping and dabbing her eyes. *Nice work, Henry! Now she can relax and learn.*

Henry works hardest, however, in my communications classes, where students give at least four speeches per semester. Though the students manage the first assignments, introducing themselves in front of the podium and then speaking for only one minute, they often become dry-mouthed and shaky for their five- and ten-minute presentations. Once again, Henry to the rescue! I tuck him just inside the portable podium where students can see or nervously squeeze him before they begin their introductions.

My students' evaluations tell me that Henry is more reassuring than I ever imagined possible. So I continue to teach with gentleness, with humor and—wherever possible—with Henry.

Oh, Master Teacher, when the learning seems hard,
remind me to laugh at myself.
—GAIL THORELL SCHILLING

Fri 4 *I know what it is to be in need, and I know what it is to have plenty. I have learned the secret of being content in any and every situation, whether well fed or hungry, whether living in plenty or in want. I can do everything through him who gives me strength.* —PHILIPPIANS 4:12–13 (NIV)

For years I've gained and lost the same twenty pounds over and over. Up, down, up, down. Then somebody (usually me) gives me a bag of chocolate-covered almonds or malted-milk balls or a bag of candy bars, and—well, you get the picture. My resistance disappears and so does the candy.

When I met Margaret at a five-day conference in Minnesota, she seemed a bit down in the dumps. Margaret was afraid she'd get adult-onset diabetes if she didn't lose fifty pounds. But like me, she'd tried many times before.

"Margaret," I said, "let's do it together. We'll e-mail each other for inspiration and for help over the rough spots. We'll be like a two-woman Overeaters Anonymous team. Every Friday we'll weigh and measure ourselves and report in. Next year when we come back to this conference, we'll be fit and healthy."

Over the next year Margaret and I e-mailed, often two or three times a week. We wrote funny poems and letters, trying to keep each other on track. We confessed our too-much-ice-cream and portions-too-big slipups. But mostly we buoyed each other up. We praised each pound and inch that disappeared. We made better food choices, ate less, exercised more and lost weight.

The secret for both of us was doing it together. I think that's the secret to many other things too.

Lord, keep me mindful that I can succeed at anything more easily when I have a friend on the journey.
—PATRICIA LORENZ

June

Sat 5 *Call to remembrance the former days....* —HEBREWS 10:32

We were driving somewhere, and my wife Sandee and I began to talk about our wretched history with automobiles. Just for fun, we started listing the cars we've owned:

- The 1969 Delta 88, the car I had on my first date with Sandee. I told her she needed to sit closer to me because the passenger window leaked. She shot me a look that said, *No thanks, bub.* It began to rain harder, and she found out I wasn't kidding.

- The 1974 VW with mismatched fenders. My father and I rebuilt it, and I wanted to show it off to my now-girlfriend Sandee. We still hadn't fixed the starter, so my dad yanked the crankshaft belt while I turned the key. It started—well, nearly. But the belt pinched off my father's ring finger—well, completely. Instead of showing off the car, I showed off how fast I could drive to the ER.

- The 1978 Chevette, so Sandee could drive back and forth to the seminary—but first she had to master the stick shift. After a particularly frustrating lesson she said, "I can't do it." I wanted to be a patient teacher, but we were in an intersection and there was a truck bearing down on us, so I gently asked Sandee if she could TRY AGAIN NOW BEFORE WE ALL DIE JUST GO GO GO . . . and she did.

Maybe it wasn't a wretched history after all. Sure, there were hard days and endless time beneath the hood with oily rags, but there were magical moments too: bringing the newborn kids home from the hospital, taking family vacations, sitting in the back with the hatch open looking at fireworks, watching the bright lights and listening to the *ooh*s and *aah*s that make up a life together.

Thank You, Lord, for those automotive time capsules and the memories they bring. And thank You for helping Sandee with that stick shift, so we could keep on making memories together.
—MARK COLLINS

Sun 6

Each one should use whatever gift he has received to serve others, faithfully administering God's grace in its various forms. —I PETER 4:10 (NIV)

Aloha," the beautiful long-haired woman said as she hung a string of shells around my neck.

"Oh," I said, a bit confused, "thank you."

Am I in the right place? I thought. It was a regular Sunday morning at my church, and I was expecting the usual ushers to hand me a program with the usual automatic "Good morning" or "God bless you." I didn't recognize the women stationed at each door. Their lovely smiles radiated warmth, and the sleepy faces of those walking in suddenly lit up as they touched the gifts they'd received.

"What's going on?" I asked a friend as I took my seat.

"It's a church from Hawaii," she said, beaming with excitement and examining her shells. "They came to lead the worship."

Lead the worship they did. In fact, our congregation felt like guests of honor in their church instead of members of our own. Boys and girls performed a Hawaiian dance, signing the words of each beautiful song with graceful hand gestures. It was as if we'd crossed the ocean and landed in the Hawaiian Islands.

At the end of the service, our visitors thanked us profusely for welcoming them into our church, but it should have been the other way around. They were the ones who showed us the true meaning of hospitality, and the necklace of shells I received that morning hangs on my door as a reminder that everyone who walks into my home should feel as welcomed as I did that day.

> *Whether I'm a guest or a host, Lord, help me*
> *to show* aloha *(love) to everyone around me.*
> —KAREN VALENTIN

Mon 7

"You shall clear out the old to make way for the new."
—LEVITICUS 26:10 (RSV)

Endings seemed to come at me all at once. During just one spring my two-year term as president of the parents' association at my children's school ended, seven years of teaching my daughter Maria's Sunday school class ended when she moved into the confirmation program, my son Ross graduated from high school, and my weekly Bible study ended when our leader moved to another city.

Everyone seemed ready to move on except me. How could God expect me to say good-bye to all these facets of my life at the same time? Friends I'd made through volunteering, the contributions I'd made to the life of the school, even my Bible study were part of my identity. *This is who I am,* I thought.

But as a little time passed, new opportunities opened up out of the old. The school hired me to work part-time, allowing me to strengthen many of the friendships I'd made and forge new ones. I was offered the opportunity to teach a Sunday school class once a month, a good fit for my working schedule. I started attending regular Sunday morning Bible classes, learning about God's Word from new teachers and new classmates, many of whom I'd never met. Nothing replaces having my son close by, but I feel a new kind of delight hearing about the fabulous musical experiences he's having in college in Nashville, Tennessee, none of which would have been possible if he hadn't been ready to move on.

I've learned that many of life's endings really are beginnings; you simply have to look a little farther down the road and know that God has something more in mind.

> *Dear Lord, give me courage to let go of the familiar and*
> *embrace the plans You have for me.*
> —GINA BRIDGEMAN

Tue 8   Give to him as the Lord your God has blessed you.
—DEUTERONOMY 15:14 (NIV)

"Only Brock," my sister Keri teased, "would travel all the way to Zimbabwe and end up in the investment business!" I had just picked up my family at the airport on their return from that country, and Keri was bursting with stories to share.

I had made the long journey to Zimbabwe the year before, visiting the farm for AIDS orphans that our family, church friends and many Guideposts readers support. While touring a clinic that serves as an awareness center for people infected with HIV, I met a young entrepreneur who refused to let AIDS affect his spirit. His name was Tapiwa, and he had helped write a book that served as an educational tool for many sick folks. He helped to fund the printing of this book by making and selling *maputi*, a popcornlike snack popular in Zimbabwe. He had dreams of expanding his business so that he could help his family.

"Back in America," I told him, "I work for an investment company and I'd very much like to invest in your business." I pressed some money into the disbelieving boy's hand and looked into his eyes. "I'll be back someday to see how we're doing."

That was that, or so I thought. On her visit to the AIDS clinic, Keri learned that Tapiwa was eager for me to return. It seems he has a lot to share with his American partner. He's turned those first dollars into a small factory where he prepares and packages his corn. He has two employees and several roadside stands. He's keeping his family afloat.

Keri laid out the entire story with great pride. "Brock," she said, "this is the best investment you've ever made!"

My sister had never been more right.

> *Dear Lord, thank You for the daily opportunity*
> *You give me to invest in others.*
> —BROCK KIDD

Wed 9

Children's children are a crown to the aged. . . .
—PROVERBS 17:6 (NIV)

I came home early one evening and noticed the flashing light on my phone, indicating that I had a message.

I pushed the button and immediately heard the sobbing voice of my six-year-old granddaughter Gabriella, who was about to lose her first tooth.

"Oma," she sputtered, "I have a very loose tooth"—deep, shaky breath—"and I'm scared." Another shaky breath. "Bye."

The next message clicked on, and her daddy's calm voice said, "Mission accomplished."

I laughed out loud as I replayed the messages. I didn't push Erase because I wanted to save this audio-memory and the other memories it triggered: *I was about Gabi's age, sitting on a kitchen stool, very late at night, crying and holding my mouth. My mother was beside me, encouraging me. I'd been in bed in the lower bunk, whimpering and fiddling with my loose tooth, when my know-it-all older sister leaned over the top bunk and told me, "It'll come out in the middle of the night and you'll swallow it and die." That did it. I got out of bed to face the ordeal of having my first tooth pulled, so I wouldn't die.*

Gabi's daddy, our son, also age six, was fearfully and tearfully peering into the bathroom mirror with his daddy behind him calmly tying a long piece of dental floss around his wobbly tooth and gently showing him how to pull both ends of the dental floss to pop out the tooth.

These memories made me smile and thank God for the gift of the generations and the opportunity it gives us to see and remember the precious milestones that mark the stages of growing up.

Lord, thank You for the many ways that children
remind me of myself—and of You.
—CAROL KUYKENDALL

<u>*Thu 10*</u>   *"The wind blows where it wishes and you hear the sound of it, but do not know where it comes from and where it is going...."* —JOHN 3:8 (NAS)

My children have always kidded me about how quickly I can fall asleep. When I sit down in my easy chair to watch a football game, my sons take bets as to how soon I'll be snoozing.

But occasionally I'll have a night when sleep will not come. Last night I turned out my desk lamp at midnight, let the dogs back into the house and was asleep before my head hit the pillow—for fifteen minutes. Then I was jolted awake, a thousand thoughts pouring through my mind: *My quarterly tax payment will soon be due; I'm nudging up on a deadline; I've got a doctor's appointment next week....*

I got up, put on my robe and wandered out into the front yard. It was a beautiful night, mild and pleasant, balanced between spring and summer. Standing beneath a canopy of water oaks, I gazed at the stars as a breeze rippled off the western prairie. Going back inside, I climbed to the second floor, opened the windows in the guest room and lay down on the bed. In the darkness, I listened to the gentle wind whisper under the eaves and watched the curtains billow in. Snuggling under covers, I felt the breeze ruffle my hair. There was a smell of sweet hay in the soft Texas night. Then sleep embraced me.

When sleep and rest will not come, I need to open the windows of my soul and let God's Spirit blow in.

Father, I cannot command the wind to blow, but I can trust that in Your good time, Your presence will be felt in my life, bringing peace and rest. Amen.
—SCOTT WALKER

Fri 11

And Jesus went forth, and saw a great multitude, and was moved with compassion toward them, and he healed their sick.
—MATTHEW 14:14

I was sitting in the crowded waiting room of St. Thomas Hospital. I was there with my son Jon, who was having some tests done and needed me to drive him. I unfolded the first of the three newspapers I'd brought and buried myself in an article on pet-sitting. The room was hot; the intercom was noisy; someone was coughing; a child was crying. I buried myself deeper in the paper.

"Patient forty-two," called the intercom. Then it called the same number again, louder.

A nurse came out to look for her patient. "Is number forty-two here?"

He was sitting alone, next to me, emaciated, in torn blue jeans and a faded flannel shirt. "I'm sorry," he said nervously. "I didn't hear."

I watched him over the edge of my paper, shuffling behind the nurse. I put down my paper and looked around, noticing—really noticing—my surroundings. There was a chunky, pasty-skinned woman clutching a walker. There was an elderly woman in a wheelchair, assisted by a stooped, frail-looking man I took to be her husband. In the corner a tired-looking woman held a small, fussy child.

As my eyes roamed, I saw a crucifix on the wall. From across the crowded room, I could feel Jesus looking at me with compassion and pleading, reminding me that even on the Cross He was present to the pain and suffering of those around Him. He took care of His mother, He prayed for His enemies and He healed the soul of the thief crucified next to Him.

What do You want, Lord? I asked. But I already knew.

> *Jesus, forgive me for my indifference. I pray for these, Your suffering ones.*
> *Bring healing and peace to number forty-two*
> *and to the woman across from me and to . . .*
> —SHARI SMYTH

Sat 12   *"Who is a teacher like him?"* —Job 36:22 (NIV)

When my six-year-old grandson Indy received his first two-wheel bike, the whole family joined in to help him learn to ride it. My daughter Misty, his mom, pushed the bike along; Indy teetered a bit while she coached him on how to balance it. His dad, his younger brothers, and my husband Johnny and I called out support along the way.

After a few tries Indy suddenly picked up speed and Misty let him go. He was off on his own, pedaling perfectly down our street. "Way to go, Indy!" we all called out as we clapped for him.

Indy made a big wobbly loop and pedaled back toward us, his face flushed with excitement. He stopped quickly, turned to his mom and said, "I have to call Miss Westover!"

Misty smiled and gave him a hug. "Great idea, Indy."

Indy ran inside to make his phone call, and I followed along. "Hello, Miss Westover? This is Indy Nebeker. I wanted to tell you that I just learned how to ride a two-wheel bike and it only took one hour!" I could hear Miss Westover responding with praise over the phone. Indy beamed with pride. "Bye, Miss Westover."

Indy hadn't asked to call his best friend, his favorite uncle or his other grandparents. The first person Indy wanted to share his big news with was his teacher.

Lord, bless our teachers and keep them aware
of the profound impact they make
in the lives of their students.
—MELODY BONNETTE

June

Sun 13

"Every scribe who has become a disciple of the kingdom of heaven is like a head of a household, who brings forth out of his treasure things new and old."
—MATTHEW 13:52 (NAS)

I thought I was familiar with all the treasures of the Gospels. But this morning I discovered a new gem, tucked in at the end of several parables: Matthew describes an ancient aspect of hosting that seems as contemporary as my modest dinner party last night.

To prepare for guests, I spread my table with a linen cloth inherited from my mother. I set six places with my collectible forest green dinnerware purchased at flea markets. To add an accent, I broke in the quirky beaded napkin rings I'd received at Christmas.

At six o'clock I welcomed five guests from church: two women friends, Penny and her husband, and a newcomer, an older man I knew only by name.

"Your home is so cozy," Penny said over appetizers. She glanced toward a grouping of framed museum prints—old masters—and then toward an expanse of fresh greenery: hibiscus, begonias, ferns.

The meal itself? Someone complimented the rice with olives. "A new recipe?"

"The slaw, yes. But not the rice. I got the recipe from my friend Wendy. She moved away about twenty-five years ago." I shared a memory of her farewell party. "She was so happy to be getting married, and yet weeping, so sad to be leaving her friends." Conversation continued, sometimes dwelling on earlier decades and then turning to an experience of last week. By evening's end my circle of friends was larger, my memory bank richer, my church bond stronger.

I like to think the kingdom of God in my neighborhood is broader today than yesterday—for my having opened my home, drawing in and setting out the new alongside the old.

Lord, You enhance my life and ministry with old and new treasures.
Thank You. —EVELYN BENCE

Mon 14

"For who has despised the day of small things?" . . .
—ZECHARIAH 4:10 (NAS)

Since Gene and I married twenty-two years ago and moved from his Oklahoma farm, we've missed the enormous flag that flew in his yard. We've talked about replacing it, but there doesn't seem to be an appropriate place in our yard in Watkinsville, Georgia.

Every Fourth of July Gene and I attend a family reunion hosted by my cousin Jo and her husband John at their getaway home, a renovated farmhouse with a tin roof. The whole scene, straight out of a Norman Rockwell painting, always lifts our spirits: the old house alive again, all spiffed up, tractors parked on a hill, the wraparound porch filled with pots of flowers, plenty of home-cooked food, excited children playing or heading for the ponds to fish with their dads, someone asleep in the hammock, old-fashioned yard flowers blooming. Gene delights in the large flag around which we all gather to recite the Pledge of Allegiance.

This year Jo added something new. Driving down the half-mile entrance, we noticed that she'd attached small flags to the winding fence. As we left the picnic, Gene hesitated before entering the highway and admired the small flags that seemed to be waving good-bye.

The next week Gene placed miniature flags at the entrance to our driveway, on the mailbox and in the barrels that held geraniums, petunias and ferns in our gazebo. He smiled that same smile he had at the family picnic—and back in Oklahoma when he looked at that huge flag.

Father, help us always to answer yes to Francis Scott Key's question: "O say, does that star-spangled banner yet wave, o'er the land of the free and the home of the brave?"
—MARION BOND WEST

June

Tue 15
Now the Lord blessed the latter days of Job more than his beginning. . . . —Job 42:12 (NKJV)

There are many good things about getting older, and one of them is that you get to see how it all turns out. Some of my classmates from school days have surprised me.

That knockout blonde who always had a dozen boyfriends is now, shall I say, seven times less appealing.

Then there was that overconfident guy I envied because I lacked confidence altogether. He has made a career of job-hopping, each one worse than the last.

The slowest boy in the class is already retired, with three sources of income.

Some of my classmates were openly hostile to religion back then, but now they have found faith in God.

All these changes remind me that "it isn't over until it's over." As long as I'm alive, I can improve or I can backslide.

I need to be more patient with people who mess up, like that minister who ran off with his secretary. He made a disastrous choice, but his life isn't over. He may get turned around and become a different person.

And it's good for me to remember that I, too, can slip up. "There's no fool like an old fool," the proverb goes. And when I do, I want people to give me another chance to get it right.

Thank You, Lord, for giving me a lot of rope. I need it. —Daniel Schantz

READER'S ROOM

I was an abused child and for many years an abused adult. Through the tears and pain, I ran to God for love and comfort. God would not let my spirit be taken from me. I was forced to hide my gifts under the basket the Bible speaks of, but now, little by little, God's light is shining brighter and brighter. God took me to the stage of Carnegie Hall. Now that is love and power! —*Florence Compher, Hammonton, New Jersey*

⚜ TWELVE KEYS TO THE GIVING LIFE

<u>*Wed 16*</u> *. . . Every man that giveth it willingly with his heart. . . .* —EXODUS 25:2

GIVE WILLINGLY

Last spring my precious dog Spanky died. Sixteen years before, I'd noticed the scraggly stray dodging cars near my house and brought him home. Spanky was by my side when my parents passed away, whenever I had a rough patch at work, when I learned I had cancer.

The morning after Spanky took his final faltering breath, I remembered the landscapers who had just finished working in my yard and were busy with other projects up the street. When I called them with the news, they offered their help right away. "Look for our truck in the neighborhood when you get home from work, Roberta. We'll find a real pretty place for good old Spanky."

My sister Rebekkah, who loved Spanky as much as I did, helped me get ready for his burial. She fluffed a pink floral towel in the dryer until it was as warm as Spanky's braided rug by the fireplace. Then we positioned him just so, as if he were stretched out for one of his Sunday afternoon naps.

The three landscapers led us to a spot by the potting shed I'd built from salvaged barn wood, Victorian fretwork and vintage stained glass. They had already dug a grave under the pink crape myrtle. At the head of it stood a painstakingly carved wooden cross.

As they lowered Spanky into the ground, my heart was suddenly full—of grief, but of thanksgiving too. All because of these gifts of kindness offered with the most willing of hearts.

> *Teach me to give Your way, Lord.*
> —ROBERTA MESSNER

Thu 17

Let the field be joyful, and all that is therein. . . .
—PSALM 96:12

Having fun doesn't come naturally to me. Being a firstborn and a type A personality, I work hard at life. Since childhood I've plodded along the path of duty, structure and routine. I know fun isn't wrong, but how could it be right to take a break with so many things to do?

I'm drawn to people who know how to laugh and play, though, like my friend Leigh Anne. "Want to go pick strawberries?" she asked me one morning.

Take time off to frolic in a strawberry field? I lived twenty minutes from a strawberry patch and had never tasted or picked a single berry. Buying fruit from the grocery store saved time, money and gas. But not wanting to be a fuddy-duddy, I said *yes* and hoped it wouldn't take long.

Still clicking through my mental to-do list, I slipped into Leigh Anne's van. I buckled up and glanced over at her. She was smiling. "You're going to love this." I nodded politely.

At the field we hooked baskets on our arms. It seemed we'd entered another world. *Oh, the smell!* The sweet aroma made me forget all about my list.

"Look at how big they are!" Leigh Anne exclaimed. Each strawberry nearly covered my palm.

After we paid for our strawberries, Leigh Anne grabbed one and took a bite. "You've got to taste them," she said. We sat awhile and laughed in the warm sun, juice trickling down our arms.

"Thank you," I said. "I never knew."

"Just wait till blackberry season," she replied.

> *Father, don't let me miss out on the joys You send—*
> *strawberries and friendship.*
> —JULIE GARMON

Fri 18

For with thee is the fountain of life: in thy light shall we see light. —Psalm 36:9

It was the end of another in a long string of hectic days, and I was leaving the office after dark again, exhausted, muttering that my wife Julee was going to kill me. I grabbed my briefcase and had just flipped off the lights in my office when I glanced out the window and saw the word *Life* emblazoned in the sky above Manhattan.

I stopped in my tracks. Maybe because I was so beat it took me a minute to figure out it wasn't a hallucination. No, the lit-up word was actually half of the MetLife logo atop its skyscraper ten blocks up the concrete-and-glass canyon of Park Avenue. Apparently the *Met* part had burned out, leaving just the word *Life* in bright red letters. Satisfied that the mystery was solved and that my sanity was reasonably intact, I started to leave again. I paused and looked back at the word suspended above the skyline. *Life.*

It hit me all at once, cutting through the headaches of the day. *What an incredible word! What an extraordinary concept!* The idea of being alive, of having life, seemed utterly startling, even improbable. We live in a universe made up of inert, nonliving matter and, overwhelmingly, empty space. We probe our galactic neighborhood for signs of life to no avail. As far as we know, life as we understand it exists only on this speck of rock and water and air we call earth. Life, against all odds, is ours. A cosmic gift.

It was getting late, and Julee was probably still going to kill me. I was still feeling tired, still a little stressed-out, but most of all I felt alive.

> *Father, of all the gifts and blessings You bestow on us,*
> *the greatest is the miracle of life. Let me find joy and*
> *satisfaction in every amazing, improbable moment.*
> —Edward Grinnan

Sat 19

The end of a matter is better than its beginning. . . .
—ECCLESIASTES 7:8 (NIV)

It was five minutes to seven on a rare Saturday morning off from work when I heard knocking on my front door. I buried my head in the pillow. *Please, God, let it just be a dream.* But it wasn't. Drowsily, I lumbered to the door and peeked out of the spyhole. My new downstairs neighbor was standing there. "Open up! It's an emergency!"

I flung open the door, wide awake now. "What's wrong?"

"Water is gushing from your apartment into my bedroom!"

We rushed around my apartment, checking the kitchen and the bathroom, flinging open closets, dropping to the floor to check for wet spots. Nothing. "Let's go downstairs," I said, "to check your place."

In her bedroom she pointed to a drip so tiny that it would have taken twenty-four hours to fill a teapot. "This is the *torrent?*" I asked. "Call the manager." I raced upstairs and went back to bed.

Five minutes later there was more knocking.

"What now?" I asked.

"I can't find the landlord's number. Please call him for me."

So I did, and finally, half an hour later, I fell into a sound sleep.

That night I told my friend Claire what had happened: "And she woke me up! And she said it was gushing! And it was nothing! And I had to call the landlord! And we searched my apartment! And it was from the roof and didn't involve me at all—"

Claire put her hand gently on my arm. "Linda, she was a frightened young woman, who's probably never lived alone. To her, the drip was a big deal. Now I'm going to write down something that'll calm you. Keep it in your wallet."

"What is it?"

She handed me a yellow sticky note: "Thank God there's no leak."

God, when I get upset over nothing, remind me about that sticky note.
—LINDA NEUKRUG

Sun 20

And, fathers, do not provoke your children to anger, but bring them up in the discipline and instruction of the Lord.
—EPHESIANS 6:4 (NRSV)

Two years ago I was offered a new job. It promised to be challenging and fulfilling and, yes, even fun—a tremendous opportunity and a blessing in every way. Well, every way but one: It was 142 miles from home, each way; 142 miles from my wife's ministry, 142 miles from my daughter's high school. Moving wasn't a viable option.

For weeks I wrestled with one key question: not salary or prestige or career tracks, but about being a dad. Was I being selfish to take the job? Didn't being a father take priority? How can you be a good father when you're not even home?

Twice I had the phone in my hand, ready to turn down the job, but hung up. Then one day I happened to find myself in the same room as someone I knew was a terrific father. I wound my way over to him and when he turned and said hello, I told him about my situation. "What should I do?" I asked him.

He looked me straight in the eye and said, "You—and your daughter—don't need my advice. You need each other. If you can give each other that, as often as you can, with as much commitment as you can muster, you'll be fine."

I took the job. It's meant being away from home two, three, sometimes even four nights a week. That's been really hard on all of us. But here's what I've learned about being a father from being away: That while kids think they need a lot of stuff, what they need most is you! And there are a million different ways to give a bit of yourself every day, whether you're home or not.

Father God, as You have given freely to me, inspire me
to give of myself to my own children.
—JEFF JAPINGA

Mon 21

Preach the word, be urgent in season and out of season, convince, rebuke, and exhort, be unfailing in patience and in teaching. —II TIMOTHY 4:2 (RSV)

"Mom, is it okay if I take Elizabeth out to dinner at the Indian restaurant?"

I stared at my twelve-year-old in wonder.

"Are you sure that's how you want to spend your money?" Mary's godmother had given each of the children twenty dollars, and I was surprised that John wanted to spend this bonanza on his sister.

"Yes. I want to do something special for Elizabeth," my son replied.

"Okay. Don't forget to leave a tip."

Off my two oldest went, practically skipping to the restaurant around the corner. They returned reporting that they'd had a great time.

A few days later, ten-year-old Mary approached me. "Mom," she said, "can I take Maggie to breakfast at the diner?"

"Are you sure that's how you want to spend your money?"

"Yes! I have enough."

The diner is only a block away, full of people we know. So off they went for waffles and juice, big and little sister beaming.

Today Maggie, who's seven, asked if she could take Elizabeth out for a "special time." Could it possibly be that after 1,786,422 attempts to instill sibling solicitude, something has finally stuck? I've been a parent long enough to savor any scraps of hope that are tossed in my direction. I guess perseverance really is a virtue.

> *Lord, do You think that maybe, someday, I'll finally grasp and live out that first commandment?*
> —JULIA ATTAWAY

Tue 22   *"The Lord will guide you always; he will satisfy your needs in
a sun-scorched land and will strengthen your frame. . . ."*
—Isaiah 58:11 (NIV)

My husband's best friend Norm fell off the roof of his house.
Complications from his injuries set in, and he wasn't expected to
live through the night. Distraught, Norm's family gathered at the hospital. Not wanting to intrude on their privacy, Wayne and I felt there was
little we could do but pray as we waited for word.

Feeling the need to do more, Wayne asked me to contact our church
to ask if one of the pastors could go to the hospital and pray with the
family. The assistant pastor went and reported back that he'd met
the family, shared the Gospel and prayed with them. He told us how
grateful they were for his visit.

Later, when we got the news that Norm had miraculously survived the
night, Wayne and I were overwhelmed with joy. But when I mentioned
our pastor's visit to Norm's wife Sharon, she sounded confused. No one
from the church had stopped by to visit or pray with them. We learned
that the pastor had met with a different grieving family. As it happened,
their family member had died that night.

Some might say that our assistant pastor made a mistake, but I don't
believe it. God sent our pastor to the people who needed Him most.

*Thank You, Lord, that You know our needs and
are always ready to meet them.*
—Debbie Macomber

June

Wed 23

Show me thy ways, O Lord; teach me thy paths.
—PSALM 25:4

There were six of us gathered around the dining room table: Al, our attorney; Janet, his secretary; Mary, my wife Ruby's companion; Eileen, Mary's field supervisor; plus Ruby and me. We had finished signing updates to Ruby's and my wills, and our business was complete.

Our conversation turned to dreams and careers. Each of us had found success: Ruby as a tax examiner and me as a technical writer. But we'd all had dreams for our lives that hadn't come true.

Al spoke of wanting to be a musician; Janet, Eileen and Ruby dreamed of being nurses; Mary wanted to be a nun; and I hoped to be a social worker. Our careers, it seemed, were not of our own choosing. Had we missed out on something in our lives?

As I listened, I remembered the words of the late Dr. Karl Menninger, who asked, "What do we need to be whole, fulfilled, healthy-minded?" His answer was, "Everyone needs two things. First, we need work to do that we consider important and someone to assure us that our efforts are indeed worthwhile. And second, we need someone to love who loves us in return."

I looked around the table and I saw that for all of us, these needs had been fulfilled. But there was something else: Scripture tells us that God often called people to serve Him in ways they hadn't expected or even wanted. God summoned Moses from his father-in-law's flocks to lead the people of Israel out of slavery; He sent Jonah to Nineveh against his will; Paul was a hardened persecutor until his dramatic conversion to Christ. As God loved them, so He loves each of us, and this love manifested itself in each of our careers and in our family and friends.

Understanding Father, our dreams were changed because You had
a better road for us to travel, one that brings us closer to You.
—OSCAR GREENE

Thu 24

Jesus said unto her, I am the resurrection, and the life: he that believeth in me, though he were dead, yet shall he live.
—JOHN 11:25

A few years ago Guideposts published *Comfort from Beyond*, a book filled with warm and wonderful stories of the encouragement and solace people have received from family and friends who have passed on. I loved the stories, but I was skeptical that such a thing could ever happen to me.

Then one day a large brown envelope arrived in the mail. I slit it open with no idea at all of what it might contain. There in my hand was a red file folder; "Brigitte" was written on the tab. A small sticky note attached to it said, "We thought you might like to have this."

Inside was a collection of poems, e-mails, photographs, a couple of newspaper clippings—everything that I had ever sent to my late friend and colleague Van Varner. Tears rolled steadily down my cheeks. *Van cared enough about* me *to save all these things?* There were painful reminders of how much I missed our bimonthly lunches at his chosen lunch spot, the restaurant in an old-line department store, where he always ordered the chicken-and-rice soup. And there was the knowledge of how steadily he had supported me both professionally and personally.

From that moment on there's been not a trace of doubt in my mind that Van is waiting for me, with his silver hair a little ruffled as he walks always on the curbside of the street "to have my sword hand free," as he used to say, though highwaymen are scarce on New York City's Fifth Avenue.

> *Comfort and sorrow make for odd bedfellows, Lord,*
> *but no one ever claimed that life was simple.*
> *And thank you, Van, for that comfort from beyond.*
> —BRIGITTE WEEKS

❊ THE GIFT OF SIGHT

Fri 25   *If therefore thine eye be single, thy whole body shall be full of light.* —MATTHEW 6:22

SACRED MOMENTS

I've made it a point to memorize my favorite photos, so I can call them up when my soul is hungry for beauty. In that same mental file is the memory of a day when our friends Jim and Nancy Pratt from London drove us out to a small English country church. Without telling us why, they asked us to remove our sunglasses before entering. We were simply awestruck by the sight of the glorious stained glass window over the altar, dominated by swaths of deepest ocean blue. The window was created by the famous artist Marc Chagall, commissioned by a family whose daughter had drowned in a sailing accident. The window shows her rising from the water and ascending on a horse to Jesus, surrounded by angels. We stood together, breathless and moved to silence by a Presence beyond our understanding. It was some time before we could bear to leave.

When darkness had fallen on our last night in London, the Pratts took us outside, where we passed through a Japanese-style wooden fence and gate. As we stood in silence, Jim went from stone lantern to stone lantern with a torch, lighting up the little Japanese garden they had created, complete with a small teahouse, a waterfall and pool, and a raked-sand-and-rock garden. This, too, felt like a truly sacred moment. The English gardens, the Eden Project, the Lost Garden of Heligan, the Chagall window, the Japanese garden with its lanterns—all of these are images I shall cherish for days and nights to come.

Sacred Creator of all things, You are the light that shows me the way through the darkness. —MARILYN MORGAN KING

Sat 26
"I, the Lord, am the maker of all things, Stretching out the heavens by Myself...." —ISAIAH 44:24 (NAS)

If you look carefully, the sky can be incredibly revealing and richly interactive. Once I saw a sun dog on a blustery winter day—two bright smears of light flanking the sun, caused by blowing ice particles reflecting its rays.

Out watching a lunar eclipse one evening, my neighbor and I waved at the moon in a teasing attempt to see our own shadows there! How humbling it was to see earth's curve creep across the moon's face.

After reading a story about a "dream pillow" cloud, my grandchildren and I had great fun selecting our favorite clouds for dreaming on.

When an Alaskan June midnight sun set on my daughter's birthday, I congratulated the glowing pink clouds, calling "It's a girl!"

How mesmerizing to watch the northern lights flash emerald across the Alaskan arctic night and imagine that emerald rainbow around God's throne (Revelation 4:3).

God has sunk His wealth in the sky, there to see 24/7. But something is not there yet. Jesus said of His return, "Then they will see the Son of Man coming in a cloud with power and great glory" (Luke 21:27, NAS). The sky will one day dazzle us with God's richest treasure: Jesus, our Majestic Savior, Bright Morning Star, Redeemer and Friend. He's the best reason to keep looking up.

"O beautiful, for spacious skies," Lord, the backdrop for my interaction with You and the panorama for Your triumphant return!
—CAROL KNAPP

June

Sun 27

"A tithe of everything from the land, whether grain from the soil or fruit from the trees, belongs to the Lord; it is holy to the Lord." —LEVITICUS 27:30 (NIV)

When I was growing up, the Communion service at our church was a very big deal. I looked forward to the day I could take the little crackers and drink the juice from the doll-sized cups, but until then I had a very important job: the offering.

Every week, as the deacons gathered to pass the plates, Dad would pull out a handful of coins and hold them in his broad, strong hand. I picked through the coins until I could find the ten best, shiniest pennies among the lot. I'd spread them down my knees, making sure that the date was legible, the surface polished and the faces scratch-free. Then I'd roll them up in my palm and deposit them with a resounding clang in the plate as it passed by my parents.

Mom and Dad encouraged all of us children to give to the church, starting when we were only old enough to pick out the best, shiniest pennies, but their lesson has lasted long beyond that. Today, my ten best pennies might be volunteering to make meals, helping out in a children's class or an extra donation on a special Sunday. Whatever they are, I'm to give my ten pennies with the same joyful heart I had during the Sunday services of my childhood.

God, give me a heart that longs to please and seek You
through the care and support of others.
—ASHLEY JOHNSON

☀ MEETING SUNRISE

Mon 28 *Jesus answered and said to him, ". . . We will come to him and make Our home with him."* —JOHN 14:23 (NKJV)

MAKING FRIENDS

I jogged to my car, dragging God with me as I zipped through my daily prayers. *Bless Mom and Dad*, I prayed, and down the list I went. Then my mind skipped to the errands I needed to run before my friend Autumn and her seven-year-old daughter Carissa arrived for a sleepover. *God, I'll catch some time with You this afternoon.*

Afternoon melted into evening and before I knew it, Autumn and Carissa were knocking on my door. My golden retriever puppy Sunrise bounded after Carissa, who ran away squealing in delight. The two tumbled on the lawn until dinner, and afterward they were at it again. We popped corn; Carissa shared hers with Sunrise. When we snuggled into blankets and turned on *Anne of Green Gables*, Carissa wanted Sunrise next to her.

During a break in the movie, Carissa tugged on my pant leg, "Rebecca, where does Sunrise sleep?" she asked.

"In my walk-in closet."

"Do you think I could sleep with her?"

Autumn nodded, so after the movie I laid pillows on the floor next to Sunrise's bed and tucked Carissa into a sleeping bag. As I glanced over at my prayer chair, I remembered my broken promise. *Oh, God, I never did get back to You!*

I looked into the closet at Carissa snuggling next to Sunrise. *God, that's what I want to be—passionate about being with You. Please be with me everywhere I go.*

Thank You, Lord, for the comfort of Your friendship.
—REBECCA ONDOV

Tue 29   *Who redeems your life from the Pit, who crowns you with steadfast love and mercy.* —PSALM 103:4 (RSV)

Our party had camped for the night at a quiet beach tucked into a curve of the Colorado River. The red-brown walls of the lower Grand Canyon rose above us toward the deep blue afternoon sky, where only a few stray clouds drifted past. We'd been on the river for ten days, and the slow rhythm of the trip had seeped into every one of us. Even me, though it had taken the first five days of the trip to trade the constant adrenaline of the workplace for the momentary adrenaline of the rapids we encountered now and then.

"I don't think I could deal with any responsibility right now if my life depended on it," I said to my husband Keith. We were sitting on the beach, listening to the gentle lapping of the river, speculating about a wire stretching overhead across it.

And then we all heard the plane. Planes are not supposed to fly below the rim of the canyon, but fliers out of Nellis Air Force Base sometimes disregard that rule.

"Where is he?" one of the boatmen yelled.

The engine noise got louder, and suddenly we saw a plane only about ten yards above the river, rounding a bluff upstream and heading toward us—and directly toward the wire. We leaped to our feet, waving frantically at the plane and screaming. It seemed that a crash was inevitable, but at the last second the flier saw the orange warning cones strung on the wire, jerked the plane up, and missed hitting it by a foot or two. In another moment he had vanished downriver.

We all stood looking after him, shocked by the nearness of disaster.

At last I said somewhat sheepishly to Keith, "It seems when someone else's life depends on it, I didn't think twice about the responsibility."

You fill me with concern for others, Lord, and
You give me strength to help them.
—RHODA BLECKER

Wed 30

Sing praises to the Lord, O you his saints, and give thanks to his holy name. . . . Weeping may tarry for a night, but joy comes in the morning. —PSALM 30:4–5 (RSV)

I woke up feeling depressed. There was no reason for it that I could think of, yet my usual cheery outlook for the day was missing. After breakfast I sat down in my prayer chair. *Lord, I'm feeling kind of down today. Please help me find a better attitude.*

Whoosh! A dragon belched fire right over our house. I knew there were no such things as dragons, but that's what it made me think of. *Whoosh!*

I jumped up and ran outside. Hanging about fifty feet above was a hot-air balloon, its red, orange and yellow stripes glistening in the sunlight. A man and a woman waved to me over the edge of the gondola.

"Hello down there!" the man called.

"Hello!" I yelled, waving back.

The man turned and tugged at something that released a small plume of flame inside the balloon. *Whoosh!* The balloon lifted higher into the air and drifted away.

"Have a nice day!" the woman called.

I raised one arm in farewell. "You too!"

I watched until the balloon became a speck in the distance and then walked, smiling, into the house. I went back to my prayer chair and said out loud, "Thank You, God! That was a unique answer to prayer!"

With spirits lifted as high as that balloon, I continued my morning meditation.

> *Lord, thank You for unexpected events that bring us joy.*
> *Today I'll watch for an opportunity*
> *to lift someone else's spirit.*
> —MADGE HARRAH

THE GIFTS I'VE BEEN GIVEN

1 _____

2 _____

3 _____

4 _____

5 _____

6 _____

7 _____

8 _____

9 _____

10 _____

11 _____

12 _____

13 _____

14 _____

15 _____

16 _____

17 _____

18 _____

19 _____

20 _____

21 _____

June

22 _____

23 _____

24 _____

25 _____

26 _____

27 _____

28 _____

29 _____

30 _____

July

*Now there are diversities
of gifts, but the same Spirit.*

—I CORINTHIANS 12:4

✿ GIFTS FROM ABOVE

Thu 1   Weeping may endure for a night, but joy cometh
in the morning. —PSALM 30:5

A GIFT OF PERSPECTIVE

S omeday this, too, will be a pleasure to recall."
When I was about twelve years old, I came across that saying,
copied it down and taped it to my desk drawer.

Many years later that same desk was loaded onto a moving truck,
headed for our new home—high on a hill, with no yard, less mainte-
nance and fewer rooms. We were simplifying.

When the truck pulled up to our new home, the driver walked slowly
into the empty kitchen, hat in hands, and said, "Mrs. Kidd, I have some
bad news. We didn't know about the hill when we packed the truck . . .
and I'm afraid the load shifted." He looked like he was going to cry.

We walked out to the truck as one of the crew struggled with its back
door. As the door slid open, I peered inside. It was as if someone had taken
all our furniture, housewares, books and clothes and put them in the spin
cycle of a huge dryer. There were boxes filled with bits of broken glass;
legs were separated from tables; bureau drawers were scattered about.

I was holding back hysteria as I returned to the house and began telling
the men where to put the furniture. In came my childhood desk. I gently
pulled open the top drawer and there was that same old saying taped inside.

Of course, I thought, *we wanted to simplify and we just got a little extra
help.*

Later that evening, the owner of the moving company appeared, a
grim expression on his face. I'm sure he anticipated a lawsuit. But my
husband and I had agreed: This move was a new beginning.

"Everything's fine," I said.

> *Father, give me the gift of perspective so that I can face setbacks*
> *with good humor.* —PAM KIDD

Fri 2   *"Please accept the present that was brought to you, for God has been gracious to me. . . ."* —GENESIS 33:11 (NIV)

On the last day of our second mission trip to a remote village in Honduras, we were surprised when the villagers asked us to join them for a picnic beside a shallow river littered with rounded rocks and boulders.

As I started to walk toward the picnic, I noticed a tiny girl named Julia with Down syndrome looking up at me. The year before, she had shyly hidden behind her mother Gloria's skirt. Now she held her hand up to me as if she'd known me all her life. I took her hand, and we made our way across the rocks together.

When we reached her mother, Gloria unfastened the small beaded necklace with a shiny rock in the center from around her neck. I froze as she reached up and firmly fastened the necklace around me. I shook my head, protesting, "No, no!" My mind told me, *I can't accept this! I have plenty of necklaces at home, but she has only one.* Yet my heart answered, *You can't refuse her gift.*

I smiled and gave Gloria a big hug, knowing that I had received more than a necklace; I'd been given the grace to receive a gift of love.

> *Dear Father, thank You for giving me Your love*
> *even though I really don't know how*
> *to accept it graciously.*
> —KAREN BARBER

Sat 3

"I will also honor them and they will not be insignificant."
—JEREMIAH 30:19 (NAS)

Each Saturday morning during early summer, you will find me in the backyard, swatting mosquitoes while I mull over which flowers to choose for a bouquet to take to church on Sunday. *Should I cut some round balls of blue allium? White Shasta daisies? Golden rudbeckia? Some of each?* Later on I deliberate over red gladiolas or mauve cosmos, stately white lilies or carnival-colored zinnias.

When I started making floral bouquets to decorate our church, it seemed that no matter how many blooms I chose or how large the arrangement seemed at home, the minute I placed it at the front of the church, it shrank into insignificance. Higher, wider, fuller—nothing seemed to make it stand out in the sanctuary.

And then one week, when I didn't have enough blooms to round out the arrangement I had in mind, I supplemented it with lots of small, bright yellow flowers, tucked in here and there to fill in the bare spots.

I was pleased when I stood at the back of the sanctuary to see how the smaller, brighter flowers drew attention to the whole bouquet. They were, I decided, much like the small loving deeds of the folks in the congregation who stay in the background but "fill in the bare spots" and help all of us focus on that One Who is the center of our worship.

Remind me, Lord, that each small service I render
enhances the beauty of church life.
—ALMA BARKMAN

Sun 4   *In returning and rest shall ye be saved; in quietness and in confidence shall be your strength. . . .* —ISAIAH 30:15

When our son John was about to turn ten, Julia and I decided that I would take our history-loving boy to celebrate the nation's birthday—and his own a few days later—in the nation's capital. I made reservations and pored over guidebooks, determined to squeeze as much as possible into what would be John's first visit to Washington, DC.

But a week before the Fourth of July, I came down with a fever that turned out to be the first sign of a painful infection. A visit to the doctor got me some antibiotics and the advice that out-of-town travel would be a very bad idea.

While John tried manfully to hide his disappointment, I went to bed to sweat out my fever in the heat. On the afternoon of the Fourth, Julia asked me if I felt up to going out. Still a little woozy, I got out of bed, showered and dressed. She had assembled the troops: John, with his wooden rifle over his shoulder, his three sisters with bags and bundles, and toddler Stephen. Our little regiment slowly made its way up the street and into the park.

Julia led us to an out-of-the-way bit of lawn with a stand of trees. Blankets were spread, and out of the bags came crisp French bread, a profusion of cheeses, a big bowl of fresh fruit salad and bottles of cold lemonade. After grace and a first assault on the provisions, our little army headed out for a brief skirmish, while I rested in the shade and watched them chase one another through the trees.

We had no pomp or parade that day, no bonfires or illuminations, just a leisurely afternoon to savor a simple meal, a beautiful spot and one another, and to remember all those whose tears, toil and treasure made it possible for us to enjoy such quiet, glorious moments.

> *Lord, no matter what my circumstances, may I never forget*
> *to celebrate the blessings of freedom.*
> —ANDREW ATTAWAY

Mon 5
*The Lord is my light and salvation; whom shall I fear?... —*Psalm 27:1

M y son Solomon was afraid of getting his head wet. Last summer when I signed him up for swim lessons, my husband and I spent many nights reassuring Solomon that he'd be fine.

On the morning of his first lesson, Solomon and I waited outside the community swimming pool. I gave him a hug and whispered, "You can do it!" Solomon put on a belt with floats and climbed down the ladder. He followed the instructor's words carefully. When she asked him to blow bubbles in the water, without hesitation he leaned in and blew.

In the following days Solomon learned to float and paddle. By the second week my concern eased, and I read a magazine as they practiced. At one point I looked up to check on Solomon and didn't see him. I raced to the pool's edge and fearfully searched the bottom. I was about to yell out to the instructor when I noticed the boy in front of me swimming gracefully with his face in the water. He was wearing the same kind of swimsuit as Solomon. *Wait, that is Solomon! Look how beautifully he glides!*

I clapped and cheered, and my eyes filled with tears as Solomon reached the edge of the pool.

Thank You, Father, for giving me the opportunity to see
my son rise above his fear and to do so with grace.
—Sabra Ciancanelli

Tue 6

And his name shall be called Wonderful, Counsellor, The mighty God, The everlasting Father, The Prince of Peace.
—ISAIAH 9:6

When I was a child, I spent summers with my Chinese grandparents in California. Each morning we'd have a time of prayer and devotion after breakfast, which, on a lucky day, would be my grandma's fried rice, eggy and dotted with little bits of Chinese sausage. We'd read the Bible, we'd pray—for our family, for friends, for the President of the United States, for the world—and we'd sing hymns in Cantonese. My minister-grandfather, who had suffered a stroke, belted them out when he remembered the words, and my grandmother's warbly voice carried us through.

As I was walking through Chinatown in New York City recently, the sights and sounds—little old ladies, sizzling street food, the barrage of Cantonese—triggered my mental time machine, and one song from our family repertoire popped into my head. It's an old Christian standard known in English as "Isn't He Wonderful?" But in Chinese, the title is translated, "Isn't Jesus Christ Really Amazingly Mysterious?"

It occurred to me that with the simple switch of language, this song gained nuance and depth that the combination of the English words and the music couldn't manage. It's not that *wonderful* is a bad word. It's just that "amazingly mysterious" said much more about the nature of the Lord—how He isn't just wonderful, but really awe-inspiring, extraordinary and beyond our understanding.

In both English and Chinese, the song continues: "Eyes have seen, ears have heard . . ." And indeed, mine were opened.

Lord, thank You for showing me that
not everything is lost in translation.
—JEFF CHU

Wed 7   *"No eye has seen, no ear has heard, no mind has conceived*
what God has prepared for those who love him."
—I Corinthians 2:9 (NIV)

"I t is what it is," a young woman told me recently with tears in her eyes, as we stood outside the aerobics class where we'd become friends. She was describing her painful adjustment to a new reality in her life—impending divorce.

Though I knew those words helped her accept her hard circumstances, I wanted to tell her how much I dislike that cliché, because it so quickly limits what "it" might become. I wanted her to believe that God could use this painful reality to grow something new and hopeful in her life, even though she couldn't possibly imagine how right now.

I know, because I've been there—not in the same circumstances but with similar feelings. My resistance to the phrase comes from years of looking back at difficult things and recognizing how God brings good out of them.

Three years ago when I was diagnosed with stage-four ovarian cancer, I faced an emotional crossroad: I could hopelessly resign myself to "It is what it is" or I could believe that "it" could become so much more than what appeared at that moment.

Once I got beyond the initial shock and grief, I began to recognize that cancer brought me opportunities and gifts that other people don't have: the gift of experiencing deeper, more meaningful relationships with the people I love; the opportunity to know and choose to do what matters most each day; the strength to cope with realities I didn't know I could handle.

As I left my friend in the parking lot, I prayed that she would receive the blessing of that same kind of hope—soon.

> *Lord, thank You for showing me that with You,*
> *"it" isn't always what it appears to be.*
> —Carol Kuykendall

Thu 8   *For by him were all things created. . . . —*COLOSSIANS 1:16

"Come on, Sheila, time to go see Doctor Nancy." I scoop up my kitty quickly, thrust her silky body into the carrier, and make sure her fluffy tail is all the way in so I don't catch it in the zipper. Sheila doesn't weigh much, so I put the carrier over my shoulder, and she looks out through the mesh as I proceed through our neighborhood of honking taxis, sniffing dogs and chattering schoolchildren.

Over the past thirty years in my Manhattan apartment, I've roomed with five cats: Catarina, Lucy and Onions, Clarence and Sheila. They've all had checkups and medical treatment at the veterinary three blocks away, where they've been cared for with kindness and efficiency.

Over the years in the waiting room, I've seen a range of other pets too. Dainty parakeets, raucous parrots and toucans, occasional gerbils and hamsters with quivering noses. One day a little girl appeared with a mouse in a small wire cage. "Hi, Mousie," the vet greeted her and placed Mousie on the weigh-in scale at the same time my cat Clarence was being lowered in from the other side. Fortunately both were withdrawn before one of the patients turned into a snack. I've also seen a rabbit with long floppy ears and a snake in a doughnut box. The other dogs and cats are quite a cast of characters too, and we pet owners often exchange stories and tissues and even hugs. "I'll pray for you," a woman with a frisky poodle said to me quietly the day I learned my Clarence had cancer.

I have a book of *Prayers from the Ark* translated from French. And as I trudge along with my kitty in her carrier in my own ark of New York City, I make one of Noah's prayers my own:

> *"Lord, what a menagerie! The days are long, Lord;*
> *guide Your ark to safety until we reach*
> *the shore of Your covenant."*
> —MARY ANN O'ROARK

Fri 9 *They shall feed every one in his place.* —JEREMIAH 6:3

Phyllis, my next-door neighbor's mother, always wore an apron. That's because she was always cooking: rolling out pie crusts for the firefighters in her picturesque New Hampshire town, shaping dozens of her famous mountain cookies for bake sales or simmering Boston baked beans for church suppers. If food was needed, Phyllis was there. When her daughter Janice invited me over for cookouts, supposedly Phyllis's day off, I'd enjoy the conversation—and Phyllis's creamy potato salad with a yummy extra something. That woman just *had* to cook.

Now Phyllis knew that I felt lonely living on the lake in the winter, especially during that first empty-nest year following my daughter Trina's graduation. So during the darkest evenings of the year, Phyllis included me at her table for a proper Sunday dinner: meat, potatoes, gravy, several vegetables and two desserts, a true labor of love whipped up by a woman nearly eighty years old and too diabetic to eat most of it. Yet how she nourished so many of us!

Then one July afternoon, God suddenly called Phyllis home. Janice found her mother near the door of the sun porch, wearing her apron. In her hand Phyllis held bread; she had been on her way to feed the birds.

Lord, thank You for the ways dear Phyllis nourished me. Use me to carry on her pantry ministry. —GAIL THORELL SCHILLING

READER'S ROOM

I wear hearing aids, and every so often after a shower I panic. *Did I take out the hearing aids?* I touch my ears to make sure. I don't want to miss the little things, like my grandsons' laughter, my sons' or husband's "I love you," or a neighbor's "Hi!" I still have problems hearing. My audiologist says that's normal. But I think I need to listen more intently, the way I listen to God. When I share everything with God, I feel His answers, because I'm tuned into Him. —*Tiffany Klappenbach, Mount Gilead, North Carolina*

Sat 10

He that findeth his life shall lose it: and he that loseth his life for my sake shall find it. —MATTHEW 10:39

I'm sitting on a park bench, reading a book while the butterflies hover over a stalk of hollyhocks and then flutter to the daylilies bending on their stems. I've come to this bench as I often do on a Saturday to escape the phone and the computer and the bills that need to be paid. I even make a point of not taking a watch. It's my sort of "staycation"—a way of getting away without going far at all.

All of a sudden my calm is interrupted by a boy, about three years old, who dashes along the path and then ducks behind a hedge. "I'm hiding!" he calls to his mother, who's pushing an empty stroller along the path behind him. "You can't see me!" he yells, his blond cowlick rising over the shrubbery like a duck's tail.

Of course she can see him and so can I. But I know just how he feels, the two of us hiding from the world. I sit on my park bench, close my eyes and feel far away from the stresses that put me off balance and make me less than the person I want to be, until I remember Whose I am and what's really important in my life.

The boy pops up from behind the hedge and greets his mother in a fit of giggles. "You found me!" he exclaims.

"I did!" she says, giving him a hug.

I watch them go and then get up from my bench, glad of my escape. Happy to be lost for a while just so I, too, can be found.

Lord, I lose myself today so that You can find me.
—RICK HAMLIN

Sun 11

And He saw a poor widow putting in two small copper coins. And He said, "Truly I say to you, this poor widow put in more than all of them." —LUKE 21:2–3 (NAS)

Here's a present-day parable: A woman visiting her mother in north Idaho took a Sunday morning walk on the local high school track. While she was walking, she found two pennies and stuck them in her pocket. She tossed the pennies into her walking shoes when she changed clothes and forgot them. The next day she flew home to Minnesota and rediscovered the coins as she unpacked. She set them on her night table.

The following Sunday she went to church. In the Bible passage that day, Jesus watched people contribute lavishly to the temple treasury, while a poor widow put in only two small copper coins. He said she had put in more than them all because they had given from their surplus, but she had given from her poverty "all that she had to live on" (Luke 21:4, NAS).

The woman thought about this widow who gave all she had. The woman was not a widow, but she was having trouble giving to her marriage. She felt poor inside, with little to offer. That evening as she walked past her night table, she noticed the pennies. God seemed to speak to her: *Give what you have, even if it seems too small to count.*

The woman took courage. She began to recognize ways she could genuinely offer what she had in her marriage. She thought if she kept giving long enough, her two coins would become a heap of treasure for her husband and for her. She didn't fear that her "two small copper coins" would run out. Hadn't God provided them on a Sunday morning walk before she ever understood why?

Elroi ("God Who sees"), I—this woman—thank You.
—CAROL KNAPP

Mon 12

"I will bless you . . . and you will be a blessing to many others."—GENESIS 12:2 (TLB)

I love to travel and, like many people who fly, I've had a few over-the-top experiences. On a flight from Chicago to Hong Kong, when we were two hours past Anchorage, Alaska, a young woman had an asthma attack and we had to turn around, dump excess fuel, make an emergency landing in Anchorage, refuel, then deice the plane before we could take off again. It added five hours to the regular seventeen-hour flight.

Another time, on a crowded plane, I was hoping the seat between me and the young woman in the aisle seat would remain empty. Just then an extremely large man plopped down, pinning my shoulder under his girth. Before we took off, the flight attendant delivered a seven-month-old baby girl to his lap, saying, "Your wife says she misses her daddy." His wife was up front with their five-year-old. Five minutes after takeoff, Daddy started whistling to calm her down. He whistled nonstop for the next hour.

Both experiences taught me that it's usually the tough stuff that happens to us that are really gifts in disguise. At the very least they make the most interesting stories later on. For months afterward I told my family and friends those flight stories with great embellishment, noting how excited I was to see Mount McKinley at sunset as we headed back to Anchorage. And about how I enjoyed my conversation with "Big Daddy" while I played with his baby girl, tickling her little toes and playing peekaboo with her small receiving blanket.

I think life is like that: interesting blessings disguised as struggles. I've learned to be more patient and actually look forward to the unusual and the unexpected when I travel. The stories themselves are worth it.

Father, when things don't go as planned,
keep my sense of humor intact
and give me patience.
—PATRICIA LORENZ

July

Tue 13

The Lord will work out his plans for my life. . . .
—PSALM 138:8 (TLB)

For the past nine years we've traveled from Copeland, Kansas, to Oklahoma City twice a year for my husband Don's post-cancer checkups. The pattern never varied: We left late in the afternoon, spent the night with my sister, saw the surgeon early in the morning and were home by midafternoon. Don always wanted to stay an extra day or two to visit friends, but I didn't want to miss work.

When Don was scheduling an appointment after I retired, he said, "This would be a great time to visit Connie and Ray. We could also see Amy."

"We can't," I replied automatically. "I have to get right home."

"Why?" Don shot back. "The house is clean, and you just mailed the grant proposal you were writing." I argued, I lost, and here's what happened:

1. The doctor said Don is still cancer-free.
2. We enjoyed a delicious lunch and a long afternoon "catching up" with Connie and Ray in Ada, Oklahoma.
3. My niece Amy told us about an annually renewable college scholarship for our oldest grandson Ryan. (He got it!)
4. On the way home we toured Alabaster Caverns, the only natural gypsum cave in the world that's open to the public. After the tour we had a marvelous Mexican lunch at a tiny café.
5. I had as much fun as Don!

It's hard to break old habits, but by God's grace—and with frequent nudges from Don—I'm embracing the awesome adventures God has planned for the rest of my life.

> *Keep reminding me, Lord, that my way isn't the only way—*
> *or even the right way.* —PENNEY SCHWAB

Wed 14

A man who loves his wife loves himself.
—Ephesians 5:28 (GNB)

Just because I've been married to the same woman for forty-six years doesn't mean I'm an expert on marriage. It's a mystery to me how married couples get along at all, considering our differences.

- Sharon loves to talk. I never miss a chance to keep quiet.
- I turn the thermostat up to stay warm. She turns it down to save money.
- At night, she pulls the covers up to her chin. I leave them down at my waist.
- She wants the fan to oscillate. I like it to blow steady.
- When we travel, she wants the windows up and the stereo off. I want the windows down and Frank Sinatra singing.
- At the buffet, she fills her plate with meat. I fill mine with veggies.
- She wants onion on everything. I want onion on nothing.
- She eats slower than a turtle. I eat like a starved lion.
- She never wants to be late. I never want to be early.
- I surf three news channels at once. She wants to watch just one.

Some of our differences are negotiable. When Sharon is in the car, I put the windows up, but I play Sinatra softly.

Some of our differences are not negotiable. Abraham Lincoln said that his wife wanted to paint the bedroom green, and he wanted to paint it yellow. "So we compromised," he said. "We painted it green."

Differences are frustrating, but they're also interesting. Who wants to be married to a clone of oneself? We have the important things in common and we can work out the little differences.

Lord, thank You for making us with the ability to adapt to our mates.
—Daniel Schantz

Thu 15

Then I saw, and considered it well: I looked upon it, and received instruction. —PROVERBS 24:32

Our little dog Dolly loves to spend time in the backyard. Sometimes she explores the bushes and flushes out lizards; other times she lies quietly in a sunny spot and sleeps. On this particular day she wouldn't stop barking. I figured she'd heard the *clink-clink* of collar tags as a dog passed by on the sidewalk, but she kept it up. I glanced outside and saw that she was barking at the grapefruit tree, so I went out in the yard to take a closer look. I didn't see anything unusual.

"Take a rest, Dolly," I said as I went back inside. But she wouldn't rest, and finally I walked outside and sat under the tree so I could get a Dolly-eye view of the branches. Sitting up there calmly was a big gray cat.

"I'm sorry I doubted you," I said as I brought Dolly inside until the cat decided to move along. I thought I had looked at that tree, but until I got into a position to see it from Dolly's point of view, I wasn't really seeing it at all.

I try to remember that when a disagreement arises at work over the best way to accomplish a job or I can't understand why a friend acts a certain way. I remember sitting under that grapefruit tree, looking up, doing my best to see things as Dolly saw them. By changing the view, I can see a problem in a completely new way, allowing a path for resolution.

Lord, make me willing to "get under the tree" when
I need to and see the world from another angle.
—GINA BRIDGEMAN

Fri 16

Whatsoever Adam called every living creature, that was the name thereof. —GENESIS 2:19

I was recently in Hawaii, where I had dinner on the beach with a quiet, grinning man, who started telling me about all the fish in the waters around us. After a while he just chanted the names of the fish, and we sat there by guttering candlelight, amazed at the artistry of the Creator. My friend sang the fish for a long time and concluded by saying, "But the best to eat are *ahi, aku, au, awa, aweoweo, kala, kumu, moano, moilii, oio, ono, uhu, uku* and *uu,*" at which point we ordered *ahi.*

Later I was standing in the sun in front of a tattered grocery store, holding fresh pineapples like prickly footballs, when a bird the size of a tent sailed over, and I gaped and said to a tiny man next to me, "Man! What was that?"

"That is *iwa,* the frigate bird, which you rarely see over this parking lot," he said, "though sometimes we do. And here I have seen *a,* the booby with the red feet, and *akikiki,* the creeper, and we also have here the *i'iwi* and *o'u'* and *nukupu,* who are also honeycreepers, and *pueo,* the little owl, and *io,* our Hawaiian hawk, and *ulili,* the little tattler who wanders, and our *o'o,* the honeyeater, and *elepaio,* the flycatcher, and *alala,* old man crow, and *huna kai,* the sanderling—her name means ocean foam. And we have *hoio,* the shearwater—he lives in caves by the sea—and *uau,* the petrel, and *aukuu,* the night heron, and *koloa,* he is our duck. And of course you know *nene,* the goose. There is one over there under the crown flower tree, see?"

"Yes, sir, I see. Thank you, thank you so much," I said, and he wandered off, smiling. I stood there for a long time, thinking that the language of the love of God comes in more colors and shapes and melodies than we could ever count.

Dear Lord, blessed are we beyond our wildest dreams.
—BRIAN DOYLE

🌼 TWELVE KEYS TO THE GIVING LIFE

Sat 17 It is more blessed to give than to receive. —ACTS 20:35

GIVE LOVINGLY

For months I'd looked forward to my niece Allison's wedding. I couldn't wait to see her walk down the aisle to the altar on the arm of my brother Robert.

When I arrived at the church, Allison and Robert were standing outside, waiting to make their entrance. The first thing I noticed wasn't Allison's long, flowing white gown; it was her unusual bouquet.

What on earth was that florist thinking, mixing purple and orange and pink and red? And whoever heard of combining tulips and carnations?

I tried not to look at the flowers as Allison made her way down the aisle. She was positively glowing, but I couldn't help feeling sorry for her. This was the day she'd dreamed about since she was a little girl. And what would that garish bouquet look like in the photographs?

At the reception, Allison radiated joy as she thanked everyone for making her day so wonderful. Then I noticed a stack of small envelopes in Allison's hand. After hugging a group of doting aunts and offering them each one, she headed in my direction. "This is for you, Aunt Roberta," she said.

I found a place to park my cake and punch and opened my envelope. Inside was a note from Allison: "My wedding bouquet represents all the special people in my life. You are one of them. The pink tulip, your favorite flower, is for all the things you've done to make me who I am."

Suddenly Allison's bouquet was no longer a hapless heap of daisies, roses, carnations and tulips. It was simply beautiful.

> *Thank You, Lord, for those who risk looking foolish*
> *to love with their whole hearts.*
> —ROBERTA MESSNER

⧗ COMFORT FOR THE HURTING HEART

Sun 18 *Jesus wept.* —JOHN 11:35

WHEN WORDS FAIL

S*omething's up,* I told myself early that Sunday at church when I noticed clusters of people talking in whispers. During the service I learned the reason: One of our brilliant, charming young women, whose incessant pain from an incurable ailment was impossible for doctors to alleviate, had taken her life the day before. Incredibly, her parents were in attendance that morning. Their grief was so deep that they'd come, seeking solace from fellow church members. I touched them both and said, "I'm so sorry." Yet I felt helpless, wondering, *What else can I do?*

Six months later I asked the father, "What was and was not helpful, especially during those first few days and weeks?"

"Most memorable was the young woman who spotted us as we came into the foyer that day. She threw her arms around my wife, and both of them cried for a long time. Her hug was just tight enough and just long enough and her tears were just wet enough to be a balm for both.

"At the same time I noticed an older mother who'd lost her daughter to a murderer and I thought, *She made it. I can make it also.*

"On the other hand, there were the people who implied our trouble was not nearly as bad as theirs. And there were those who wanted details that they could feed into the gossip stream.

"The manner of our daughter's death wasn't anywhere near as important as this one fact: We had lost our child. We ached like everyone else who's bereft of a loved one."

Dear Lord, show me how to best comfort those who are grieving.
—ISABEL WOLSELEY

❈ THE GIFT OF SIGHT

Mon 19   *I was eyes to the blind.* . . . —JOB 29:15

EYES FOR OTHERS

I was excited when the letter came from Recording for the Blind and Dyslexic. Ever since I was in high school, I had wanted to read to blind people and I'd prayed to have the opportunity someday. Now, with the latest recording equipment, special software and volunteer readers, I'd be able to do it. My husband Robert also liked the idea, and we decided it was something we really wanted to do. So we learned how to use the software and began recording two hours a week at a library an hour's drive from home.

We had been recording for a couple of years when I started stumbling in my reading, skipping lines and losing my place on the page. Why was I making so many mistakes? The more it happened, the more my confidence fell.

At my yearly eye exam I learned that the macular degeneration in my right eye was becoming worse. The doctor suggested new lenses, but they were worse than my old glasses.

Still I resisted the idea of giving up recording, until the problem became so severe I was having to stop, back up the recording and rerecord several times in a page. Finally one day, in frustration, I just turned the remainder of the session over to Robert and wrote an e-mail to the woman in charge, telling her I couldn't continue.

My heart sank as I wrote. I had prayed for the chance to help others; now I found that I might need help myself.

> *Healing God, may I have the courage to ask for help when*
> *I need it and the grace to accept it when offered.*
> —MARILYN MORGAN KING

Tue 20   The thief comes only to steal and kill and
destroy.... —JOHN 10:10 (RSV)

Summer, 1944. Somewhere in North Africa." That's all the details my
letters home were allowed to provide, that third year of the war. In
fact, we enlisted men didn't have much more information ourselves, other
than that we'd been waiting for weeks here in this dry, hot staging area.
The camp was a *repple-depple*, army slang for a replacement depot, and
what we'd be replacing was dead and injured soldiers.

There was one unofficial source of news, however, that we listened to
whenever we could. "Evening, fellows," said the sultry voice over the radio.
"This is Midge at the Mike, calling from Radio Berlin. I'll be bringing
you some Glenn Miller to remind you of home. Don't you wish you could
go dancing tonight instead of fighting a losing war?"

Axis Sally we called her, this American girl now living in Germany.
How in the world did she get her authoritative information? She said we'd
come over on a Cunard Line troopship (that was true) and that we would
soon join the 141st Infantry Regiment, Gen. Mark Clark's Fifth Army,
in Italy (which also proved to be true). "Most of you will get killed," she
said. "Too bad."

We tried to laugh at Sally. But as I lay sweating in my army-green
underwear on my canvas cot, I knew I was scared about what lay ahead,
and listening to Axis Sally didn't help.

Today, as I approach my eighty-eighth birthday, bad news is still broad-
cast over the airwaves: fearful stories of wars, natural disasters, economic
downturns. This is when it's helpful to remember Axis Sally. The facts,
like Sally's, may be accurate. But when I let myself focus on these things,
I'm rendered fearful and ineffective. It's how the spiritual enemy works.
A steady diet of negatives leaves us demoralized. Why not listen instead
to the Good News, which empowers us to reach out with love and hope
to a hurting world?

*Father, help me hear Your voice today above the clamor of
bad news reports.* —JOHN SHERRILL

Wed 21 Seek ye first the kingdom of God, and his righteousness; and all these things shall be added unto you.
—MATTHEW 6:33

Midway through a busy week, trying to manage too many things, I raced to pick up Mary at her ballet intensive. For once I arrived early. Breathing a sigh of relief, I peeked into the studio. Mary's class had begun *pointe* this week, and this was their third day. The going was rough; normally graceful girls hobbled to and from the bar, their usually smooth routine chopped into painfully short segments. As I watched, Mary's half of the class went up on *relevé* and tried to balance. It was a long way from graceful.

I knew *pointe* was supposed to be painful. But it had never dawned on me that my daughter, who stood independently at eight months and immediately tried to jump, would ever have trouble finding her balance. The thought gave me pause.

For weeks I'd been trying to figure out how to bring order to all the things I had to do. I'd told a friend I felt like a juggler trying to keep an ill-assorted array of items in the air: plates, bowling pins, the occasional butcher knife, and now and then a medicine ball. Watching my daughter, I thought I'd been using the wrong analogy. Perhaps I wasn't juggling but trying to find my center of gravity.

The fact is, if I live my priorities—God, family, community—and keep them in order, an awful lot of things fall off my to-do list on their own. The challenge is figuring out how to do whatever is set before me gracefully, without losing my centering in Christ. I'm sure Mary will be secure *en pointe* long before I get that lesson down pat.

Lord, may You always be at the center of everything I do.
—JULIA ATTAWAY

Thu 22 "Here on earth you will have many trials and sorrows. But take heart, because I have overcome the world." —JOHN 16:33 (NLT)

Rose Kennedy has given us a legacy of faith and courage, and I frequently find myself inspired by the strength she showed throughout her life.

I was desperately trying to hold together the raw and ragged edges of a hurt that wouldn't knit itself together and heal. My thoughts were jumbled by grief and tears and became the only language I could speak. Then came a lifeline from something Mrs. Kennedy once said: "It's not the tears that make the pain more bearable, it's determination!" *Determination.* That one word gave me stamina, resolve and resilience.

As a young girl, during the contemplative moments of a Lenten retreat, Mrs. Kennedy thought of the joys and sorrows, difficulties and griefs that inevitably come into all our lives. Whatever happened, she determined, "I will hold my soul forever free!" She refused to let her faith be bound by circumstance; instead, she placed unshakable trust in the goodness of God, which encircled her with an aura of peace.

Keeping in motion gave her emotional ventilation. Daily she plunged into the ice-cold waters of Cape Cod for a swim, and then went for a walk, praying and making up her mind that she was not going to be defeated by the tragedy of losing three sons. Senator Edward Kennedy said of her, "Mother believes that if there are rays of sunshine in a stormy sky, focus on the light, not the darkness."

Each year on this day, Rose Kennedy's birthday, I pause to give thanks for the strength she has given me.

> *When I'm twisted up with worries and fear, set my soul free,*
> *O blessed Holy Spirit. Steady my faith, strengthen my heart*
> *and wrap me in Your gift of peace.*
> —FAY ANGUS

Fri 23

From now on every road you travel will take you to God. . . . —PSALM 25:10 (MSG)

One afternoon we were in Chicago, packing to return home to Austin, Texas, from a meeting. I'd been very inspired by the speakers and felt that God was calling me back into action somehow. Although we were tired, we decided to save the cab fare and take the subway to the airport. We had two large bags with rollers, a computer case, a carry-on and a briefcase.

Within ten minutes we realized we were in trouble. The train tracks were being repaired, and we were rerouted under a good bit of Chicago, carrying our bags up and down stairs and having to hold them on our laps in the train so people could stand, sit or get by us. Then there were twenty minutes on a hot and crowded bus. Several times people stopped and grabbed our bags to help us.

By the time we got to our departure gate, we were sore all over and exhausted. I looked at my wife Andrea, who's younger than I, and said between deep breaths, "Honey, you're a real trooper!"

With a twinkling eye and a grin, she replied, "You are too!"

It was only then that I realized how strange I must have looked heaving those heavy bags up and down all those stairways—a skinny, white-bearded, old man of eighty-one, who had completely forgotten he wasn't a youthful seventy-five anymore.

> *Dear Lord, thank You that some of Your favorites didn't get*
> *their assignments until they were at least my age.*
> *If there's anything You'd like me to do,*
> *You don't have to test me anymore.*
> *I think I'm ready.*
> —KEITH MILLER

Sat 24

He will be the sure foundation for your times, a rich store of salvation and wisdom and knowledge....
—ISAIAH 33:6 (NIV)

It's county fair time here in the Midwest. Cows, pigs, rabbits, tractor pulls, corn-on-the-cob, funnel cakes—the fair has it all!

Yesterday I took my grandsons for an afternoon of rides and snacks. As we entered the midway, I spotted my favorite ride: the merry-go-round. Soon I stood between Drake and Brock, both of whom were mounted on impressive painted ponies.

As we gained speed and the music reached its crescendo, the ponies went into their gallop. "Nina," Drake squealed, "it goes up and down!" Again the horse lurched. And again Drake squealed, "It goes up and down!" Over and over, his verbalized delight at the sudden rise and fall of his mount never waned.

Later, as we walked the rest of the midway, I kept thinking about what Drake had said. *Carousel horses aren't the only things in life that go up and down. There are my weight, my hopes (sometimes for my weight), my investments (okay, so it's been awhile since I saw those in the "up" position), my mood, my self-esteem. Even my spiritual life has its ups and downs. One day I feel close to God and the next I become like an Old Testament prophet crying out, "Where are You, Lord?"*

The thing I love best about merry-go-rounds, in addition to those galloping horses, is that they go 'round and 'round. All that whirling reminds me that even the down times, even the doubts, don't last forever. Happiness could be just a half-turn away. All I have to do is hold on, stay on the horse and with God's help, try to enjoy the ride.

> *You, Lord, are the constant in my whirling circumstances.*
> *I will trust You and hang on tight.*
> —MARY LOU CARNEY

🐚 WORDS FROM THE SEA

Sun 25 *The Lord gave Job twice as much as he had before.*
—Job 42:10

DAY 1: CONSOLATION

Here near our friends' house the shore is all rocks, with no place to walk. But a short path along the bluff leads to a long, sandy beach. Or it did, in other years.

Even before unpacking the car, John and I set out down that path, eager to stretch our legs after the five-hour drive. We were stopped short by an impassable jumble of rocks left by a winter storm.

The blocked beach access, I thought, was just one more example of how cherished things can be snatched away. The recent death of a close friend had made me extra sensitive to any loss—like our dogwood tree back home, killed by invading beetles. Even the closing of a favorite bakery seemed part of the pattern.

A few days later we found a roundabout way down to the beach. Finally we could make our customary walk to the outlet, our reluctant turnaround point, a broad stream where a swamp emptied into the ocean. But . . .

"Surely," said John when we'd walked for twenty-five minutes, "we should have come to the outlet by now!" But the beach stretched on unbroken; before us lay miles of sandy coastline we'd never before explored. The same storm that had blocked the bluff path had sealed off the outlet and opened a new walking route.

When God takes away something precious, the ocean tells me, He sends another gift in its place.

Father, I have lost my friend. What new avenue
of love will You open to me today?
—Elizabeth Sherrill

✿ WORDS FROM THE SEA

Mon 26 *There is the sea, vast and spacious. . . .*
—PSALM 104:25 (NIV)

DAY 2: AWE

Today from the porch the ocean is speaking to me about vastness—about a horizon stretching beyond the limit of sight.

Our home in suburban New York is at the bottom of a hill. Except for a wedge of sky above the trees, everything you can see is close by. The lawn, some shrubs and the houses on either side make up the view.

But here on the coast! To the left the shoreline curves away into the distance; to the right, on clear days, you can make out the low silhouette of an island. Everywhere else is a boundless expanse of water—blue or gray or silver—beneath the immense dome of the sky.

Reluctant to leave the porch this morning, I've brought a pad and pencil with me to write out my shopping list. It's a long drive to the nearest stores and, with the price of gas, we keep trips to a minimum. Bread, milk, eggs, paper towels . . . we're low on all these things. A birthday card. Suntan lotion. Laundry detergent. If I don't write it all down, I'll forget something. But somehow I don't pick up the pencil.

Not yet. Not while my eyes are gazing at a world stretching to infinity. Not while my mind is staggered by the immensity of God's creation.

Of course, I'll make that list: food, cleaning supplies, a birthday card—these are the details of living that Jesus made important by living our daily lives with us. It's just that amid the thousand details there also needs to be time to exclaim with the angels:

Holy, holy, holy Lord!
—ELIZABETH SHERRILL

🐚 WORDS FROM THE SEA

Tue 27 There the ships go to and fro.... —PSALM 104:26 (NIV)

DAY 3: CONNECTEDNESS

From the beach this afternoon I spotted a majestic schooner far offshore, tall white sails tilting in the wind. I watched it through binoculars till it was out of sight, bound, no doubt, for Newport.

Newport is nearby, at least by water. By land it's a long, slow, twisting route following the coast. And watching that schooner skimming straight to its destination, I suddenly saw the ocean not as the place where roads end, but as the open highway that first connected the earth's far-flung people. Long before reliable roads were built, the sea and the rivers flowing into it were the principal route for conquest, trade, settlement.

Three months earlier I'd also stood on a beach watching boats at sea. The sea was the Gulf of Thailand, and the graceful women walking past spoke a language I didn't know. We give names to particular stretches of water—South Pacific, Indian Ocean, North Atlantic—but, of course, it's all one ocean, one great waterway circling the earth.

It's twilight now, and I've walked down to the point to watch the setting sun lay a golden trail across the water. Maybe, I think, one of those Thai women is watching this sun rise over the ocean this very moment. Maybe she, like me, is murmuring a prayer to the Creator of land and sea.

> *Help me see all the people of the world, Father, held in*
> *Your single embrace as Your single ocean enfolds the earth.*
> —ELIZABETH SHERRILL

✿ WORDS FROM THE SEA

Wed 28   *Let us not become weary in doing good, for at the proper time we will reap a harvest if we do not give up.*
—GALATIANS 6:9 (NIV)

DAY 4: PERSISTENCE

It was warm enough this afternoon to pull off my shoes and go wading—gingerly. I hadn't gone barefoot in a long time, and stones and pebbles were hard to see in the swirling water. Every time I stepped on one, it hurt.

Afterward I sat on the sand, letting my feet dry, watching the gentle rush and retreat of the waves, listening to the rattle of stones in the surf. Those stones, I thought, were like the hard, hurting things in my life: the job that wouldn't go right no matter how long I worked at it; the relationship that remained broken no matter what I did.

There's something mesmerizing about waves. Instead of getting up, I nestled deeper into the soft sand, hypnotized by the water's motion. Pressing forward and withdrawing, advancing and retiring, endlessly dragging the stones back and forth; all day, all night, through years and centuries, rolling the stones over and over.

Making sand.

Of course! It was this ceaseless advance and retreat of the ocean, wave after wave, never stopping, never giving up, that had turned hard stones into the yielding sand where I sat. I stood up and started back to the house . . . to the waiting task, to one more effort at reaching out.

> *Whatever job confronts me, Father, let the waves remind me*
> *that quitting is the only sure way to fail.*
> —ELIZABETH SHERRILL

🧠 WORDS FROM THE SEA

Thu 29   *There is the sea . . . teeming with creatures beyond*
number—living things both large and small.
—PSALM 104:25 (NIV)

DAY 5: LIFE

A few hundred yards offshore this morning, a whale broke the surface of the water. I saw its dark rolling back for only a single tantalizing moment. But the thrill of that brief sighting has had me thinking all day about life in the ocean.

Evidence of it lined the beach where I went walking: quahog shells, mussels, slippers, limpets, periwinkles; shore creatures feeding on the ocean's bounty; tern diving for fish; a gull feasting on the carapace of a horseshoe crab; a flock of sanderlings chasing the retreating waves. People too were harvesting the sea's riches, from the man in wading boots casting for bluefish as I passed to the lobsterman I watched as he checked his pots.

But there were other things on the beach today besides signs of life. By the end of my walk I'd picked up two bottles, a plastic ring-holder from a six-pack, a deflated beach ball and the remnants of a Styrofoam cup. And this before the season here begins; where there's been, yet, no oil spill; where, though overfished and partly contaminated, the sea still yields a small but precious catch.

I thought of the satellite photo of our ocean planet that hangs on my office wall—a startling blue jewel in the blackness of space, the only place in the universe we know of with liquid water. *What have you done*, the ocean asked me, *with this unique creation, God's laboratory of life, His incomparable gift?*

> *Father, show me how to cherish, protect and preserve the world on which You've lavished the water of life.* —ELIZABETH SHERRILL

🌸 WORDS FROM THE SEA

Fri 30   *Thou changest them like raiment, and they pass away;
but thou art the same, and thy years have no end.*
—PSALM 102:26–27 (RSV)

DAY 6: CHANGE

The seascape here is never twice the same, not just from one day to the next, but minute to minute. Seconds ago the whole surface was pewter gray, now it shimmers like silver. It can be as smooth as the "glassy sea" of Revelation or a churning froth of whitecaps.

This morning I sat on the porch, watching long, slow swells roll in to explode against the large rock just offshore, now lashing the base of the rock, now shooting straight up, now cascading clear over the top, chasing away the cormorants who settle there to dry their outstretched wings. No two encounters of wave and rock are alike.

Yesterday an artist set up her easel on the beach. I watched as, with her watercolors, she captured a split second in a wave's onward rush, stopped it, held it motionless forever. *That's what I'm always trying to do*, I thought, looking at the living ocean before me, *with the circumstances of my life. As though stasis, things-as-they-are, were God's plan for His world.*

Everything in that world, of course, tells me the opposite—tells me that no created thing stays the same for long. And nowhere does God speak to me so clearly of His forever making all things new as here beside His ever-changing sea.

> *Help me rejoice in the newness of Your world today, Father,
> in the serenity of knowing that You are the same—
> yesterday, today and forever.*
> —ELIZABETH SHERRILL

🐚 WORDS FROM THE SEA

Sat 31 One thing I ask of the Lord, this is what I seek . . . to gaze
upon the beauty of the Lord. . . . —PSALM 27:4 (NIV)

DAY 7: BEAUTY

The bedroom windows here face east. Through them come the sound of the surf, the salt air of the sea and, of course, around 5:00 AM, the light of the rising sun. Usually I groan and reach for my eye mask.

Today, though, a Carolina wren sang so urgently somewhere nearby that I threw off the covers, dressed and headed down the road to my favorite vantage point at the water's edge.

On the dunes the rugosa roses were in bloom. I caught their fragrance before I saw them—white, pink, maroon. The tide was ebbing, leaving behind a carpet of glistening stones. I sat on a flat-topped rock and watched the incoming waves rise, curl, spill over. For an instant, as each wave crested, the early sun shining through it turned it translucent emerald green.

Beauty—the sheer, extravagant beauty of God's creation is what the ocean is calling me to see today. Tomorrow we have to leave this house by the shore, and I've wondered how I can bear to say good-bye to the salt air and blue water. The ocean is speaking to me about just that. *Open your eyes!* it says. *See the beauty of a raindrop as well as the beauty of a wave, a chipmunk as well as a whale, the potted plant in your kitchen as well as a wild dune rose. You've learned to look keenly here by the sea; look as keenly back home.*

Let me never call unlovely, Father, anything You've made.
—ELIZABETH SHERRILL

THE GIFTS I'VE BEEN GIVEN

1 _____

2 _____

3 _____

4 _____

5 _____

6 _____

7 _____

8 _____

9 _____

10 _____

11 _____

12 _____

13 _____

14 _____

15 _____

July

16 _____

17 _____

18 _____

19 _____

20 _____

21 _____

22 _____

23 _____

24 _____

25 _____

26 _____

27 _____

28 _____

29 _____

30 _____

31 _____

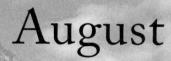

August

*Thanks be unto God for his
unspeakable gift.*

—II Corinthians 9:15

❀ GIFTS FROM ABOVE

Sun 1   *The joy of our heart is ceased; our dance is turned into mourning.* —LAMENTATIONS 5:15

A GIFT OF SERVICE

The early sun was dancing through my kitchen as I checked e-mails on my laptop. The words I had been dreading flashed across the screen: "Prince is gone."

Prince lived in rural Zimbabwe, in a one-room shack with a bed and a glow-in-the-dark star that hung from the ceiling. Like thousands upon thousands of children, he was a victim of AIDS. His mother and brother had already died; his father, also HIV positive, was doing his best to make sure his son had at least one meal a day.

After our first meeting I came back to Nashville, Tennessee, loving this little guy. I wondered how I might make things better for him. *Books*, I thought, *and food*.

I e-mailed Paddington, who directs our work with AIDS orphans in Zimbabwe. Yes, he said, he'd make the long journey to Prince's village to look out for him. On our next trip to Africa, we brought Prince gifts from America: a windup radio, a flashlight and a soft blanket of his very own.

By the time I received the news of Prince's death, many people knew his name, and his sweet smile had fueled interest in our work in Zimbabwe.

Think of Prince gazing at his plastic star and me in my comfortable American home. Only a very clever God could have put us together and engineered the gifts that followed:

For Prince, food, books, a windup radio, and the knowledge that a great many people had come to love him and that his life mattered.

For me, a chance to follow God's call, to touch His hand and to share the depth of His laughter and His tears by loving a little guy named Prince.

Father, in my dancing and in my weeping,
let me be one with You. —PAM KIDD

Mon 2   *I lavish my love on those who love me and obey my commands, even for a thousand generations.* —EXODUS 20:6 (NLT)

Like many parents, I care about the faith of my children and grand-children. I pray for them and hope they will always love God. But it's easy to wonder how future generations will respond when it's time to make their own decisions about following Christ.

That made me pull out our family's genealogy, an almost-1,200-page tome printed in 1928 titled *Descendants of Jacob Hochstetler,* which includes the history of my Swiss Amish ancestor as well as lists of the hundreds of family lines descended from him. My dad Ira is among those whose names appear in the book.

What struck me most about Jacob was his faith. His family had fled Switzerland and come to America in the early eighteenth century because of religious persecution. Like the rest of the Amish, he took the com-mands of God literally—he wouldn't kill other human beings, even in war. During the French and Indian War he refused even to defend himself when Indians attacked his Pennsylvania home; he was wounded and lost his wife, a son and a daughter. As he and his two remaining sons were captured and about to be taken to separate villages, his parting advice was "Do not forget the Lord's Prayer."

Jacob and his sons survived the war and went on to spread the Hostetler (there are various spellings) lineage westward until, today, you can find us throughout the United States. Most of us are no longer Amish, but in our Jacob Hochstetler Family Association's newsletter I've read of many Hostetlers down through the years who have gone into the ministry or otherwise heeded God's call. What a legacy!

Father, may the generations that follow me seek You and find You and truly experience the love You have for them.
—HAROLD HOSTETLER

August

Tue 3

"Because of your great compassion you did not abandon them in the desert...." —NEHEMIAH 9:19 (NIV)

My husband Keith and I had prepared to backpack into the Grand Canyon for a solid year before our trip. But most of that conditioning had been with only partially filled packs and on flatter surfaces than we would encounter on the canyon trails.

On our second day of the real hike, on the Tonto Platform between the Hermit Trail and the more primitive trail at Boucher Creek, we were already very tired. A couple of hours of walking didn't quite match up to eight hours a day of hard hiking.

We were plodding along the trail on the Tonto, a little after noon on the second day of the trip, when we suddenly noticed that there was no trail in front of us. Somewhere, we had taken a wrong turn.

"Stop walking," Keith said.

I already had, but my heart was pounding with far more than just exertion. "What do we do?" I asked.

"We need to find out where we walked off the trail. Let's retrace our steps."

We doubled back the way we thought we'd come, but there was really no way of knowing if we were going off in a different direction. The land rose and fell around us without breaks or landmarks.

Suddenly, silhouetted against the sky at the top of a fold of land to our left, I saw a cairn (smaller rocks piled on larger ones). "Look!" I yelled. Keith turned and saw it too. Someone had marked a place where it was easy to walk off the trail, and now it was easy for us to make our way through the scattered brush and climb the slope to pick it up on the other side.

Thank You, Lord, for the kindness of strangers more capable than I am.
—RHODA BLECKER

Wed 4 Lift up thine eyes round about, and behold. . . .
—ISAIAH 49:18

"Wait just a moment. I'm missing something."

It was our first full day in London, and Carol and the children couldn't wait to leave the hotel and start sightseeing. But first I had to find my walking shoes. The shabby sneakers that I'd worn on the airplane wouldn't stand up to city pavements; my feet would be aching in no time flat. I needed sturdy shoes, but I couldn't find them anywhere. Finally the truth dawned on me: I had left my shoes back home in Massachusetts.

Crestfallen, I told my family that we'd have to spend our first day in London shopping for shoes. My wife and children are good sports and didn't complain, but I could see that they were disappointed.

A half hour later we arrived at Oxford Street, the main shopping thoroughfare of central London. We pushed our way through the jostling crowds, ignoring the sights, intent on finding a shoe store. I was fuming, berating myself for my forgetfulness, when Andy shouted out, "There goes a double-decker bus!" Sure enough, one of those magical red vehicles drove right past us.

A minute later Carol said, "Look, kids, there's a restaurant that serves steak and kidney pie!"

As we looked in the window at the diners and their unusual food, our frowns melted away. The Tower of London could wait until the afternoon; right here on Oxford Street, we discovered the heart of Merrie Olde England! We spent the rest of the morning strolling this wonderful street, enjoying the bowler hats, umbrellas, British accents and huge black taxis. And we also managed to find me a pair of good, stout shoes.

Lord, teach me to discern the wonders that always surround me.
—PHILIP ZALESKI

Thu 5

Casting all your care upon him; for he careth for you. —I PETER 5:7

At first we thought the neighbors were landscaping the vacant field behind our house. A week later a large construction vehicle rumbled onto the field, and within days a track was formed and filled with teenagers riding motorcycles and recreational vehicles.

The loud hum of motors echoed through our house for hours at a time. I closed the windows and tried to ignore the unnerving noise, but it was no use. My home office, once a peaceful room with gorgeous views, was now an impossible place to work.

My husband and I, along with other neighbors, approached the owners of the land and pleaded with them to stop. Dozens of calls to the zoning board and the police left us feeling helpless. I began to think about moving. *Please,* I prayed whenever I heard the noise, *make them stop.*

Months later I noticed my neighbor from across the street looking at the track. It had been raining for days, and there were large puddles everywhere. When I went out to see what was the matter, he shook his head. "The track is ruining my pond," he said. "The mud and oil from their vehicles are running under the road, into the pond, and killing my fish."

In less than an hour, the owners of the track and my neighbor were in front of my house. My neighbor talked about calling the environmental authorities if nothing was done. For the rest of the day and well into the evening, my husband and I watched the owners plant seeds and cover the track with hay. Now when I look out my office window, I see the peaceful landscape of answered prayer.

*Thank You, Lord, for assuring me that no situation is ever hopeless—
and for the peace and quiet!*
—SABRA CIANCANELLI

Fri 6

He who is kind to the poor lends to the Lord. . . .
—PROVERBS 19:17 (NIV)

The phone rang one evening; it was a neighbor calling to tell my wife that she had found someone who had 250 basketballs and soccer balls to give away. "Rosie," she asked, "do you think the ministries that your foundation supports could find a use for these balls?"

"Yes, of course!" Rosie was overjoyed.

The ministries were overjoyed too. For some of the children in their programs, it would be the first time they'd be playing with a new ball. And all of us were touched that our neighbor had gone out of her way to find a donor to provide these balls because she knew that they would be a blessing to the kids.

Even in times of general hardship, there can be a great gap between those who have and those who have not. It makes such a difference when people are concerned enough to see the need in communities that would be easy for them to ignore—and then reach out with the love of God.

Lord, I know in my heart that if I am kind to the poor, You get glory.
Help me to be alive to the opportunities to help,
which are all around me.
—DOLPHUS WEARY

August

Sat 7

Wondrously show Your lovingkindness, O Savior of those who take refuge at Your right hand. . . . —PSALM 17:7 (NAS)

The dog run where I take Millie for her exercise and canine social life is also an interesting place to observe people. The other day I overheard a conversation between two women sitting next to me on a bench.

Older Woman: What day is it?

Younger Woman: Fifteen.

OW: Congratulations.

YW: Thanks. I never thought I'd make it, especially last night. I really wanted to.

OW: But you didn't.

YW: No. But I'm ashamed of myself for wanting to. I just kept praying and the urge passed. I went to a meeting first thing this morning and talked about it to the group.

OW: What will you do the next time the urge hits you?

YW: Pray. Pick up the phone. Find a meeting.

OW: You're going to be all right then. Don't be ashamed. The one thing you can always do is pray. God understands.

YW: I never believed in God, let alone prayer, before. Now it's saving my life, I guess.

OW: I'm praying for you too, dear. Lots of people are.

The older woman rose and retrieved her dog, and the younger woman pulled out a book. I watched Millie chase another golden retriever in a big circle until they skidded to a stop. Then I stole a peek at what the woman was reading—the Big Book, the Alcoholics Anonymous spiritual blueprint for recovery from alcoholism, a day at a time. She turned the page, and I closed my eyes. She had one more person praying for her.

You are there for us, God, as our highest power in our hardest times.
—EDWARD GRINNAN

Sun 8 *"I the Lord do not change. . . ."* —MALACHI 3:6 (NIV)

When I was a child, tent revivals held by traveling evangelists came along at least once every summer. The wooden folding chairs, the sawdust floor, the breeze under the tent flaps and the birds in the rafters are still alive for me, as are the powerful images of the preachers themselves.

There was the musician who played a jumble of instruments, including the marimba and the musical saw. His wife sang. The words of one song especially stand out:

> *Wonderful grace of Jesus,*
> *Greater than all my sin.*
> *How shall my tongue describe it,*
> *Where shall its praise begin?*
> *Taking away my burden,*
> *Setting my spirit free. . . .*

Then there was the chalk artist who sketched his sermons on a huge spotlighted canvas. Every night a different picture poured from his fingers. The one I remember best was a narrow, dirt road that ran through the Cross and empty tomb and ended in the bright lights of eternal life.

And there was the poetic evangelist with the bigger-than-life, gravelly voice. Every night he thundered out a different theme with the same solution woven through: "When despair knocks, send Jesus to the door." "When doubt knocks, send Jesus to the door." "When temptation knocks, send Jesus to the door."

Today those tent revivals have gone the way of black-and-white television. They're miles and years removed from my busy, more complicated world. Yet, the same simple, undiluted Gospel message still holds: "Grace greater than all my sin" rescues me and keeps me on the path to eternal life.

> *Lord Jesus, thank You that Your power is still the answer to*
> *temptation, despair and doubt.* —SHARI SMYTH

Mon 9

Therefore I will boast all the more gladly about my weaknesses, so that Christ's power may rest on me . . . For when I am weak, then I am strong.
—II Corinthians 12:9–10 (niv)

They were words no amputee ever wants to hear: "Based on your X-ray, I'd say your foot is fractured."

As a professional motivational speaker, I'd frequently put my safety at risk to keep the audience's attention, hopping up on chairs and tables or jumping off stages. In fact, it was one such jump from a six-foot-high stage that had brought me to the doctor's office.

"So do I have to be in a wheelchair?" I asked.

"No," the doctor said. "It's a unique type of fracture that actually resets itself. You just need to walk very cautiously for the next two months."

It was good news and bad news: not spending two months in a wheelchair—good; walking very cautiously—bad. How could I captivate my audiences if I had to keep still while I spoke?

I went home, sat down and felt sorry for myself for several hours. *It just isn't fair!* Then I thought about the great speakers I had seen over the years. None of them had ever jumped off the stage. How did they hold the audience's attention? The answer was obvious: great material and effective delivery.

So I got back to the basics, honing my presentation skills and the content of my speech, and over the next two months my performances grew stronger—along with the bones in my foot.

Lord, thank You for perfecting me through my imperfections.
—Joshua Sundquist

Tue 10 *And God said, Let us make man in our image, after our likeness: and let them have dominion over the fish of the sea, and over the fowl of the air, and over the cattle, and over all the earth, and over every creeping thing that creepeth upon the earth.* —GENESIS 1:26

When, forty years ago, we were preparing to leave Ohio to move to New Mexico, an acquaintance said to us, "I can describe Albuquerque in one sentence: Grass is a status symbol."

That was true then, when everyone in this desert city, including us, worked to keep our lawns green and well-trimmed. But the population of Albuquerque exploded through the years, and we now have a water shortage. More people have turned to xeriscaping, which means doing away with grass and creating landscapes out of colored rocks, gravel and native plants that require little water.

I've noticed that the people around me are becoming more aware of the need to preserve other natural resources too. They're buying fuel-efficient cars; recycling their metal cans, newspapers and plastic products; helping to protect endangered species; and finding ways to cut down on the pollution of our air and rivers. I think when God gave us dominion over all the earth, He didn't mean we had the right to exploit and destroy His handiwork. I think He meant for us to be responsible caretakers of His Creation.

Thank You, God, for this beautiful world!
Today, on this fortieth anniversary of Earth Day,
I'll look for more ways to help
protect our environment.
—MADGE HARRAH

Wed 11

When I consider thy heavens, the work of thy fingers, the moon and the stars, which thou hast ordained. . . . O Lord our Lord, how excellent is thy name in all the earth!
—PSALM 8:3, 9

Today's mail brought a nice note complimenting me on something I'd written for *Daily Guideposts.* The devotional had hit a chord, and the reader felt compelled to write. I'll answer with a letter thanking her for her thoughtfulness. I've observed that some people don't know how to respond to a compliment, maybe because they're so rare. But a simple thank-you is always appropriate.

The head of a large company once told me he was reluctant to give compliments, fearing that his employees would become complacent. "I pay them well. That should be enough." I ventured to tell him that both pay and compliments might be in order, if his goal was to create more loyal, productive workers.

Oscar Wilde once remarked, "An acquaintance that begins with a compliment is sure to develop into a real friendship." And some of King David's most memorable offerings to God (like the one above) are full of praise, which it could be said is part and parcel of a good compliment.

Thank You, Lord, for Your creative hand,
Designer of beauty throughout the land.
—FRED BAUER

Thu 12

The right word at the right time—beautiful!
—PROVERBS 15:23 (MSG)

I desperately needed a few words from my son Jon. For months he'd been in prison and didn't answer my letters. He had been struggling with addictions, and I felt relieved that he was now safe, following rules. But I hounded him in my letters: "Why don't you write?" There was no response. But he finally phoned one day to tell me he could receive small amounts of money to be spent at the prison store.

I wrote back with fifteen statements I'd come up with. Each contained a blank for him to fill in. "Complete these, Jon, by simply filling in the blanks, mail the sheet back to me and I'll pay you two dollars for each answer." In three days a letter from my son appeared in our mailbox! I kissed it, standing there in the sweltering August sun, and marveled over his handwriting. Then I traced my address with a finger, smiling. Here's a sample of the words he wrote.

1. Mostly I feel: excited about what the future holds for me.
2. What I anticipate is: more funny times with Jesus.
3. The most important thing I've learned during the past months is: that you can never give up on your dreams.
4. One of my favorite biblical truths is: how Paul got his vision back after being blinded.
5. My strong points are: my good looks.
6. The last funny thing I recall is: me and my detail officer laughing about this questionnaire, Mom.
7. The best part of each day is: when I get to shower after working all day in the sun.

Oh, Father, I'm singing, "Beautiful words, wonderful words, wonderful words of life" (Phillip P. Bliss).
—MARION BOND WEST

August

Fri 13

*Then Job answered the Lord: I know that you can do all
things, and that no purpose of yours can be thwarted.*
—Job 42:1 (NRSV)

When you're faced with a decision or you need to do something you
haven't done before—a new job or a new Bible study group or
planning next week's menu—how do you approach it?

My default mode is to be cautious. I want to know what other people's expectations are, the rules I need to follow. I don't want to make a
mistake because I don't want people criticizing me. No criticism? Then
all is well.

Shortly after I started my new job a couple of years ago, I had a cup
of coffee with a colleague. I was telling him about my cautious approach
to the new work. He got a quizzical look on his face and said, "Don't you
believe the Bible?"

My first thought was, *Oh no! The most brilliant Bible scholar I know is
criticizing me. What have I done wrong?* Then he smiled and gave me a pat
on the back. "The Bible is clear," he said. "God loves you, God has gifted
you and God watches over you. If that doesn't give you the confidence to
be creative and courageous, I don't know what will."

I'll probably never be a bold, caution-to-the-wind person. But since
that day I've tried to be a more biblical person, trusting more in God and
less in my own abilities. I must say, it's a great way to go.

*Lord, give me the faith to stand up on my own
and try something new.*
—Jeff Japinga

❁ TWELVE KEYS TO THE GIVING LIFE

Sat 14   *Thou shalt love thy neighbour as thyself.*
—LEVITICUS 19:18; GALATIANS 5:14

GIVE EXPECTANTLY

My great-nephew Trenton was turning eight, and his parents had invited his friends to a party at the local YMCA. As the guests shot hoops on the gleaming oak floor, Trenton's father Alex signaled that it was time for the birthday boy to begin opening his gifts.

Soon I heard a boy with shaggy brown hair whisper to the child standing next to him, "He's opening my gift now!" The box contained a Spiderman wristband, which was greeted by a chorus of "Cool!" "Way to go!" and "Bend your wrist, T. It squirts awesome webs!" The enthusiastic reaction repeated itself as Trenton opened the rest of the presents.

Alex wrapped his arm around my shoulder. "Aren't children terrific when it comes to giving gifts, Aunt Roberta? They're as excited as if they were getting a present themselves."

That evening I drove to the store to pick up a gift for an upcoming bridal shower. *I'll have to paste on a smile,* I thought, *and laugh at the mindless banter while the bride-to-be gushes over mixers and bath towels.* But then I remembered the birthday party I'd just attended. *What if I choose a gift that I can really get excited about?*

I filled a basket with a few of my favorite little household things, like the microfiber cloths that make dusting a breeze and a candle that smells like linen hung on a clothesline in June. When Maria, the bride-to-be, reached for the shrink-wrapped basket tied with a jaunty pink-checked bow, I nudged the woman seated next to me. "That's my gift," I said, and I was really smiling.

When it comes to giving, Lord, make me ever childlike.
—ROBERTA MESSNER

Sun 15

But by His doing you are in Christ Jesus, who became to us wisdom from God. . . . —I CORINTHIANS 1:30 (NAS)

Some of my dearest friends are people I've never met. Many are poets, gone long before I was born but intensely alive when I read or hear their words.

Though we lived centuries apart, John Keats and I met when I was in college. In Keats I discovered a young man deeply enchanted with the beauty of life and swept away by love for a young woman he could never marry. In his twenties Keats realized that he would die from tuberculosis before he was thirty. On the night I read his anguished poem "When I Have Fears That I May Cease to Be," I keenly realized that every day of my young life was a precious gift, a priceless opportunity to create, to love, to work and to be.

Now in my fifties, I am awed by the poetic craft of Alfred, Lord Tennyson. To read "Ulysses" for the first or thousandth time is to know that though half of my life is over, it is not too late "to seek another world . . . that some work of noble note, may yet be done."

But above all, the poetry of the Bible is a sumptuous feast for the wise and the simple. The beautiful metaphors of the Psalmist accompany us through every moment of our day and night. And to read the Gospels and hear the parabolic poetry of Jesus is to glimpse the ultimate truth of God.

Take time to read, reflect and ponder the poetic wisdom of the ages. And above all, listen to the words of Jesus. His voice reveals God's truth.

Father, may the wisdom of the past introduce me to present truth.
And in all things may I hear the voice of Jesus. Amen.
—SCOTT WALKER

⧗ COMFORT FOR THE HURTING HEART

Mon 16   *"You have covered yourself with anger. . . . You have covered yourself with a cloud so that no prayer can get through."* —LAMENTATIONS 3:43–44 (NIV)

WHEN HURT TURNS TO ANGER

One day I spotted an acquaintance and privately prided myself on remembering her name. "Hi, Ingrid," I said. "How nice to see you again."

Ingrid returned my smile with a scowl and a fierce retort: "Nobody asked me if I wanted to be included in any of the women's circles. Just take my name off the list!" Then, without another word, she stalked off.

My surprise turned into anger. *What was that all about?* Granted, we attended the same church, but I'd had nothing to do with assigning anyone to a specific circle group. *I greeted her nicely. She had no right to snap at me like that!*

I was still seething when, a week later, I learned that Ingrid's husband had left her. Her unexpected response had nothing to do with me; I merely happened to be there when her anguish erupted. I should have followed her and said, "Ingrid, let's have lunch, and you can tell me what's the matter."

Lord, help me to remember that when someone has an uncharacteristic flash of anger, it often means that person needs a kind word of comfort.
        —ISABEL WOLSELEY

Tue 17 *And forgive us our debts, as we forgive our debtors.*
—MATTHEW 6:12

I haven't been inside a bank in years. I do nearly all of my banking after hours, nearly always in an absolute rush.

Last week was a little different. Before I stopped at the ATM, I happened to listen to a news story about credit-card production. Apparently certain credit cards are mass-produced in a sweatshop somewhere— somewhere far from me, across the ocean in countries that have no ATMs, in countries that have no credit.

At the machine I opened my wallet—a sea of colored plastic. I found myself staring at the number pad, unable to remember my password, my mind littered in plastic cards that may have been churned out by a small boy at the stamping machine, filling my wallet with its chronicle of debt.

I became totally flummoxed, thinking about some boy I would never meet in a village I would never visit, cranking out little plastic cards for pennies a day.

A line had formed behind me as I struggled at the ATM. The crowd seemed to chafe at the wait, wondering how anyone could be so insensitive.

And I was wondering the same thing myself.

> *Lord, when I ask forgiveness for my debts,*
> *please know that I mean all of my debts,*
> *those known and unknown.*
> ### —MARK COLLINS

Wed 18   And their joy was very great. —NEHEMIAH 8:17 (NIV)

For the last several months my four-year-old grandson Drake has been intrigued by the tall pile of ice cream that comes in a cone—and, of course, by all the licking involved. After years of cups and spoons, it seemed the time had come. So today, while his little brother was napping, I took him to the ice cream store.

Drake ordered in a loud, clear voice: "I want an ice cream cone. Not a cup." When the teenage girl behind the counter handed it to him, he gripped it firmly in one hand—too firmly, I feared. And his smile! It was literally ear-to-ear.

We sat down, and Drake began to lick . . . and lick. Only once did I have to take a lick to prevent the sticky white stream from dripping down his hand. (I did, however, have to get more napkins!)

Lick, lick. "This is good, Nina." *Lick, lick.* "I am a big boy, so I can have a cone." *Lick, lick.*

Finally his tongue scooped up the last of the towering frozen treat. Now came the cone itself. "I like this crunchy part." *Bite, bite.* Then a revelation: "Oh, Nina, there's more ice cream inside!" followed by giggles of delight.

One dollar and six cents and twenty minutes of my time. I drive home pondering the power of simplicity and the rejuvenating quality of joy.

Simplicity. Joy. I must remember how often those two are found together. Next time, I'll get a cone too.

> *Dear Jesus, keep me from making life—and contentment—*
> *more complicated than it needs to be.*
> *And thanks for ice cream!*
> —MARY LOU CARNEY

Thu 19

Cast me not off in the time of old age; forsake me not when my strength faileth. —PSALM 71:9

My father gets around with a walker these days, and he doesn't get around much. But he was there when the whole clan—twenty and counting—gathered for a week at the beach, staying at a rental on the sand. We sailed, we surfed, we rode bikes on the boardwalk, swam out to the buoy and kayaked in the bay. Dad seemed to enjoy having everybody together, but even from under the umbrella on the porch, he got frustrated at not being able to do half of what he once could.

Late one afternoon I suggested a walk. "I'm not sure how I can do it with this walker on the sand," he said.

"Let's try," I said. "You can hold my hand if you need to."

He made his way down the beach, leaning on the walker or me. We stopped to watch some sailors bring their boats to shore and take down their sails. "Hey, Mr. Hamlin!" one of the guys called. "How are you doing?"

"Just fine," he said, his hands on the walker.

We trudged back next to the water, choosing the hard sand. A pelican dipped past us and plunged into the bay, picking up dinner. A kayak cut across the smooth water, a fish leaping in its wake. The shadows of the palms lengthened across the sand in front of us. "The shadows lengthen," Dad observed.

They do, I thought. The years go by, and you don't know where they went. Age brings its struggles. But at the end of the day there are still beauties to be found in a setting sun and a slow walk on the beach, father and son.

> *All those years my father took care of me, Lord,*
> *may I now take good care of him.*
> —RICK HAMLIN

$\underline{Fri\ 20}$ *"But for you who fear My name, the sun of righteousness will rise with healing in its wings. . . ."* —MALACHI 4:2 (NAS)

Poking through a thrift shop, I bought a small plaque with a motto I liked: "A heart that has lost the will to sing is like a butterfly with a broken wing" (Harriette B. McCormick). Some time later I found a beautiful monarch butterfly with a broken wing. Dismayed, I watched it fluttering, straining to lift itself and fly, only to fall back to the ground.

I tried to set the butterfly in my flower bed, amazed by the strength of its clinging to my finger. It continued to flop among my marigolds. I longed for it to have another chance at flight, like the one God had given me. For a time my heart had "lost the will to sing." I must have appeared to God much like a wounded butterfly struggling to become airborne.

My wing repair has taken time. It has been a complex work. Occasionally I falter in flight, weighed down by grief, remorse and regret. I tremble on the ground until God reminds me that I can fly, that He has remade my wings even stronger than before.

Lord, my Healer, repairer of all I bring to You, keep me believing that You will again give my spirit flight. —CAROL KNAPP

READER'S ROOM

My grandmother started sending me *Daily Guideposts* more than twenty years ago. We often talked about the daily devotional over the phone. She died two days before her ninety-fourth birthday while I was holding her hand and reading *Daily Guideposts* to her. A year later, I ordered *Daily Guideposts* for myself for the first time. It arrived on August 20, the birthday I share with my grandma. I knew she was smiling at me from heaven and wishing me a happy birthday.

—*Cathy Wiszowaty, Hickory, North Carolina*

Sat 21   *The earth is full of the goodness of the Lord.* —PSALM 33:5

When I answered the doorbell one afternoon, two smiling women greeted me. "I'm Barbara," one of them said, "and this is my daughter. We only have a moment. We were at the charity bookstall and we picked up this book. Inside we found a letter to your wife." Then she handed me an autographed copy of *Pearl's Kitchen* by Pearl Bailey.

Pearl's Kitchen was one of Ruby's favorite books. Pearl Bailey had given it to Ruby after a concert, and Ruby cherished it. She had asked me to put the book in the attic for safekeeping, and in my haste to find books to donate, I had included Ruby's without really looking at it. Fortunately, Barbara had sensed the book had special meaning. Now I had to face Ruby.

Ruby was delighted that her book had been returned. She put it beside her bed to enjoy during quiet moments. And instead of scolding me, she just said, "Oscar, be careful when you give away books."

In their quiet ways Barbara and Ruby taught me lessons in kindness and forgiveness. Barbara went out of her way to return a gift to a stranger, and Ruby forgave my carelessness. I'll still be donating books I don't need, but from now on I'll try doing it with a little more prudence.

> *Father, in my zeal to do good, let me always remember*
> *to use good common sense.*
> —OSCAR GREENE

Sun 22

O Lord, how long shall I cry, And You will not hear? . . .
—Habakkuk 1:2 (nkjv)

Just once in my life, Lord, I'd like to have a conversation with You. Sure, I'm glad You hear our prayers, but it's really hard to have a relationship with someone who never responds, You know?

It would be really great if just once we could have a back-and-forth, where I say something like, "How are things in heaven?"

And then You say, "Things are always fine in heaven."

And then I say, "Well, things are not so fine down here. Our friend has cancer, and all summer we've had floods. Do You have anything to say about that?"

"Have you read my book Habakkuk?"

"Habba what? Is that in the Old Testament?"

"So you haven't read the things I've already said?"

"You got me, but I would just like to hear the sound of Your voice and see the expressions on Your face. You know . . . body language."

"Do you like thunder? My voice is like that. Can you stare at the sun? I dwell in unapproachable light."

"But if You could sort of disguise Yourself as a man and come down here for a visit . . ."

"I did that long ago. I went to weddings and funerals. I taught in the marketplace and schools. I played with children. But not everybody liked Me. Remember, I hear every prayer you utter and I think of you every day. I look forward to visiting with you in heaven even more than you do."

It's so hard to live by faith, Lord, and not by sight. Give me patience!
—Daniel Schantz

Mon 23

"Come to me and I will give you rest—all of you who work so hard beneath a heavy yoke."
—Matthew 11:28 (TLB)

Two years ago I flew to Hong Kong with my brother Joe and sister-in-law Linda. One day we decided to explore the Central Mid-Levels Escalators, the world's largest outdoor covered escalator system—over 2,600 feet long, more than twenty-five escalators, flat walkways and travelators (moving sidewalks) that connect the Central and Mid-Levels areas in mountainous Hong Kong's Western District.

As the open-air escalators took us up, up, up past houses, apartments, stores, restaurants, gardens, tiny shops and tearooms, we got a bird's-eye view of the way the people live. Most of the buildings were just five or six feet from the escalators, so I felt as if I was watching a slow-motion documentary of life in Hong Kong. Most of the residents had their drapes, blinds and windows wide open, inviting nosy tourists like me to peek inside.

They were boiling water for tea, reading the newspaper, talking to their loved ones, cleaning up. As we traveled up past their homes I thought, *Is this how God sees us? Scurrying about doing our daily mundane things, unaware we're being watched?*

Secretly I was wishing one of those old women in the tiny apartments would wave me inside to join her for a cup of tea. I wanted to know more about what her life was like. *Is that what God wants of us too*, I wondered, *to be invited in?*

Father, during my busy days give me the grace to stop, make a cup of tea and settle in for a warm, friendly conversation with You.
—Patricia Lorenz

❊ THE GIFT OF SIGHT

Tue 24　*I can do all things through Christ which strengtheneth me.*
*—*Philippians 4:13

A MATTER OF ATTITUDE

My former neighbor Carla Gallemore had become blind as a result of "twilight sleep," an anesthetic technique used during childbirth in the early twentieth century. "At one time I felt sight was my most precious gift, but I was wrong. Attitude is," Carla said, and she proved it. Using a Braille typewriter, she wrote a very successful book, *Once I Was Blind*.

One day Carla called me and said, "Did you know *The Miracle Worker* is showing at the Fox? I'd like to see that movie."

"See it?" I asked.

"Yes. I've learned to 'see' with my ears and through other people's eyes. I can follow a movie pretty well by listening. When I can't, I'll tap your arm and you can whisper to me what's happening on the screen."

So we went to the movie—the story of the young Helen Keller and her teacher Annie Sullivan—and found it to be extremely inspiring. I think Carla got more out of *The Miracle Worker* than I did, even though she had no sight. "It's all a matter of attitude," she said. "Keeping a hopeful mind and heart makes all the difference, whatever one's handicap is."

Help me, Comforter, to keep a positive attitude through faith and
trust in You and through a feeling heart.
*—*Marilyn Morgan King

Wed 25

*O Lord, you are my God; I will exalt you and praise your name, for in perfect faithfulness you have done marvelous things, things planned long ago. —*ISAIAH 25:1 (NIV)

As I grow older, I've come to recognize God's hand in my life more and more. For instance, the night I met Wayne, I had a date who canceled at the last moment. I was dressed and ready to go, only to have my plans dashed. No more than a half hour later the phone rang again; it was a friend of my roommate's who was looking for a date to take to a movie. That was how I met my husband.

This last summer something occurred that had God's fingerprints all over it. I was in Phoenix on tour with a number of events scheduled. My travel plans are arranged a year in advance and my schedule on the road is usually jam-packed, but for some inexplicable reason, that particular morning was open.

As it happened, the son of one of our dearest friends was to be buried that day in Phoenix. I'm convinced that God knew and prepared the way for me to attend Michael's funeral. I was able to be in church to love, support and comfort our friends.

God's intervention is evident in every corner of my life; I call these "divine appointments." Often, I don't recognize these intersections of time and eternity until much later. Often, what seems to be happenstance shows me once again that He is in control of every detail.

Open my eyes, Lord Jesus, to Your divine appointments.
—DEBBIE MACOMBER

Thu 26

Whoever watches the wind will not plant; whoever looks at the clouds will not reap. —ECCLESIASTES 11:4 (NIV)

Since I began writing, I've been able to talk to other would-be writers about how to begin. Most of them have fantasies about how it will be when they write. They imagine themselves sitting next to picture windows that look out over forests or crashing waves.

I started writing under a waterfall. The brown water leaked from a hole in my living room ceiling. Shortly after I began my first project, the ceiling caved in. As I sat at my hand-me-down computer, water trickled through the light fixture above where I sat. Some of the water I caught in a bucket; the rest soaked the carpet around me.

All of my delusions about what writing would be like evaporated for me and my family as my papers and equipment took over the bottom floor of the two-story house we rented. As the summer arrived, the damp carpet and the heat—we were unable to use the air conditioner because it was the source of the leak—created our own special but unwanted sauna.

My children Lanea and Chase and I laugh about it now. Best of all, at the end of the discomfort was a book. It changed our lives.

"There's no perfect place or time to begin anything you want to do," I tell the students—though I see in their eyes that they don't believe me. Like them, I still dream of a haven that overlooks a beach or a lake. But I'll settle for the air-conditioned living room I work in now. Cool and dry, it seems like paradise.

God, help us to honor and make use of the imperfect day.
—SHARON FOSTER

Fri 27 It is better to eat soup with someone you love than steak
with someone you hate. —PROVERBS 15:17 (TLB)

Anyone who says the Bible is irrelevant probably hasn't read it. At
least they haven't read Proverbs. It's loaded with good advice and
amazingly accurate observations on life. I read the one above not long
ago, and it immediately reminded me of an experience I'd had at work.

Newly employed at my daughter Maria's school, I was required to
attend the employees' retreat before school started. I enjoyed getting to
know the other new people as well as the teachers and staff whom I'd
known only in my role as a parent. We shared a lot of laughs, especially
in the relaxed atmosphere of mealtimes. About a week later a few of us
were talking about the retreat at lunch and a teacher who hadn't attended
asked, "How was the food?" The woman next to me and I answered
simultaneously, only she said "Awful!" and I said, "Great!"

Everyone laughed, and later I thought about why I answered as I did.
The food wasn't great, but I was focused on the good company; maybe
that actually made the food taste better.

Food is a gift from God to nourish my body, not to entertain me.
Realizing this in recent years has made me a healthier, happier person.
God's better gift is His people—their stories, their laughter, their love in
my life. They make soup taste like steak and always make me return to
them for seconds.

Dear God, bless my food, but bless my friends more.
—GINA BRIDGEMAN

Sat 28 The young man saith unto him, *All these things have I kept from my youth up: what lack I yet?* —MATTHEW 19:20

Our move was almost complete, except for the attic. All four members of the family had sorted through their personal things, so I didn't expect to find much up there. On this final day my father had come up from New York City to help us finish the move.

My body was tired and sore and my spirit yearned for some summer fun, but I kept thinking, *This is it. This is the last hurrah of moving.* I walked up to the attic with my dad; the heat made it almost unbearable. We were dismayed to find that it was filled with boxes of all kinds and sizes, all of them empty.

"You have more boxes here than a store," my father said. Dad had worked for thirty-five years in the fabric retail business; he knew about boxes. "How did you end up with so many?"

We'd been saving them since we arrived in Carmel, New York, seven years ago—for the big move. And here we'd almost finished it without remembering they were there. Dad walked around, picking up boxes and repeating his question. I started laughing. It became the joke of the day.

The experience got me thinking about some of the things in my life that hold me back. It's been a long time since I've taken inventory of the things that are stored in my heart. What have I been holding on to that is no longer of any value or benefit? What do I need to remove, so I can grow in my faith?

Lord, help me to examine my heart and to let go of things that take up space that could be filled with Your love and grace.
—PABLO DIAZ

Sun 29

*"But I tell you who hear me: Love your enemies, do good to those who hate you, bless those who curse you, pray for those who mistreat you." —*LUKE 6:27–28 (NIV)

I've been deeply concerned for my friend. Her teenage daughter has moved in with her older boyfriend and his dad. The boyfriend and his dad treat my friend with hostility. To make matters worse, my friend's ex-husband has joined them in their anger at her. Together they've leveled false accusations against my friend and have alienated her daughter from her.

Over the past months my friend has poured out her despair to me. Tonight, however, when I phoned her, I heard an amazing change in her voice. "I feel as though a huge weight has been lifted off me," she said.

"What happened?" I asked incredulously.

"Well, when I heard the Gospel reading at church this morning—to love your enemies and to pray for those who persecute you—I knew that somehow I had to do what Jesus said, even though it seemed impossible."

"Considering how you've been treated, it does seem impossible to respond that way."

"I felt that I couldn't but that God could. For the rest of the service, I prayed for them. When I came home, I still felt overwhelmed by my hurt and anger, so I prayed more. Instead of praying for them to change, I simply asked God to do good to them.

"Suddenly, everything inside me changed. I felt a lightness I've never felt before. I know that somehow everything will work out. I'll keep praying for them and trusting God. I finally have peace."

Thank You, Lord, for helping my friend—and me—
to obey Your Word, even when it seems impossible.
—MARY BROWN

Mon 30

How can a young man keep his way pure? By guarding it according to thy word. With my whole heart I seek thee; let me not wander from thy commandments!
—PSALM 119:9–10 (RSV)

David Denny founded the city of Seattle in 1851. I know the man well; I wrote six books about him and his Sweetbriar Bride Louisa. With only twenty-five cents in his pocket, he went on to become the city's third richest man, with assets of three million dollars. In the Panic of 1893, his brother begged that he shut down his enterprises to weather the terrible recession.

"I can't," he replied. "A hundred families will starve." David instead mortgaged everything, and the recession rolled in. He and Louisa celebrated their fortieth wedding anniversary in an empty mansion and then moved to a log cabin he'd once given his daughter Abbie. He died ten years later with less than twenty-five cents to his name but with a reputation worth more than gold. Seattle loved Honest Dave.

Before he died, he wrote: "If I could live my life again, I'd still come West, I'd join the same church and marry the same woman. But I'd endeavor to be a better Christian."

This summer Theron, one of his great-grandsons, invited me to go through an old trunk of David's. I happily examined artifacts, manuscripts, photos and letters. "You're welcome to take anything you'd like," Theron offered.

"Do you have one of David's Bibles?" I asked. He handed me a Bible, open to the flyleaf: "D. T. Denny, Jan 15, 1900." David's grandson Laurie had added: "Grandpa died at 3:06 Wed morning of Nov 25, 1903.... Grandma held his hand and he passed away."

Louisa had an addition of her own for Laurie, who inherited the Bible: "The battle is over and your grandpa had the victory."

Lord, thank You for this unexpected and priceless gift, a reminder to be the better Christian David truly was—a pauper who won the victory. —BRENDA WILBEE

Tue 31

"I am sending you to them who are stubborn and obstinate children, and you shall say to them, 'Thus says the Lord God.'"
—EZEKIEL 2:4 (NAS)

Stephen burrowed his way into a rack of clothing and sat belligerently on the floor. "I *hate* those pants!" he said with a scowl. "I'm never going to wear them!"

I'd thought Stephen, my youngest, would enjoy choosing his own clothes, since he's lived entirely in hand-me-downs. Ah well, wrong again. Nonetheless, we had to buy long pants before school started.

Arguing with an annoyed five-year-old tends to be unproductive, so I moved as far away from Stephen's sulking spot as prudence allowed. Five minutes later I ventured to comment, "Here's a pair of really soft pants." (Stephen is sensitive to textures and seams.)

"I won't wear them! The only pants I want are short pants!"

Ah—a hint of progress. "You do like shorts, don't you? But after school starts the weather will get colder, and you'll want long pants."

"It's too hot for long pants!"

I took one of those deep cleansing breaths they taught me in Lamaze class. "Okay. Let's look. I'm not sure if they even have shorts anymore because it's so close to fall."

Stephen emerged reluctantly from his cave. We looked at the sale rack. What was left wasn't what he had in mind.

"Here, Mom! This is what I want!" Stephen pulled out a pair of size-twenty-four-months sweatpants farther down the aisle.

"Those aren't shorts, honey. They're long pants for a baby."

Stephen insisted. I considered my options. "All right, here's the deal: I'll let you try those on. If they fit, I'll buy them *if* you also get two pairs of long pants."

After a bit of haggling, Stephen agreed. We headed toward the dressing room. Darned if those baby pants didn't fit my guy! Sold!

> *O my Jesus, when I'm stubborn, keep trying!*
> —JULIA ATTAWAY

THE GIFTS I'VE BEEN GIVEN

1 _____

2 _____

3 _____

4 _____

5 _____

6 _____

7 _____

8 _____

9 _____

10 _____

11 _____

12 _____

13 _____

14 _____

15 _____

August

16 _____

17 _____

18 _____

19 _____

20 _____

21 _____

22 _____

23 _____

24 _____

25 _____

26 _____

27 _____

28 _____

29 _____

30 _____

31 _____

September

Give me understanding,
and I shall live.

—Psalm 119:144

🦋 GIFTS FROM ABOVE

Wed 1   *That which I see not teach thou me. . . .* —JOB 34:32

A GIFT UNSEEN

A ll my life I've heard about the amazing virgin forest that lies tucked away in a recess of the Cumberland Plateau near Sewanee, Tennessee. There, deep in Savage Gulf, lies a five-hundred-acre wood, which, like a warp in time, gives travelers a glimpse of the New World as the first settlers saw it. I've always longed to see this national natural landmark, but the same inaccessibility that saved it from generations of loggers makes visiting difficult.

So it's no wonder that a headline in our local newspaper piqued my interest: "Two hundred acres of virgin woods have been identified within Nashville's city limits." *Unbelievable*, I thought as I continued to read the article.

And then the shocker: The property that has sheltered the forest for hundreds of years, owned by generations of the same family, surrounds our neighborhood! Now plans are underway to make it a part of our city's park system. A hidden virgin forest literally in my own backyard!

At first I was enthralled by the news, but then the truth hit home: The forest has been there all along, a gift waiting to be discovered. I thought of some of the things I long for: *A visit to a virgin forest? Well, I can check that one off. The time to go out and photograph this beautiful late summer day? Who's stopping me? The chance to be a great philanthropist? I can be a great giver to at least one person.* The trick is to look beyond my longings and see—really see—the gifts that wait to be named and claimed.

> *Open my eyes, Lord, to the gifts that are all around me.*
> —PAM KIDD

Thu 2 *My cup runneth over.* —PSALM 23:5

A few years ago the quilters of Gee's Bend, Alabama, hit the headlines. For generations, the women of the community had been making quilts from the scraps of their husbands' work clothes: corduroy, denim, twill. Their children grew up sleeping under piles of patchwork every winter, since most of the houses in the town—populated almost entirely by still-poor descendants of slaves—had no heat. Then an art dealer came to town and told the ladies that their quilts were really something else: They were art.

Within months Gee's Bend quilts were selling for hundreds, even thousands, of dollars. An exhibition toured museums. The designs— beautiful geometric patterns that resembled modernist paintings—were slapped onto coasters and ties and rugs and note cards.

Awash in newfound celebrity and unprecedented wealth, some of the quilters bought furniture, cars, a new stove for the first time in thirty years.

Then the distrust began to build. There were lawsuits. There were allegations that the dealer wasn't passing profits on to the women. There were claims of financial mismanagement.

One day I went to talk with one of the oldest quilters. We sat on her rickety front porch, on one of those suffocatingly hot Southern afternoons. I went into nosy-journalist mode, all my questions revolving around one theme: She clearly hadn't gotten rich, but didn't she want to be? Wasn't she upset?

Gazing out at the dusty road, she told me about the old days, about the civil rights movement, about how poor the town had always been, about God's faithfulness throughout. Then she stopped talking. All I could hear was birdsong. Finally she turned to me. She had an answer to my questions, a favorite Psalm she wanted to share: "The Lord is my shepherd." She paused and then continued, stopping after each word for emphasis: "I. Shall. Not. Want."

Never let me forget, Lord, that my truest riches lie
in knowing You. —JEFF CHU

Fri 3   *How good and pleasant it is when brothers live together in unity!* —PSALM 133:1 (NIV)

After packing a bag with toys, diapers, baby clothes, bottles and who knows how many other things, my son and I head out the door for a weekend in the country. Like most city moms, I have no trouble lifting the hefty stroller up and down the subway stairs, and at Penn Station I purchase a ticket for the train that will whisk me away from Manhattan. After one transfer and more stairs, I settle into my seat for the two-hour trip.

As I look out the window, skyscrapers give way to mountains and trees, and I know that the long, troublesome journey will be worth it. Much more than the country air, it's the family waiting for my arrival that I'm looking forward to. My cousin will honk his horn with a wave, my sister will jump out of the car and tackle me with hugs, and my niece and nephews will run straight to the stroller, shouting my son's name.

When I was growing up in Brooklyn, every day was crowded with the sweet chaos of family, and I'd always envisioned my own children as part of it. But slowly, everyone moved away—my parents to Florida and every-one else hours north of New York City. I miss the family circus and long for my son to experience the abundance of love I enjoyed as a child. So when the voices of my husband and I are not enough and the apartment seems too quiet, I pack a bag and take the train to the love and noise of my family.

Thank You, Lord, for all those who love me and for Your love that surrounds me wherever I am.
—KAREN VALENTIN

Sat 4

*Jesus spoke to them and said, "Take heart, it is I; do not be afraid." —*MATTHEW 14:27 (NRSV)

I was cleaning up the debris from Hurricane Gustav. Although I'd breathed a sigh of relief, it wasn't over yet. Hurricane Hannah had turned toward the East Coast, but Ike was on its way into the Gulf and Josephine wasn't far behind.

Lord, I prayed silently as I picked up broken branches, *watch over us. I'm afraid.* As my brief prayer ended, I heard voices coming from the tennis courts across from my backyard pond.

Two women were playing. As they hit the ball back and forth, one called out, "God always sees us through."

"Yes," her partner called back, "we just have to let go of our fear and latch on to our faith."

What a perfect message for me today, I thought.

The next morning in church, I listened to the story of Jesus calming His disciples on the stormy Sea of Galilee. "Do not be afraid," Jesus had said.

That afternoon I walked outside and gazed across the pond. My fear was gone.

Father, thank You for the words that comfort me
through the storms in my life.
—MELODY BONNETTE

Sun 5

Work hard so God can say to you, "Well done"....
—II TIMOTHY 2:15 (TLB)

On the Sunday nearest the first day of school, St. Mark's Episcopal Church in Altadena, California, holds a Blessing of the Backpacks. Students—and their teachers—come forward at a designated time in the service to have their backpacks blessed.

Also brought forward are packs filled with supplies that people in the parish have donated throughout the year to give to children who may not be able to afford them. Both the backpack and the child who will be carrying it are blessed.

"It honors a transitional moment that students and teachers sometimes approach with a certain amount of uncertainty," Mother Betsy, the associate rector, told me. "The backpacks are blessed as symbols of the hope, excitement, work, friendships and possibilities that the new school year holds."

Here is a prayer from the service at St. Mark's:

*Dear God, as we begin a new school year, we ask You to bless these backpacks
as symbols of our study and ministry in schools, the friendships that
will grow, the knowledge and skills to be gained. Help us to learn
and to share Your love with those we see each day,
in the name of the One Who is the source of all wisdom,
our Lord Jesus Christ. Amen.*
—FAY ANGUS

Mon 6

"It is enough for the disciple that he become like his teacher...." —MATTHEW 10:25 (NAS)

I received a surprising faith boost through my job selling baked goods at the farmer's market. I had a tent and tables to set up, heavy racks of bread to load and unload, long hours standing in the weather-of-the-day and waves of people eager to hear me explain my wares.

Mothers came with children to buy their favorite cookies. Men stopped by on their lunch breaks to pick up pepperoni rolls. Summer customers wanted sweet breads for the cabin or buns for the outdoor grill. Autumn shoppers purchased scones to go with morning coffee and savory loaves to have with soup. One woman preparing a Greek dinner for friends bought the spinach feta; a man on a bicycle liked his granola with raisins; a curmudgeonly man counted on his sourdough.

Somewhere in the middle of my job, the joy hit me: the unexpected joy of serving people, matching the right breads to their needs and watching them walk away satisfied.

I formed a new picture of the Son of Man, exuberant in sharing God's message, excited to serve others: Jesus providing wine for the wedding guests in Cana (John 2:1–11), touching the hand of Peter's mother-in-law so that the fever left her (Matthew 8:14–15), giving sight to a man born blind (John 9:1–12), restoring life to a twelve-year-old (Luke 8:40–42, 49–56), welcoming children into His arms (Mark 10:13–16).

How Jesus must have celebrated with the recipients of these wonderful works! What joy He must have felt every morning, anticipating the great things He would do, the words of life He would teach!

Jesus, like You, let me be jubilant in serving.
—CAROL KNAPP

September

Tue 7 *You have proved yourselves . . . in sharing. . . .*
—II CORINTHIANS 9:13 (NIV)

I always liked going to our neighborhood lumberyard. The whine of saws and the smell of fresh-cut pine reminded me of working with my father to build a toolshed when I was a boy. I also liked the guys who worked in the yard, men with safety shoes on their feet and sawdust on their clothes. But no matter how often I tried, I'd never been able to strike up a conversation with one of them.

Then one afternoon I came in with an extremely small order, just one running foot of cedar. "You making planked salmon?" the man at the front desk asked. When I said "Yes," he shook his head. "I wouldn't use cedar, if I was you. Taste's too strong for salmon."

"Yeah," said one of the yardmen as he picked up an order sheet. "White oak is better, but you got to soak it good."

In no time two other men from the yard had joined us, a muscular guy with tattoos the length of his arms and a teenager with a shaved head. Soon the discussion turned to more complicated cooking talk—the creative use of leftovers, the right way to fold an omelet.

Back in our own kitchen, I put the white oak plank down on the counter, marveling at the change in attitudes during my lifetime. When I was a boy, cooking—except for professional chefs—wasn't considered manly. I'd always enjoyed food, cooking it as well as eating it, the perfect change of pace from a job centered on words. But for decades I kept my culinary adventures a kind of guilty secret. Men got together to talk about football, not share recipes.

Sharing is one of the reasons, of course, that men love football. And today, thank God, we can share many more interests than we could a few years ago. Football and building and cooking . . . and yes, how to sing a lullaby and change a diaper.

Give me the grace, Father, to reject every stereotype.
—JOHN SHERRILL

Wed 8   He that dwelleth in the secret place of the most
High shall abide. . . . —PSALM 91:1

I was tired of living with fear. Day after day, anxious thoughts raced
through my mind—problems in my family, a health issue, a broken
relationship. Finally, I decided to see a counselor.

During my first visit with Blenda, I talked quickly, making sure she
understood how serious my problems were. She smiled, nodded and her
brown eyes softened with empathy. Almost everything she suggested
made sense: Replace negative thoughts with positive ones, practice letting go and letting God, learn to breathe deeply. Then she told me to do
something that seemed impossible.

"Is there a comfortable spot in your home?"

One place came to mind, a place where I'd never spent any time—our
hammock on the wraparound porch. I had often glanced at it as I carried in groceries or as we pulled out of the driveway. When I wanted to
sit out on the porch, I would choose a chair, never the hammock

"Your homework is to spend five minutes a day in the hammock," she
said. "While you're there, practice deep breathing. Allow your mind to
relax. After a couple of weeks, lie there for *ten* minutes."

*Do you realize what you're asking? Anything but this. I make things hap-
pen. I get things done. I can't be still and quiet.* Nevertheless, I nodded
obediently.

Late that afternoon, I went out to the porch and touched the coarse
rope of the hammock with one finger. Cautiously, I crawled to the middle and stretched out. I looked up; hints of color dappled the trees. I con-
centrated on my breathing: *in and out, in and out.* And slowly, slowly,
peace covered me and shooed worry away.

> *Lord, You are my secret place, my hammock.*
> —JULIE GARMON

Thu 9

"Give to him freely, and your heart shall not be grudging when you give to him. . . ." —DEUTERONOMY 15:10 (RSV)

I t isn't easy to get kosher meat in Bellingham, Washington. Since we've moved here, I've had to make two trips a year into Seattle, several hours and a lot of traffic away, to make certain we have kosher chicken for Passover and the High Holy Days.

Then, between my husband's surgery and mine, there just wasn't time to get that far south, and now we were approaching the High Holy Days without any chance of making the trip. I'd already decided we would have to do the ten days with fish and vegetables, and the few packages of kosher soup I had left. I knew I could do it without too much trouble, but it wouldn't make Keith happy because he's a world-class carnivore. That long a time without chicken was asking an awful lot, especially since he did all the cooking.

Then, shortly before the holidays, I got a call from someone in the congregation. "I have to take my son into Seattle for a day," Barbara said, "and I'm going to be stopping at one of the markets that carries kosher stuff. Do you need anything?" I asked if it wouldn't be an imposition, and she kept telling me she'd be happy to do it. She was able to get everything on our list.

As I tried to thank her, she reminded me that two years before, when she had been out of the country prior to Passover, I'd shopped for her. I'd completely forgotten about it.

It was no big deal to me to give; it was certainly a big deal to receive.

God, please help me always to give without expectation of return
and remind me to be grateful beyond measure
when someone does the same for me.
—RHODA BLECKER

Fri 10

Lo, I am with you alway, even unto the end of the world. . . . —MATTHEW 28:20

September 11 is a date whose imprint on our national consciousness will take generations to fade. But it's September 10 that stays with me somehow. It's just the other side of a line of demarcation, perhaps the last day of an era.

September 10, 2001, was a perfect late-summer day, like the infamous day that would follow. New Yorkers went about their business, absorbed by the daily trials and rewards of life in the city. I took a good friend to lunch for her birthday. We groused that the restaurant had run out of the crab cakes we'd wanted to order. How could they? The baseball pennant races were on, important enough to make the front pages of the tabloids. The last thing I did that day at work was to make plane reservations for a business trip the following week. I didn't give it a second thought. Why should I?

Since then, nothing has been quite the same. But on that September 10 —on any day of my life, really—I could not possibly have known what the future held. I am not given that knowledge. That's what stays with me about this day, haunts me even—the complete uncertainty of tomorrow.

Yet I am given a knowledge far greater than the ability to see the future. I know, with the utmost certainty, that whatever unlooked-for events the next day may bring, God is with me, today, tomorrow and forever.

> *Lord, Your love and protection is the one true thing that I can count on.*
> *It's always ahead of me, guiding my way through all uncertainty.*
> —EDWARD GRINNAN

Sat 11

If your enemies are hungry, give them bread to eat;
and if they are thirsty, give them water to drink.
—PROVERBS 25:21 (NRSV)

We probably all know someone who has been affected by violence or war. You may have lost a son or daughter, a niece or nephew or grandchild in Iraq or Afghanistan. Or you may have been there in support of a friend who lost someone. If my friend Bill hadn't experienced this sort of loss himself, I don't think that a Bible verse could have possibly made him as angry as this one from Proverbs did.

Bill lost his son in the fighting in Afghanistan almost four years ago. Not a week goes by when he doesn't break down in tears—the sort of thing that Bill had never done before tragedy entered his life.

Bill and I were in Bible study together, and our leader was reviewing all of the passages in Scripture that talk about loving and praying for our enemies. In addition to the verse above, we also heard, "But I say to you, Love your enemies and pray for those who persecute you" (Matthew 5:44, NRSV). Even though those words come from the Sermon on the Mount preached by Jesus Himself, they infuriated Bill for a long time.

I'll tell you what: God works miracles. After weeks of seeking God's help, Bill is praying once again, and he tells me that praying for the men who killed his son has begun to heal his own wounds.

Dear Jesus, when sorrow makes me feel like lashing out,
grant me the gift of forgiveness.
—JON SWEENEY

Sun 12

I am mindful of the sincere faith within you, which first dwelt in your grandmother Lois and your mother Eunice, and I am sure that it is in you as well.
—II Timothy 1:5 (NAS)

Today—the first Sunday after Labor Day—is Grandparents Day and has been since 1979, when President Jimmy Carter signed a special bill making it official.

When I was little, my paternal grandparents lived nearby, and each time we drove to town Dad turned the car into their driveway "to see if Pa or Ma need anything from the store."

As I recall, Grandma's hands were always floured from rolling bits of cookie dough into balls for the next tray to go into the oven. "Scoot into the breakfast nook to eat one while it's still hot," she'd tell me. "Use that pillow to sit on, so your chin is above the table." Mostly, though, I remember sitting between them in the pew on Sundays. Grandpa wore a flower (he called it a "posy") in his buttonhole. His bass voice rumbled during the hymns while Grandma's hankie wafted lily-of-the-valley perfume.

"Pillars of the church," people called Sam and Kate. "Good folks . . . work hard for their living." For a half century they'd stuck together, never doubting God nor His goodness. Even back then, their faith was viewed by some as old-fashioned, but that faith lasted them through thick and thin.

My grandparents are gone now as You well know, Father, but thank You for having put them in my life. Today I remember and honor the legacy they left behind. Their example started, enriched and deepened my faith in You.
—Isabel Wolseley

Mon 13

Don't be afraid of your enemies; always be courageous, and this will prove to them that they will lose and that you will win, because it is God who gives you the victory.
—PHILIPPIANS 1:28 (GNB)

I was watching a nature show about some photographers who were trying to get close-ups of lions in the wild. It was a nail-biter.

To get near enough to get good pictures, the photographers had to put themselves in danger. Whenever a lion would go into a crouch, the guide would whisper, "Don't act like prey. Don't run or look scared. It will trigger an attack."

Good advice, but tough to follow. The first year I taught college, I was a Daniel in a den of young lions. I was, frankly, scared to death, and I prayed that the students wouldn't ask too many questions. I did a lot of acting brave and eventually I began to develop more confidence.

I once heard a TV actor say, "When I'm directed to play the part of a strong, confident character, I find myself beginning to feel strong and confident just from taking that pose."

So whether you're facing a job interview, an angry client or final exams, I think it helps to stand tall and not run away.

Lord, You disguised me as a big, strong man, but You know how small and frightened I can be deep inside. Help me to be brave when I'm terrified.
—DANIEL SCHANTZ

Tue 14 *For whether we live, we live unto the Lord; and whether we die, we die unto the Lord: whether we live therefore, or die, we are the Lord's.* —ROMANS 14:8

Today I threw away a pair of house shoes. They were ratty, really, the insides threadbare and tattered. In several places the sole had completely separated from the shoe. Their blue fake-fur lining was matted and mashed down. So why have I kept these slippers so long?

Because they were a gift from my mother who's been dead thirteen long years. They look exactly like something she'd have picked out: Purple flowers cover the entire shoe, and they are very, very warm. These house shoes—now so battered from wear—were one of her last gifts to me, and letting them go is like losing yet another bit of her.

My mother was not a collector of precious things. When I cleaned out her house, I took her china, her books and her wedding ring. I also inherited several quilts she had made. I cherish these things. They were hers. Now they are mine.

But these house shoes touch us both. Mother picked them out for me. I wore them with gratitude and, after she passed, with a sense of finality. When they wore out, there would be no other pair coming from her.

Still, they are a mess. If Mother were here, she would laugh at my sentimentality. "Goodness, Mary Lou, get those filthy things out of the house. And get busy doing something worthwhile."

Whatever you say, Mother.

Still, I hope the trash truck comes soon. I've already begun to reconsider.

Remind me, Lord, that nothing is ever lost as long as I know where it is . . . and I know Mother is with You.
—MARY LOU CARNEY

Wed 15 *Two are better than one . . . .* —ECCLESIASTES 4:9

The jog I take a couple of times a week from our house to the park, down through the Heather Garden and up around the museum— oh, that hill—doesn't seem to get any easier. When I think of the hundreds of times I've done this short run, I don't see why it should be such a challenge, but in the morning when I punch the alarm clock and pull on my sweatpants, it's as though I'm about to climb Mount Everest. The first few yards out of the driveway and up to the corner mailbox are excruciating.

Then something happens. I pass a neighbor walking her dogs and wish her good morning. I see a friend taking his two children to school and marvel at how tall they've grown. I notice the marigolds and dahlias that some intrepid urban gardener has planted beneath the sycamores. I wave to a hearty trio of walkers coming down the hill I'm about to climb. "Keep it up," we tell one another. Just when I don't think I'm going to make it, I hear footsteps behind me. "Hey, stranger," a voice says. It's Michael, one of the neighborhood dads I've hardly seen since our kids graduated from Little League. "Can I join you?"

We do the loop around the museum and take in an extra loop for good measure, something I would have never done without his encouragement. We stop at the playground for a few pull-ups.

"How was your run?" my wife Carol asks when I get home.

"Great," I say. "I caught up with the neighborhood." They're the ones who keep me in shape. You can always travel faster and farther when you're with friends.

I thank You, God, for the friends who give me
encouragement and help me on my way.
—RICK HAMLIN

Thu 16 *To search out a matter is the glory of kings.*
—PROVERBS 25:2 (NIV)

When our son John headed off to college, I knew there would be independence issues—mine. I've always depended on him for all things electronic. Before John left, I lamented, "What am I going to do without you? I've always relied on you to help me when I don't know how to do something on my computer."

"Do what I do," John replied. "If you can't figure something out, look it up on the Internet."

I was stunned at this simple remedy, which I'd never thought to try. I'd always figured there was something in the younger generation's blood that made them computer whizzes.

John had been gone only a week when I couldn't figure out how to make my e-mail program send an automatic reply saying that I was out of the office. I clicked every bar and looked at menus with no luck. I was about to call John, but instead I tried what he suggested: I typed my question on the Internet search page. A few more clicks and I had printed out instructions. I followed the steps. Bingo! My auto-reply was all set up.

I guess it's never too late to learn more independence and resourcefulness. Even if you have to learn it from your own teenage son!

Father, for too long I've relied on others to take care of parts of my life that I should be handling myself. Help me take practical steps toward healthy independence.
—KAREN BARBER

☸ TWELVE KEYS TO THE GIVING LIFE

Fri 17   *But lay up for yourselves treasures in heaven. . . .*
—Matthew 6:20

GIVE ETERNALLY

This past year Greg, one of my friends and coworkers, died in the line of duty as a volunteer firefighter. At his memorial service, the chaplain of the Gallipolis, Ohio, Fire Department, shared a story that touched me deeply.

On a hot September day Greg and some fellow firefighters had been tearing down a house that didn't meet the building code. Thirsty from his work, Greg drove the fire truck to the nearby *Gallipolis Daily Tribune* office for a drink of water. On his way he honked the fire truck horn as he passed a waving boy.

What happened next remains a blur. Greg collapsed at the *Tribune* office. Sirens filled the air; concerned onlookers gathered. The boy ran all the way home and then begged his mother to take him back to the scene. He just had to check on that firefighter.

"Is he going to make it?" The boy pressed his mother for details, but she had no answers. "He's my hero," the boy told her. "Someday, I'm going to be just like him."

"We can all be somebody's hero," the chaplain told the mourners at Greg's memorial service. "Everyone's circle of influence is different, of course. But in all our lives, in the simple things we do every single day, each of us, like Greg, has the opportunity to make a real difference."

Dear God, through our acts of giving, we lay up treasures in heaven that
will last forever. Help me to live—and die—a giver.
—Roberta Messner

Sat 18
   Let us then with confidence draw near to the throne of grace,
   that we may receive mercy and find grace to help in time
   of need. —HEBREWS 4:16 (RSV)

I live in a townhouse. This means there's just a wall separating me from my neighbor, an older woman who isn't as strong or steady as she used to be. I'm her Lifeline® contact person; I try to watch out for her and listen for any calls of distress.

So I was surprised at her report at noon one Saturday, when I knocked on her door, delivering a taste of my cooking: "I fell off a chair this morning. I didn't hurt myself, but it took me an hour to *scootch* across the room and pull myself up."

"What? Why didn't you yell or bang on the wall?" I asked.

"Well, I didn't want to bother you."

"It's not a bother. You were in trouble," I said.

"Well, I didn't think you'd hear me—if you were in the kitchen or upstairs or . . ."

"Why didn't you push the Lifeline button, so I'd get an emergency call?"

"Well, I know I gave you a key, but . . ." She hesitated before continuing. "Do you really know where it is? I figured you wouldn't be able to find it."

"Yes, I know where it is." I smiled and tried to make light of the situation. "Next time give me a chance. Holler!"

As I recall this conversation, I hear myself as the one who is weak or has fallen but finds an excuse—my independent spirit, my lack of confidence—for not asking God for help. And then I hear God having the last word: "Next time give me a chance. Pray!"

> *Lord, in my time of need, give me confidence in Your ability to hear*
> *my prayer and Your willingness to grant mercy and grace.*
> —EVELYN BENCE

Sun 19

"See, I am sending an angel ahead of you to guard you along the way and to bring you to the place I have prepared."
—Exodus 23:20 (NIV)

Would you speak at Linda's funeral on Sunday?" a friend asked in a phone call early one morning.

I could hardly answer; I was still reeling from the fact that Linda's cancer had returned so suddenly and viciously, metastasizing in her liver. Within a month my friend was gone. I wasn't sure I had the strength and composure to speak at her funeral.

Linda and I had worked together at MOPS International (Mothers of Preschoolers), and a couple of years earlier, we'd gone through chemotherapy at the same time, she with breast cancer, I with ovarian cancer. We were faithful comrades, watching each other and sharing our determination. I appreciated Linda's honesty and feistiness. Like me, she was not about to let this disease take her away from the life she loved with her family, friends and grandchildren.

But in the last month, I'd seen a change in Linda. As she faced this final part of the journey, her feisty fight turned into gentle strength, her reluctant acceptance into confident anticipation. I was grateful for the hopeful example she gave us. So I agreed to speak, even though I wasn't sure I could make it through my message.

On the day of her funeral, when my turn came, I got up, took some deep breaths and described the miraculous transformation I'd seen in Linda. "Her example reminds me and all who knew her that God gives us exactly the strength we need to endure the circumstances we face—not months or weeks ahead of time, but exactly when we need that strength. So, very well done, my good and faithful friend."

I sat down and then the tears came.

What precious evidence of Your love, Lord, that You give me the strength to meet the challenges in my life, both great and small.
—Carol Kuykendall

Mon 20   *"I will also hold You by the hand and watch over You. . . ."*
—ISAIAH 42:6 (NAS)

Every family develops its own special vocabulary, words and phrases that have a unique history and meaning. After more than thirty years of raising golden retrievers, our family knows exactly what it means when one of us says, "Hold my paw."

Beau, our twelve-year-old "pappa dog," has just wandered into my study. His vision is growing dim, but he still knows his way around. He often sleeps near my chair as I work, but tonight he sits down next to me, lifts a big hairy paw and puts it gently on my knee. In the midnight dimness, I drop my right hand from the computer keyboard to Beau's outstretched paw, gently squeezing the rough old pads that have walked and run hundreds of miles with me. I understand what Beau wants: reassurance that I'm with him, that our lives are joined and that I haven't let go of him.

The simple power of touch goes far deeper than words. Tonight as I hold Beau's paw, I'm reminded that God hasn't let go of me. Both of us, human and animal, yearn to know that we're not alone.

Father, let me feel the gentle touch of Your presence in my life this day. —SCOTT WALKER

READER'S ROOM

On the very day I was registering my children at a new school for the fall, I opened my *Daily Guideposts* and read Harold Hostetler's devotional, reminding us that God is with us as we leave our comfort zones. The prayer for that day was "Father, we look to You to take care of us as we move into the unknown." That was the perfect prayer for me. I'm always amazed at how God lets me know that He is with me through all the rough spots and transitions of life. —*Joni Dintelmann, Belleville, Illinois*

September

Tue 21

Each man has his own gift from God. . . .
—I Corinthians 7:7 (NAS)

When I was in high school, I longed to be a majorette like my friends. But the rules stipulated that majorettes must play a band instrument. The long-suffering band director finally suggested, "Try the triangle, Marion. Anyone can play it."

Not me.

So I went out for basketball. Of the thirty who wanted to play, only two of us didn't make it.

I tried cheerleading next—until I discovered that I couldn't smile and cheer at the same time.

An observant English teacher asked, "What's wrong, Marion?"

"I can't be a majorette, a basketball player or a cheerleader. I'm a . . . nothing."

He sat down in the empty seat in front of me. "You've gotten *A*'s on all your essays, despite your spelling. Maybe your gift is simply different. What do you really enjoy?"

I was always delighted when he assigned an essay, beamed when everyone else moaned. I'd waited on the cold granite steps for the library to open each summer morning. Books had become the brothers and sisters I didn't have, keeping me company while my mother worked. Sometimes I would lie in bed, thinking about words I enjoyed, like *tapestry*, *September*, *pristine* and *pensive*, and authors I adored: Pearl S. Buck, W. Somerset Maugham, Edgar Allan Poe, Sinclair Lewis, Emily Dickinson. Tiny Tim, Heidi, Nancy Drew, Tom Sawyer and Lassie were cherished friends.

The batons, musical instruments, basketballs and pom-poms are long gone. My own gift from God remains alive.

Oh, Father, here's a long, overdue, deep-down thank You for knowing,
even way back then, the gift for me!
—Marion Bond West

Wed 22 *Like newborn babes, long for the pure spiritual milk, that by it you may grow up to salvation; for you have tasted the kindness of the Lord.* —I Peter 2:2–3 (rsv)

Here's a note on the nuttiest gift we have ever been given by the Coherent Mercy: diapers.

Imagine a world without them, without the first parents back there at the dawn of time, even before cassette tapes, realizing *whoa!* they better use some of that cedar underbark for infant hygiene or else! So they did, and then came burlap, and cotton, and a thousand kinds of plastic, and such engineering marvels as diaper pins, and those deft little adhesive flaps, and such entrepreneurial feats as potty chairs, and cartoon and college logos on pull-up pants, and sweet insanities like talcum powder in a tin as big as a refrigerator, and small white tables specially designed for changing diapers on small wriggling people, and buckets with cool little foot pedals.

Who would have thought I would ever in a million years say that I miss changing diapers, after a million hours changing diapers? But this morning, just for a moment, I do miss the wrestle and redolence, the powder and burble, the motions and gestures of the ancient craft, the fresh-bread smell of your tiny crazy naked children, the way you rubbed your capacious nose in their bellies to make them do that walrus laugh, those infinitesimal utterly intimate moments between you and your kids. Now they are gone forever, and you'll never have the chance to tickle your grinning child the size of a sneaker, and stare, and wonder what incredible generosity handed you this joyous soul.

Dear Lord, for all the gifts that we never see clearly or understand much or appreciate hardly at all, bless You.
—Brian Doyle

☼ THE GIFT OF SIGHT

Thu 23   *Sing, O heavens; and be joyful, O earth; and break forth into singing, O mountains: for the Lord hath comforted his people, and will have mercy upon his afflicted.* —ISAIAH 49:13

SUNRISE, SUNSET

This afternoon I received an e-mail from my friend Lucinda, who hasn't been well for some time. Some days she just can't even get out of bed. Yet the final paragraph of her letter reads:

> I think I shall dress so that I can drive to the park to watch the sunset if there is one . . . of course, with all the buildings I can only see the upper part of the sky, but even that can be glorious. I have not seen a sunrise or sunset for many years, and I do so miss them.

Lucinda's letter made me realize something. Right now in my life, I'm able to watch the sunrise nearly every day, yet I often fail to notice it. We live in a little valley with mountains in the north, west and south, so we rarely have a chance to watch a sunset. But every morning, unless the sky is overcast, I can watch the sunrise. As my eyesight becomes more and more precious to me in its long good-bye, I must remember to value the beauty I can see now.

Tomorrow morning I'll not miss the sunrise as it streams in through our breakfast-room window, spilling colors on the table like a prism. And like Lucinda, I might even drive up out of the valley in the early evening to watch the sunset.

I am so thankful, Creator, for the beauty of sunrise and sunset.
As long as I have eyes to see, may I truly value the wonders
and the mysteries of Your world.
—MARILYN MORGAN KING

Fri 24   *Then he took the book of the covenant and read it in the hearing of the people; and they said, "All that the Lord has spoken we will do, and we will be obedient!"* —EXODUS 24:7 (NAS)

Since my wife retired from her job as a school librarian, she has more time to do volunteer work, and sometimes I join her. One of Shirley's volunteer jobs—surprise!—is helping out in the local elementary school library. Recently she signed us up to tutor some students who were having trouble with their reading.

Seeing children struggle to sound out look-alike words, such as *wind* in a storm and *wind* a ball of string, made me realize how difficult reading can be. The kids' problem, I saw, was akin to my trouble learning a foreign language. I've studied both French and Spanish with limited success.

Have you ever stopped to think how blessed you are to be able to read? For one thing, without that skill you couldn't study the Bible. In all likelihood, Jesus' twelve disciples were illiterate. With few exceptions, only the priests and rabbis could read the Torah in biblical times. Of course, the Apostles didn't have to read to believe. They saw Christ's miracles with their own eyes. But even then they had trouble understanding some of Jesus' sayings. And so do we. Knowing the truth and living it, we all can testify, are two different things—to feel the *wind* of the Spirit, for example, or to *wind* up a doubting Thomas.

Thank You, God, for the gift of reading,
and for Your Holy Spirit's leading.
—FRED BAUER

Sat 25

Every way of a man appears right in his own eyes, But the Lord weighs the heart. —PROVERBS 21:2 (NKJV)

A t a physics conference dinner with my husband Alex, I sat next to a man I'll call Clayton. Clayton dominated the entire conversation by talking about himself. He had solved problems no one else could; only his views were right; other researchers' work was inaccurate or unimportant. Extremely irritated, I planned to avoid Clayton in the future. In fact, I resolved never to have another conversation with him.

A few days later I was in an education class. Our professor explained how one child can become the class scapegoat and target of the other students' ridicule. "Usually it's because the class sees their own weaknesses glaringly magnified in the odd student. They don't want to admit the similarities, so they mock and exclude the student. The behavior of both the class and the excluded student is caused by personal insecurity."

As I took notes, suddenly I thought of Clayton. It struck me that I have many of the same faults. How easily I dominate a conversation and leave others out. I, too, sometimes feel that only my opinion is right. My concerns or work easily seem most important. As my professor had described, I reacted negatively to someone in whom I experienced my own weaknesses.

I changed my resolution. Instead of avoiding Clayton at future functions, I'll try to listen patiently with the same kindness and acceptance that I need.

Lord, help me to see myself more honestly and
other people more positively.
—MARY BROWN

Sun 26 *Thy faithfulness is unto all generations. . . .*
—PSALM 119:90

I just wrote the latest entry in my birthday book: Jack Ryan McMahon, a cousin born in Seattle on September 25. The baby who arrived and was duly noted before Jack was Paisley Jean O'Roark, my great-niece born in Columbus, Ohio. And when I flip the pages to January 29, there's my own name, but this entry is in my Grandmother Paisley's neat handwriting. She wrote my name there some sixty years ago.

The book is called *Natal Memories: A Scripture-Text Birthday Book*. As an introductory page explains, it was given to my grandmother in 1947 by Alexander and Elizabeth Fleming, the minister of the church that our family attended in Steubenville, Ohio, and his wife. There's a page for each day of the year with a Scripture verse at the bottom. I imagine my grandmother's concentration and satisfaction as she recorded birthdays of family and friends in a steady and loving hand, and committed many of the verses to memory.

My grandmother died when I was ten years old, and the book must have been swept into a box of her belongings, where I found it many years later and tucked it into a drawer of my own. Recently I discovered it again. And now I'm the one who smiles as I add new births and make note of those who are now here—and were here—and should be celebrated.

Lord, thank You for the little book that somehow anchors the generations of our family in what it calls Your "great unchanging heart of love."
—MARY ANN O'ROARK

Mon 27

"You're blessed when you can show people how to cooperate. . . . That's when you discover who you really are, and your place in God's family."
—MATTHEW 5:9 (MSG)

When statewide inoculations started in Oklahoma during the Depression, my first-grade class was one of the first to be given shots. My mother came to school that day to help the teacher and the nurse calm us.

When the first girl got her shot, she screamed and then sobbed. Many of the other children started crying too. I slipped toward the back of the room, hoping they would run out before I got up there.

I saw my mother talking to the teacher and the nurse. Then she walked briskly toward me and whispered, "Keith, everyone is afraid. It would help so much if you would go up there and say you want to get your shot now. It only hurts a little. You can do it."

It was the last thing I wanted to do. I didn't care how the other kids felt; I felt terrible. But I had to do it. So I calmly walked to the nurse, looked her in the eye, rolled up my sleeve and said, "I'll go next." Somehow I managed not to cry or scream. Then I rolled my sleeve down and calmly walked back to my desk.

I learned something that day: Maybe the heroes my mother had read to me about were sometimes afraid. *Even courageous people have fear*, I thought.

Lord, thank You that even though You asked three times to be excused on Gethsemane, You went ahead anyway. Give me the courage to love enough to follow You wherever Your adventure leads me.
—KEITH MILLER

Tue 28   *You have made known to me the path of life. . . .*
—Psalm 16:11 (NIV)

O ne evening I sat petting my cat, thinking about my checkered career as a high school teacher, office worker, technical writer and now bookseller. "You're a cat," I whispered in Prince's gray ear. "You're supposed to have nine lives. But shouldn't my one life have gone in a straighter path?"

Prince kept his thoughts to himself as he gazed up at me. Suddenly I remembered an incident I hadn't thought of in a long while. I'd gotten Prince from the Animal Rescue Foundation in Walnut Creek, California. In the newsletter they gave me before I'd lugged my wonderful eighteen-pound cat home, I learned that ARF had been started by a local man named Tony La Russa who had a passion for rescuing stray animals.

Not long after that, I was at work, shelving books, when I heard a low buzz coming from my coworkers. It got louder and louder, and sorting out the words, I heard: "Oh my, that's Tony La Russa!" "Can you imagine? Tony La Russa is shopping here!" "I'd love to ask for his autograph, but I haven't got the nerve!"

I can't believe so many of my colleagues are that involved with animal rescue! I thought.

Of course, Tony La Russa is also the World Series–winning manager of the Oakland A's and St. Louis Cardinals, a fact known to everyone but me apparently. He got involved with rescuing animals after a stray cat wandered onto the baseball field; he took it home.

I turned back to Prince. "You know, if God gave me the gift of being adaptable to my many job situations, maybe that's not such a bad thing. After all, if you and Tony have had more than one exciting life, why can't I?"

> *God, who says a straight and narrow life is better than a curvy and*
> *wide one? Especially if You're beside me, guiding me.*
> —Linda Neukrug

September

Wed 29

The Spirit of the Lord God is upon me . . . he hath sent me to bind up the brokenhearted. . . . —Isaiah 61:1

How's John doing?" a woman from my prayer group asked. I hadn't touched base with her in a while. We changed my son's anxiety medication over the summer, and instead of improving, my twelve-year-old spent two weeks in the hospital.

"He's up and down. Some days he seems fine, and he is. Other days he seems fine, and a minute later we're wondering if we should call 911."

There was a pause in the conversation. Then, gently, my friend commented, "The unpredictability must be hard."

It was my turn to pause and collect my thoughts. "Yes," I said, "but I don't focus as much on that now. What I'm finally beginning to grasp is that part of the point is learning to say *thank you* each day my son is alive." Still another pause. "It took me a long time to get there," I added.

"How do your other kids handle it?" my friend asked.

"They pretty much know to go to another room and entertain themselves when John starts to blow. They enjoy him when he's able to be fun and keep themselves safe when he's not."

"I'll keep praying for you."

"Thanks. It's hard, but it's harder to be John. He's a great kid with some really difficult problems. He thinks he's horrible. I wish he could know fully just how precious he is to God—and to us."

My friend nodded. There wasn't much else to say, but a lot to pray for.

Lord, people suffer. Let me hold them up to You
before I cry out for myself.
—Julia Attaway

Thu 30 This is my memorial unto all generations.
—EXODUS 3:15

Last week I tried to sharpen a mechanical pencil. Last year I sent my youngest grandson a card that read "To My Great Niece." And no family gathering passes without the Halloween story: I filled a bowl with candy, turned on the porch light and waited expectantly for trick-or-treaters—on the last day of September.

But there's a reason I'm not always attentive to details: family tradition. My mother once gathered a colorful fall bouquet for the dining table, only to discover (painfully) that she'd picked poison sumac. My sister Amanda bought and wore a belt several times until a church friend pointed out that the "lovely designs" were skulls and crossbones. Amanda hadn't noticed; she was wearing the belt upside down.

But good traits run in our family too. My banker-grandfather made an all-day trip to return mortgage papers to a struggling farmer after an overzealous employee at the bank refused a fifty-dollar seed loan without them. Grandma taught me about Jesus by patiently teaching me hymns of faith. Daddy bought gasoline so our pastor could make hospital calls. Neither friend nor stranger ever left our house hungry. At Mother's funeral a friend remarked, "I always envied the love in your family."

Some family traditions, like inattention to details, should end with me. But others—compassion, patience, generosity, hospitality, love—need to be cultivated, cherished and passed on. I hope that my children and grandchildren will continue to laugh and forgive my foibles. I pray that they will nurture and keep the spiritual gifts lived out and handed down from previous generations.

Thank You, Lord, for the blessed heritage that is mine!
—PENNEY SCHWAB

THE GIFTS I'VE BEEN GIVEN

1 _____

2 _____

3 _____

4 _____

5 _____

6 _____

7 _____

8 _____

9 _____

10 _____

11 _____

12 _____

13 _____

14 _____

15 _____

16 _____

17 _____

18 _____

19 _____

20 _____

21 _____

September

22 _____

23 _____

24 _____

25 _____

26 _____

27 _____

28 _____

29 _____

30 _____

October

Ask, and it shall be given you;
seek, and ye shall find; knock, and it
shall be opened unto you.

—LUKE 11:9

🎁 GIFTS FROM ABOVE

Fri 1
Keep your mouth shut and show your good sense.
—PROVERBS 17:28 (NEB)

A GIFT OF DISCRETION

"I *cannot* believe what I just said," I told my husband as I walked into his study. "I was talking to Mildred on the phone, and she asked me if I had met the new family that moved in down the street. I said, 'Yes, and they are about the rudest people I have ever seen.'"

"So, what did Mildred think?" David asked.

"She said the new couple just happened to be her brother and sister-in-law and hung up." I sat down, totally defeated. "Oh, David, will I ever learn to keep my big mouth shut?"

I've had this same problem ever since I was a kid. I don't know how many times I heard my daddy say, "Just try to remember, honey, engage your brain before putting your mouth in gear."

"Let's face it," I said, "I've been working on my spiritual journey for some time now, but this is one area where I seem to be going backward."

I guess David recognized my sincerity in wanting to improve, because a few days later as we were sitting down to dinner, he said, "I was leafing through Proverbs, and I came across a verse that certainly hit home for me. I thought you might be interested in it, too, so I wrote it down: 'Even a fool, if he holds his peace, is thought wise; keep your mouth shut and show your good sense.'"

Today I'm taping that verse to the dashboard of my car, the bathroom mirror and, oh, most definitely, over the telephone. Who knows? I might just learn to engage my brain after all!

Father, give me the gift of keeping my mouth shut and
my brain working. —PAM KIDD

Sat 2 *How great are his signs, how mighty his wonders! His kingdom is an everlasting kingdom, and his sovereignty is from generation to generation.* —DANIEL 4:3 (NRSV)

Okay, I admit it: I like sports—a lot; probably too much, if you ask my wife Lynn, especially in the fall, when it's football season. I'll be watching at least one and probably three or four games today and reading about ten others on the Internet.

But if that sounds like a waste of time, then you don't know some of the football people I've come across over the years. Not the big names, the stars of the game, but ordinary people, like Marc Fagot, the assistant football coach of the Geneva High School Vikings.

Why is an assistant high school football coach in Illinois noteworthy to someone in Michigan, like me? Because of the extraordinary thing an ordinary guy like Marc did. (Hint: It wasn't the fact that his team made it all the way to the finals of the state playoffs.) He coached the Vikings while battling a rare form of lung cancer. Every day, even as the disease was eating away at his body, he was on the field, coaching a group of young men.

This is what the head coach told his team the day all the coaches shaved their heads as a show of support after Marc's hair fell out from the chemotherapy: "Our shaving our heads is not about dying, it's about living. It's not about feeling sorry for anything, it's about doing the best you can with what you've got in front of you."

Most of the time, football is just football, a few hours of fun in a busy life. But occasionally, whether or not you know what a touchdown is, a football story becomes a life story. That's the game I live for every fall.

Help me make the most of the day
You have given me today, God.
—JEFF JAPINGA

Sun 3　　*Because there is one bread, we who are many are*
one body, for we all partake of the one bread.
　　—I CORINTHIANS 10:17 (RSV)

After growing up Catholic, I attended a nondenominational
Christian college where grape juice was served at Communion in
small, individual glasses. Instead of receiving wafer bread, we passed a loaf
around the pews and tore off a piece. Later, when I began attending a
Lutheran church with my husband, we received Communion by "intinc-
tion," dipping the wafer in the wine.

If you look at the celebration of the first Eucharist, described in
Matthew, Mark and Luke, you'll find a few basic elements: shared bread
and wine, giving thanks, and Jesus' prophecy that His body would be
given up and His blood would be shed for the forgiveness of sin. He
added, "Do this in remembrance of me." There are no other directions.

On this World Communion Sunday, people all over the world celebrate Communion as a sign that in spite of our outward differences, we
are one body. We come in many colors and Christ's words are repeated
in many languages, but we are all celebrating being one in Christ. Jesus
asked that we do this to remember Him. But perhaps He also hoped that
this celebration would bind us together, no matter where on earth we
may be.

Lord Jesus, thank You for the great gift of Communion with You
and with each other: one bread, one body,
one Lord, one people in Christ.
　　—GINA BRIDGEMAN

Mon 4 *It is better to trust in the Lord than to put confidence in man.* —PSALM 118:8

When I walked into my favorite supermarket, few of the customers were smiling. Overnight there had been a change: The items on the shelves had been relocated. I went down aisle fourteen looking for canned fruit, but I didn't find it until I got to aisle two. Only the meat and fresh produce were in their usual places. To add to the confusion, the old signs still hung above the aisles. It was like arriving in an unfamiliar city with a map and finding the street signs had all been moved. I felt helpless.

The manager had assigned someone to direct shoppers to the right locations, but he was soon overwhelmed by customers with long shopping lists. It was a few days before new signs were installed and shopping slowly returned to normal.

During my life I've been through overnight shuffles, diversions, vacillations and downturns. But through it all, I've had the Bible. Unlike the signs in the supermarket, the Word has never changed and the One Who gave it to us is neither confused nor overwhelmed.

Dear Father in heaven, Your Word is always there
to bring guidance and comfort.
—OSCAR GREENE

Tue 5 "*Be careful, keep calm and don't be afraid. Do not lose heart. . . .*" —ISAIAH 7:4 (NIV)

In my 130-gallon aquarium is a school of large, round, flat fish called red hooks. They get their name from a red fin that curves like a hook. Highly nervous creatures, they react to unfamiliar noises or movement with a mad dash to the other end of the tank.

One of them is a "poster fish" for making things worse than they need to be; Leaping Larry, I call him. When Larry is startled, he jumps out of the tank. While the others are swimming back to normal, there's Larry, flopping on the carpet. You'd think he'd learn, but the next time a strange shadow crosses the tank, Larry's over the edge again.

I can't be too hard on Larry because I also tend to jump out of panic. Years ago, when my husband Whitney was laid off from work, I jumped into a low-paying job I hated, punishing both myself and my family. If I'd stopped, prayed and listened, I might have heard God beyond my panic, Who had a better provision for us.

I've jumped into other things out of fear too: volunteering when I don't have time; exhausting myself with cleaning at the news of last-minute company; leaving multiple phone messages for a daughter who hasn't called when I thought she should. Fear can run my life, if I let it. The key for me is to stop, pray, listen to God. He is always ready to help me get back in the tank.

> *Lord, when fear knocks, help me to keep still*
> *and let You answer.*
> —SHARI SMYTH

Wed 6   *"I am leaving you with a gift—peace of mind and heart. And the peace I give isn't like the peace the world gives. So don't be troubled or afraid." —*JOHN 14:27 (NLT)

Up at five o'clock and driving in the rain to the airport, I became filled with anxiety about my trip. As I got on the plane, I sat by the window and watched the rain pool on the corners of the glass. I thought of my sons. They were awake now, watching television, eating cinnamon-raisin toast. How I wished I was right there beside them, drinking a warm cup of tea.

I opened my book and tried to read, but my mind raced: *Rent the car, find the hotel, meetings tomorrow, a presentation and then home.* The plane took off and I sighed.

As we rose in the sky, I looked down at the landscape. The traffic, plots of land and clusters of houses seemed like an elaborate model. Up we went, farther and farther, until we were above the rain. Looking out the window at the calm white landscape of clouds, I felt completely at peace. My worries about the trip, about tomorrow, fell away, seeming small and unimportant.

The business trip sped by. In a flash I was home, but the peace of being in the sky has stayed with me. Sometimes, when I'm making a mountain out of a molehill, I take a little trip back to that morning when I rose above the storm and everything fell into place.

> *Father, I may not be able to change the situations*
> *that cause stress in my life, but I know that You can.*
> *You are the comfort above the storm.*
> —SABRA CIANCANELLI

Thu 7

Remember his marvellous works that he hath done. . . .
—I CHRONICLES 16:12

The other day I got a note from a *Guideposts* reader that was particularly poignant. Emma was a longtime subscriber who had "lived a life full of happiness and the Lord's blessings." And indeed she had: seven kids, a raft of grandkids and a great-grandchild on the way. She'd lost her husband after fifty-three years of marriage and one son in an accident, but had leaned on her faith to get through those heartbreaks. "I'm in a nursing home now and don't get out much, but don't worry about me. I'm as happy as ever, and I have my memories."

How sad, I thought. *Such a rich life and now . . . only memories.*

Or was it so sad? I'm old enough now to have a pretty full store of memories myself. I remember my mother's giggle and my father's frown, and my late brother's goofy walk. I remember the day my family moved from Philadelphia to Detroit—the big John Ivory moving van parked in front of our house—a day charged with both sadness and the wild anticipation of an eight-year-old boy setting out for the frontier. I remember my first date (I took her to Detroit's historic Greenfield Village, where we watched a blacksmith make a horseshoe, then ate Stroh's ice cream till we were sick). I remember my first day at Yale and being dumbfounded by how old and ivied the architecture was (I learned soon enough that most of it was of fairly recent vintage made to appear older). I certainly remember the day I got my current job.

Good memories are blessings, a gift to sweeten our lives. Reading Emma's letter, I understood how fiercely I held on to mine, as fiercely as one holds on to anything precious. And as Emma knows, there's nothing sad about that.

Lord, the best memories of my life are the blessings You've given.
—EDWARD GRINNAN

Fri 8   *For where two or three are gathered together in my name, there am I in the midst of them.* —MATTHEW 18:20

I often make big dinners for my extended family. We began calling these events "parties" for the little ones. "Nina, are we having a party tonight?" my grandson Drake would ask if I stopped by his house. And his little brother Brock would join in: "Party! Party!" Not long ago, I bought a little neon light. It spells out the word *party* in a rainbow of colors. Once everyone has arrived for dinner, the grandchildren gather 'round while I plug it in.

Last night my daughter Amy Jo called to see if I could take care of the boys for the evening. Drake and Brock and I dined alone on spaghetti and meatballs that I'd pulled out of the freezer. As we settled down at the table, Drake suddenly sat up and pointed. "The party light, Nina. We forgot the party light!"

"But it's just the three of us . . . ," I began.

Drake smiled. "But it's still a party!"

So I plugged in the light. And in the autumn twilight it glowed soft and inviting. We ate in silence, the only sound was the slurping of spaghetti into small mouths.

I think I sense God's presence most during these simple times, times when I find myself standing in a small oasis of gratitude. There I recognize how blessed I am, that I—and those I love—are not alone on this earthly trek.

Come, Sweet Jesus, into every moment of my life.
—MARY LOU CARNEY

Sat 9

But we have this treasure in jars of clay to show that this all-surpassing power is from God and not from us.
—II Corinthians 4:7 (NIV)

My wife Carol wanted to attend a gourd festival at a farm in Fallbrook, near where we lived in Southern California. She persuaded our daughter Laurel and granddaughter Kaila to go, too, but I was reluctant. *What's so wonderful about gourds?* But I finally agreed to do the driving, and on a sunny October afternoon we took off over a winding road into the backcountry.

When we arrived at the festival, the others hurried to the colorful craft booths positioned underneath a canopy of live oak trees. I strolled off and found myself among tables of soil-encrusted, moldy gourds and tan gourds that had been scrubbed clean. These were not the colorful garden-variety gourds; these were dried, hard, hollow shells with seeds still rattling around inside. Some resembled huge pears and exotic jungle fruits; others were round or cucumber-shaped; still more were "jewelry sized."

Carol spotted me and motioned me over to the craft booths. There I saw cleaned and polished gourds, carved and decorated, transformed into things of beauty. The side of one had been cut away and a candle placed inside. Another was intricately carved with an overall walnut-shell pattern that made it appear light as a feather. And I couldn't miss the one with the Last Supper etched on its side.

While Carol bought three small polished gourd ornaments, brightly painted with poinsettias and other Christmas designs, I sat down on a tree stump near the middle of the festival and breathed in the atmosphere. The day was warm and sunny; the live oak trees lent their comforting shade. Gourds, and the artists who work with them, I decided, are pretty wonderful after all.

Father, how beautiful are the creations of Your hands, as You take the common things of earth and turn them into works of art.
—Harold Hostetler

Sun 10

*For He has not despised . . . the affliction of the afflicted;
Nor has He hidden His face from him; But when he
cried to Him for help, He heard.* —PSALM 22:24 (NAS)

An early autumn sun lit a pale sky at the retreat grounds. Most of the trees had shed their leaves. An outdoor prayer labyrinth bordered with stones curled toward a small tree. I sauntered along the winding path, pausing to listen for a woodpecker and look at the sunlight in an oak's bare branches.

Halfway into the labyrinth, I spotted a browned oak leaf pocked with holes. I picked it up and twirled it between my fingers as I walked. Through its holes I could see glimpses of earth; when I lifted it toward the sky, I caught pinpoints of blue; when I tilted it, the holes filled with flecks of sun.

These aren't holes, I thought, *they're windows. Through them I can see loveliness beyond the leaf.*

I made the leap from the leaf to my life. Recent battles over choices and direction had left gaping holes. I understood the Psalmist's cry: "I am benumbed and badly crushed; I groan because of the agitation of my heart" (Psalm 38:8, NAS). But hadn't new glimpses of God's love and mercy emerged? Hadn't I seen how patiently He journeys with me (Psalm 138:8), how deep His fountain of forgiveness (Psalm 86:5), how unshakable His power to sustain (Psalm 55:22)?

An epiphany in an oak leaf: wounds becoming windows revealing God.

*Father of lights, only You can open a window to reveal to me
"the depth of the riches both of the wisdom and
knowledge of God!"* (Romans 11:33, NAS).
—CAROL KNAPP

Mon 11
"See, I am doing a new thing! . . ."
—Isaiah 43:19 (NIV)

"Remember Columbus!" It's what my husband John and I say whenever one of us gets too certain about how things will turn out.

That cautioning phrase came into our vocabulary after we visited the harbor on the southwest coast of Spain from which Christopher Columbus set sail in 1492. Today exact replicas of the *Nina*, *Pinta* and *Santa Maria* are anchored there.

From the harbor we climbed up the hill to the Franciscan monastery of La Rabida, where in 1485 Columbus brought his motherless young son and his dogged hopes. For seven years he'd waited in Lisbon, trying to persuade the king of Portugal to let him reach the riches of Asia by sailing west. No, the king's astronomers concluded at last: Columbus' calculations were flawed; Asia was too far away.

Penniless and exhausted, Columbus turned to Spain. For seven more years, while the monks of La Rabida housed him and his son, Columbus petitioned the Spanish monarchs. At last the long-sought ships were granted. The monastery walls recount the triumphant story. In the final painting the monks watch proudly from the shore as the three ships' sails fill with wind.

But Columbus' own story ended not in triumph but tragedy. This steadfast man spent his health, his fortune and his chance at happiness trying for the rest of his life to prove that the land he'd found was indeed Asia.

For, of course, the astronomers who'd said no to Columbus' proposition were right: Asia was much too far west for the ships of that day to reach. Others soon recognized that what Columbus thought was Asia was a new world.

Columbus did not. So wedded was he to his own conception that he was unable to see the reality before his eyes. To John and me, "Remember Columbus!" means, "Make plans, but hold them loosely!"

Open my eyes, Father, to Your world filled with surprises.
—Elizabeth Sherrill

Tue 12   *A wise son maketh a glad father. . . .* —Proverbs 10:1

Afriend of mine claims that it's the job of a parent to give a child both roots and wings. Well, when Timothy went off to college and Carol and I no longer had any boys at home, I was worried that maybe we'd overdone it in the wings department.

I mean, for the first week Tim didn't even call, and after that we'd get only nuggets: He loved his classes, he had great friends, he was playing Frisbee on the lawn and working hard. But in my empty-nest stage, I kept wondering: Didn't he miss us even a little? Didn't he miss our fall rituals, like shopping for apples at the green market, going to a Columbia football game, carving a jack-o'-lantern, planting the spring bulbs? Every November we'd put in tulip bulbs and daffodils and crocuses. Now I'd have to do it on my own.

"I'm glad Tim's happy," I'd say in my prayers, "but fall feels empty without him."

Then one day I came home from work and Carol said, "There's a package for you on the dining room table." A sizable cardboard box from some unknown address, it smelled faintly of damp earth. I opened it. On top were an order form and a card. "Happy Father's Day a little late," it said. "Love, Tim." There in the box were bulbs—spring bulbs to plant in the autumn.

"What a great present, Tim," I told him on the phone. "I'm glad you didn't forget."

"Sure, Dad," he said. Wings and roots: It takes both.

> *May my children remember where they're from as*
> *they spread their wings and fly.*
> —Rick Hamlin

October

Wed 13

You became imitators of us and of the Lord....
—I Thessalonians 1:6 (niv)

The Clearwater Marine Aquarium, ten miles up the road from my home in Florida, takes wounded or sick dolphins, sea turtles, otters, sharks, stingrays and fish, and nurses them back to health so they can be returned to the ocean. My favorite mammal at the aquarium is Winter the dolphin, who lost most of her tail in a crab trap and had to be fitted with a prosthetic fin with an extra-sensitive silicon sleeve. Developed just for Winter, it can be suctioned to her body so that she can dip up and down the way dolphins normally do.

Watching Winter swim with her artificial tail reminds me of the fifteen years when I had to wear reading glasses. Then my eyes changed, and I could read and see without glasses for about five years. I felt as free as a fish in the ocean. But then, slowly, reading anything became impossible. The eye doctor put me back into wear-them-all-the-time bifocals. All those years of not needing glasses and feeling free, and then suddenly I felt like Winter must have felt every time they strapped that prosthetic fin on her tail.

Sometimes there are other things I resist just because I don't want to be encumbered, like my helmet when I go biking, or a life jacket when I'm in a kayak or snorkeling, or my daily vitamins, or the seat belt when I'm in the backseat of someone's car. But I know these things, like my bifocals, are gifts that keep me safe, healthy, and feeling and acting normal. And so I strap it on, buckle it up, take the pills, put on the bifocals and like Winter, I'm ready to flip my tail!

> *Lord, as I get older, help me to accept*
> *Your aging-gracefully gifts*
> *with gusto and grace.*
> —Patricia Lorenz

Thu 14

And the King shall answer and say unto them, Verily I say unto you, Inasmuch as ye have done it unto one of the least of these my brethren, ye have done it unto me.
—MATTHEW 25:40

I was walking past the Islamic Center of Pittsburgh when I encountered an older gentleman in rough clothing and even rougher condition. "Disheveled" would be a kind description; it looked as if he hadn't seen the inside of a laundry or shower stall in some time. Showing my gift for instant judgments, I guessed that the cup he held contained either loose change or an adult beverage.

Seemingly out of the blue, he looked toward the Islamic Center and yelled, "No! Not you! No way! No!"

Here it comes, I thought, *a rant against Islam or non-Westerners or you name it. It'll be ugly and uncomfortable.* I walked away quickly, not wanting to be associated with him.

From the corner of my eye, I spied a young man emerging from the Islamic Center, moving toward the older gentleman . . . and smiling.

"Where've you been, bro?" the young man said with easy familiarity.

"It *is* you!" the older man said. "I've been waiting to see a smiling face." And then they embraced.

Sometimes I wonder what God wants from me, and sometimes God makes it easy to see: He wants me to be the smile that people are waiting for. He wants me to end my quick, useless judgments. He wants me to embrace rather than walk away.

Lord, help me never to turn away from the least of my brothers,
from any of my brothers.
—MARK COLLINS

October

Fri 15

*Nevertheless God, that comforteth those that are cast down,
comforted us....* —II Corinthians 7:6

When my husband Jerry was diagnosed with inoperable brain cancer back in October 1982, I couldn't imagine how I would continue to live. Fear and pain accompanied me everywhere, even in sleep. I wasn't angry with God; I would go on if only I knew how, but I didn't. It seemed that I was totally helpless and no escape was possible. Family, friends, God's Word, prayer, phone calls, visits, casseroles, books of inspiration, hugs—nothing comforted me.

I almost stopped eating, rarely slept, never laughed, couldn't read or concentrate. On one particular horrific night when Jerry was back in the hospital, the fear arrived promptly at three o'clock in the morning. I actually fled my bedroom to a guest room, I curled into a ball and cried out, "God, give me something—or I can't go on!"

God planted just one word in my pounding heart. *Nevertheless.* Eventually, I discovered it's used in the Bible more than two hundred times. I figured out that God isn't a God of *what if* but of *nevertheless.* Two months later Jerry died, but the power of "nevertheless living" got me through.

I've come to agree with the astonishing statement of Gene Edwards in his little gem *The Inward Journey*: "Thank you, friend pain."

*Father, in the name of Jesus, I pray for life-changing comfort
for anyone who needs to hear from You right now.*
—Marion Bond West

⊛ TWELVE KEYS TO THE GIVING LIFE

Sat 16   *Every man shall give as he is able, according to the blessing of the Lord thy God which he hath given thee.*
—DEUTERONOMY 16:17

GIVE WHOLEHEARTEDLY

A few years ago Wanda, one of the patients at the hospital where I work, stopped by my office. "I heard that you have breast cancer, Roberta," she said. "We're having a healing service at my church Saturday night. I was wondering if you would go with me."

For forty years I'd prayed that God would deliver me from the neurological disorder that caused me constant pain. God's answer always seemed to be a firm *no.* But now I was desperate and afraid.

On Saturday night I trudged down to the altar with Wanda while my family and friends stayed behind, praying and believing; I could do neither. Wanda put her arms around me and whispered her own faith-filled prayers into my ear.

"Jesus" was all I could mutter.

All of a sudden, an intense heat filled my chest. A current coursed through my upper body and down my arms. The minister motioned for me to come forward. "You had cancer when you came here tonight," he said, "but God healed you while the choir was singing."

When I returned to my doctor the following week, tests confirmed that there was no cancer. That continues to be the report to this day.

That night, as I left the altar to return to my pew, the minister looked into my eyes and said, "Don't leave this world with anything clutched in your hands that God meant for you to give."

It's true, Lord: In this life the only thing I really keep is what I give away. —ROBERTA MESSNER

Sun 17

*Rejoice in the Lord your God, for he has given you . . . both autumn and spring rains. . . . —*JOEL 2:23 (NIV)

My wife and I decided to gather some aspen for firewood this season. I parked our truck next to some standing dead trees and said, "Thirty years ago someone would already have taken these trees. I wonder why so few people cut firewood in the fall anymore. We didn't see any other vehicles on the road today."

It was a beautiful fall morning. The yellow leaves of the healthy aspen trees all around us looked fiery against the brilliant blue sky. Instead of being sad about the dying tradition of gathering firewood, we decided to celebrate the fact that we were able to eat a quiet lunch together after our hard work. No other woodcutters meant no other noisy chainsaws and no dust from other trucks. Who can mourn for the past when the present has so much to offer?

By Sunday the rains had come, and it was wet and dreary. It was tempting to focus on the problems besetting our church, especially the dwindling number of young people who attend our services. But in spite of our problems, we were still able to worship God. Later that week I would meet with our vision team and wrestle with the difficulties our church faces. Meanwhile it was time to rejoice.

Thank You, God, for the gifts of the past and the present.
—TIM WILLIAMS

READER'S ROOM

I fell and broke my knee, needing surgery and long and painful recovery time. The women at the Bible study, where I fell, came to visit and help every weekday for two months and my choir family sent food. After three months of going to church but not being able to sing with my choir family, the sopranos came down and carried me up to sing with them. I will always cherish that moment. —*Bonnie Pula, Sanford, Florida*

❊ THE GIFT OF SIGHT

Mon 18   *Walk in the ways of thine heart, and in the sight of thine eyes.* . . . —ECCLESIASTES 11:9

THE SHADOW

M y first thought when the new moon-shaped shadow obscured the vision above my left eye was *Oh, it must be these new glasses!* But when I took them off, the shadow remained.

As he shined a piercing white light into my dilated eye, my ophthalmologist said, "It's probably just a floater."

A week later my left eye could see only fuzzy shapes through a dull gray curtain. This time when the doctor examined my eye, he said, "You have a hole in the macula" (the part of the eye that sees). He sent me to a surgeon who discovered a detached retina and told his assistant to give me his first available surgical appointment.

My husband Robert held my hand as we walked back to the car, tears sliding down my face onto my teal shirt. It wasn't the surgery I feared; it was the possible loss of sight. The diagnosis of macular degeneration in my right eye had been on my chart for three years. But this was my left eye! I remembered Dr. Bode's words: "It may not happen for a long time, but if you live long enough . . ."

Well, this is it. I must have lived long enough for my left eye to become affected!

Seeing has always been one of my most valued gifts, and blindness my greatest fear. Now it was happening.

Creator God, it seems the time has come.
Please lead me through the dark.
—MARILYN MORGAN KING

Tue 19

What man knoweth the things of a man, save the spirit of man which is in him? . . . —I CORINTHIANS 2:11

Uncle Paul was the grouch in our large extended family. He was short and wiry, with a harsh voice and unpolished ways, and he loved to argue. For some reason his ornery streak really came out around Christmastime. If his brothers and sisters suggested turkey for the big family dinner, he would insist on ham. If everyone wanted to go ice-skating, he would clamor for a movie. One Christmas things got so bad that his siblings put some coal in his stocking. Uncle Paul didn't see the joke.

Nonetheless, I liked Uncle Paul. He was a good fisherman and taught me how to bait a hook and reel in a catch. He was also a skilled story-teller, with vivid anecdotes of his early years on the island of Malta. I mourned him when he died some twenty years ago, and when I thought about him, I'd usually shake my head in sorrow, remembering this bright, resourceful man who wasted his years complaining.

That was my view of Uncle Paul until one day, when poring through a box of family memorabilia, I came across an envelope that had scrawled on it, in my mother's handwriting, "Uncle Paul." Opening it, I found the usual odds and ends—a ring, a pen, a set of keys—and something unexpected: a certificate from a Maltese charity, thanking Uncle Paul for his many generous gifts of time and money. An accompanying photo showed Uncle Paul receiving the certificate at a large banquet, a beatific smile on his face.

Uncle Paul the Grouch? I had discovered Uncle Paul the Giver.

> *Lord, teach me not to judge, for none of us knows*
> *what goodness lies hidden in our neighbor's heart.*
> —PHILIP ZALESKI

Wed 20
O God, You have taught me from my youth. . . .
—Psalm 71:17 (nkjv)

Children are voracious learners, and I think it's because they have pure motives. They are not pursuing a degree or a six-figure income. They just want to know how the world works. They are driven by the passion of curiosity.

I hand my grandson a shoe box. "Here, Abram, you can have this." The rest of the day he "studies" the box. He will fill it up and empty it out twenty times. He will throw it through the air, float it on a mud puddle and pull it around the yard with a string. At the end of the day, he has a PhD in shoe boxes and then he will move on to the study of paper clips or bricks.

One of the best students I ever had in my classes was an early retiree who had always wanted to go to college. He had heart trouble, but he was the first one on campus every day and the last one to leave. His hand was always in the air with questions and he hung around after class to learn more. His heart gave out before he could graduate, but he died a very happy man.

As I get older, I find myself returning to the way I learned as a child. I bought some old high school textbooks at a sale, and at bedtime I'm reading with fascination the history I hated in school because of tests and homework.

Out in the garage I've been tinkering, hoping to invent something like, oh, cold fusion. So far the only fusion was when I Super-glued my fingers together. Go ahead and laugh, but I'm having a blast just being curious, experimenting and exploring the way I did when I was six.

Thank You, Lord, for giving us the gift of curiosity.
—Daniel Schantz

October

Thu 21 *The Lord is the strength of my life....* —PSALM 27:1

When I moved to New Hampshire to be near my elderly parents, I found that one of the dilemmas of working part-time was having no employer-paid health insurance. Then I discovered that I could purchase a short-term "bridge" policy, which could cover me for unexpected health crises while I tried to work and help my parents downsize to a retirement village. But the cost! Even a bridge policy would take a chunk out of my meager income as an adjunct English instructor.

I picked up the phone book, made a few inquiries and settled on a slow-talking insurance agent who offered several options. First, I had to answer a few questions to determine my eligibility and rate.

"Okay, Gail. Do you have any problems with heart, circulation or blood pressure?"

"No."

"Any diabetes?"

"No."

"Any respiratory conditions?"

"No."

"Any mental or nervous conditions? Any addictions?"

"No. No."

"Cancer?"

"No." I paused. "I'm really pretty lucky, huh? Just short on cash."

The agent paused for a moment. "Yup. I'd say if you have your health, that's all you need."

Within twenty minutes we found a policy, and I didn't flinch at the premium. Instead, I finally remembered to thank God for the gift of health.

Creator God, how wondrously You have made me.
Please forgive me when I forget to say thank You.
—GAIL THORELL SCHILLING

Fri 22   *The Lord is my shepherd....* —PSALM 23:1

The bleakness of the fall day was magnified by a slow, steady rain that merged asphalt and buildings into a gray, lifeless landscape. As I drove down one of Nashville, Tennessee's busiest streets, the traffic crept along and then came to a standstill as the light in front of me went through a complete cycle from green to yellow to red. "I should've gone the back way," I muttered under my breath.

Just then a pedestrian caught my eye. He was walking on the edge of the sidewalk, swinging a white cane back and forth on the concrete. The blustery wind seemed to be blowing him a little off balance as he methodically searched for objects in front of him with his cane. Directly ahead was a telephone pole; he quickly tapped his cane and stepped around the pole as if he could see it. Still snarled in traffic, I watched him make his way forward, never missing a step, relying on his cane to show him the way.

The traffic began to move again, and as I pulled away, I thought about what I'd just witnessed. That blind man finding his way on a rainy street was a sign that I could move in a more positive direction. I'd let myself become the victim of a dreary day, not seeing the Shepherd, staff in hand, Who waits to guide me.

> *Dear God, help me to remember that when*
> *I follow You, goodness follows me.*
> —BROCK KIDD

EDITOR'S NOTE: *Monday, November 22, will be Guideposts' eighteenth annual Thanksgiving Day of Prayer. Please plan to join the members of our Guideposts family in prayer on this very special day. Send your prayer requests (and a picture, if you can—but remember that we won't be able to return it) to Day of Prayer, PO Box 5813, Harlan, Iowa 51593-1313, or visit us on the Web at OurPrayerThanksgiving.org.*

Sat 23

*Be patient, then, brothers, until the Lord's coming. See how
the farmer waits for the land to yield its valuable crop
and how patient he is for the autumn and spring rains.*
—JAMES 5:7 (NIV)

*Last eve I saw a beauty contest brief
Between a rainbow and an autumn leaf.*

I wrote those lines in a book many years ago, and they came to mind this morning as I looked out the living room window and saw the crimson, golden and pumpkin-colored mosaic of leaves that carpeted my front lawn. Soon they will need to be raked and carted off. The city has a huge machine that vacuums them up and takes them to be composted.

Fall and winter are not my favorite seasons. (Old bones, I've discovered, creak in cold weather.) "But you enjoy football, don't you?" I can hear someone ask. And the answer is *yes*, and Penn State's Joe Paterno, the ageless coach (he's in his eighties), who lives down the street from us, has told me that this is his favorite time of the year. And my friends who ski think that there's nothing more beautiful than a foot of fluffy white snow.

So when I lament the falling of the leaves and mourn the denuded branches of my seventy-five-year-old maple, I should remember that it's just resting. In the ripeness of time—God's perfect time—buds will emerge, and behind them verdant, shading, air-cleaning leaves.

*Fill us with hope, Lord, trusting that
the dying leaves on earth's cold floor
will resurrect and green the trees once more.*
—FRED BAUER

Sun 24

The stranger that dwelleth with you shall be unto you as one born among you, and thou shalt love him as thyself. . . .
—LEVITICUS 19:34

All of our children are now in college or graduate school: Drew, a student at the University of South Carolina Law School; Luke, a senior at Samford University; and Jodi, a sophomore at Furman University. Over the years many older friends told us that our children would grow up before we realized it. They were right!

But we have anything but an "empty nest." My wife Beth is the international student relations adviser at Baylor University. One of her responsibilities is to find host families in our community of Waco, Texas, who will befriend international students. This year we have adopted three students: Lulu, a predentistry student from Singapore; George, a prelaw student from the Philippines; and Lian, a graduate student in photojournalism from China.

This afternoon I received an e-mail from George's father. Tonight Lulu ate dinner with us and is spending the night. Yesterday Beth had lunch with Lian. Our life is enriched by our friendship with these wonderful young adults from Asia. They are now a part of our family.

Beth and I are discovering that when we extend friendship and hospitality to God's children, we receive far more than we give. And when we embrace people from around the world, God is able to multiply goodness and love between cultures and nations.

God's greatest gifts to us have been Drew, Luke and Jodi. We just didn't know that He would also give us the surprise package of Lulu, George and Lian.

Father, help me to know that all children are my children
because they are Your children. Amen.
—SCOTT WALKER

Mon 25 *But my eyes are fixed on you, O Sovereign Lord. . . .*
—PSALM 141:8 (NIV)

While hurrying to an important meeting recently, I stopped at a red light and quickly pulled my mascara out of my purse. Just as I swiped the black wand across my eyelashes, the light turned green. The car behind me honked, and I dropped the wand straight down the front of my white shirt, leaving a large, gloppy black line.

For the next two hours I fixated on the stain, hoping that it might look less obvious with the third or fourth glance down at it. I pointed it out to others, assuming my acknowledgment would somehow make it better. And, of course, I didn't think as much about the subject of the meeting as I did about the mascara on my shirt.

Driving home, I was reminded of a story about Elisabeth Elliot, whom I've admired for her courageous choices in life and her focused perspective. After her missionary husband Jim was brutally murdered by the Auca Indians he was trying to befriend in Ecuador, Elisabeth and her infant daughter returned to the jungle, despite its hardships, to continue trying to reach these people with the love of Jesus. One day, while tending her baby, she saw a scorpion on the window.

Elisabeth realized she had a choice: She could either focus on the scorpion and her fears, or look beyond it to the people on the other side of the window and the vision she and her husband had shared for reaching them. She looked past the scorpion, stayed in the jungle for two years and made an eternal difference in the lives of many of the Aucas.

That's a long way from mascara on a white shirt but a powerful reminder to me to keep my fixations in perspective.

Father, help me always to look at the bigger picture
and what matters most to You.
—CAROL KUYKENDALL

Tue 26

I am the light of the world: he that followeth me shall not walk in darkness, but shall have the light of life.
—JOHN 8:12

It was going to be a long day, an hour's drive to get to the train and then another hour and a half to get to the city. Although it was late autumn, I was still getting used to the dark mornings.

Driving to work, I thought of the day's important meeting and went over the points I wanted to cover. My mind shifted to worries about things at home. *I should have paid the bills yesterday,* I thought. *I think one will be late.*

Traffic was bad. Finally I pulled into the train station and rushed to the parking meter. Both slots were broken. *Great, now I'll get a parking ticket,* I thought. With no time to spare, I got on the train.

Although I'd planned to use the train ride to prepare for the meeting, I found myself scribbling a list of worries. The parking ticket I hadn't yet gotten was on the top of my list. The rest of my day was filled with disappointments. My meeting left me feeling as if I'd let everyone down.

On the train ride back, I got nervous about the ticket I was convinced would be on my windshield. But when I got off the train, I sighed with relief—no ticket.

On the drive home, the trees lining the road sparkled in glorious hues of gold and auburn. The fall foliage was at its peak and its beauty was stunning. How had I missed this on the drive down? And then I realized, *Of course, it was dark! And when I focus on my dark thoughts and worries, I miss the beauty that's right here on the path in front of me.*

> *Dear Lord, when things around me seem dark,*
> *help me to focus on Your light.*
> —SABRA CIANCANELLI

October

Wed 27 *The Lord direct your hearts....* —II Thessalonians 3:5

O f all the birds flitting about in our backyard, my husband Leo and I find the bright yellow and black goldfinches most captivating. I tried to attract them to our bird feeders one way and another for several summers, but to no avail.

Browsing through a bird book, I noticed that goldfinches prefer one particular kind of seed, so I bought a bag. I filled a tubelike feeder with the tiny black seeds and hung it in the young willow tree that had sprung up at the edge of our vegetable garden. And then we waited.

And waited. One month, two, three.

"You know, I think that willow sapling has to come down," Leo remarked one morning in late summer. "Its roots are depriving the tomato plants of moisture."

I agreed. "Not only that, but it's grown so big, it's soon going to shade too much of the garden."

Leo picked up his ax, and I followed him. *So much for our goldfinch project*, I thought as I stretched up to remove the bird feeder, hanging it a few feet away at the edge of the carport.

Busy with fall cleanup, I forgot all about it until one morning the sight of yellow and black feathers caught my attention. There at the feeder, gorging himself, was a male goldfinch.

Lord, help me remember that sometimes all it takes to attract people
to You is a small move in the right direction.
—ALMA BARKMAN

Thu 28 Great are the works of the Lord; they are pondered by all who delight in them. —P SALM 1 1 1:2 (NIV)

Perfection, according to the ancient rules of Chinese landscape paint-ing, equals mountain plus water. You've seen those paintings: They always have some soaring peak and some rushing river, perhaps with a pagoda for a little extra visual something. That's the formula: mountain + water = perfection.

I thought of that one day last fall as I hiked with a friend in Scotland. It was a cold day, and to our north loomed the highest mountain in Great Britain, the formidable Ben Nevis. As we navigated the valley below, we passed terrain that seemed straight out of *The Lord of the Rings*—babbling brooks, humongous boulders, gurgling waterfalls, hillsides ablaze in autumnal yellows, browns and reds, polka-dotted with the furry white of dozens of sheep.

A couple of hours into our hike, we rounded a bend and the land opened up. Tall grass waved in the breeze, welcoming us into a wide open meadow ringed on one side by an arc of river. My eyes followed that river ahead of us to a cliff. Dancing down it was an enormous waterfall. As we took in this majestic sight, snow started to fall, as if God had decided that would be the perfect moment to embellish His creation with a little lace. My buddy turned to me and said, "Where's the unicorn?"

We laughed and then started talking about how awesome the scenery was, how anyone who saw this would have to ask how in the world it could have just happened on its own: this mountain, this river, this perfection.

Lord, thank You for that gorgeous landscape that shows me the power of Your creative hand.
—JEFF CHU

October

Fri 29   *Give us this day our daily bread.* —MATTHEW 6:11

"Your blood pressure is a little high," my doctor said as he made notes on my chart. "Losing a few pounds should take care of it."

I'd first gained weight when I was eleven and now I was approaching sixty. So for nearly half a century I'd struggled to "lose a few pounds," trying one fad diet after another, taking up elaborate exercise plans that never lasted more than a week, and always returning to the high-calorie comfort of chocolate chip cookies and peanut butter sandwiches.

"I give you good, nutritious food at home," my wife would say. "Where is all that weight coming from?"

I knew the answer well enough: from donut and muffin breakfasts, fast-food lunches and junk food snacks. When it came to bad eating, I was an undisputed champion. But now I was paying a price, and I didn't want to pass that price on to Julia and the children.

The doctor's assistant gave me a piece of paper with a name. "Marilyn is a nutritionist," she said. "She'll help you lose the weight."

It's been more than a year since I started seeing Marilyn, and some things have happened to me that I could never have expected: I've grown fond of salads and fresh fruit and fat-free yogurt; I've become a regular on the two-mile walking route through the parks of upper Manhattan; I've lost fifty pounds; and, yes, my blood pressure has gone down.

But most important, I've learned that whether it's prayer and Bible reading to grow my soul or diet and exercise to slim down my body, being faithful—one day at a time—to a simple regimen can do more for me than I could ever have imagined.

> *Lord, if I rely on my willpower, I know I'll only go backward.*
> *Give me Your grace today to grow in health of body and spirit.*
> —ANDREW ATTAWAY

Sat 30   *Lord, you establish peace for us; all that we have accomplished you have done for us.* —ISAIAH 26:12 (NIV)

Recently my wife Rosie and I attended a board meeting in Denver. As we sat around the table at lunch, people began to talk about their occupations and accomplishments. One woman, the wife of another board member, seemed reluctant to join the conversation. "I don't have any special gifts," she said.

Eventually in the course of our discussion, we learned that she had visited missionaries in Africa and was working on a study guide on the Gospel of Matthew for them. She had already written study guides for two other biblical books. We were amazed at her accomplishments.

"For a person without any special gifts," I said, "you surely are a blessing!" It was such an encouragement to meet someone who was being used by God in such a powerful way. But it also got me to thinking: Sometimes I may fail to celebrate the ways God is working in my life because I'm so focused on other people's accomplishments that I can't see my own. So now, whenever that happens, I pray:

Lord, in whatever I do, help me to glorify Your name.
—DOLPHUS WEARY

Sun 31

The wolf will live with the lamb, the leopard will lie down with the goat, the calf and the lion and the yearling together; and a little child will lead them. —ISAIAH 11:6 (NIV)

A few years back I was on a plane, seated next to a teenage boy who was the talkative sort. We struck up a conversation and chatted for a good part of the flight. I talked to him about my work and then showed him my current knitting project. Both are passions of mine, and so, of course, is my family.

Although we'd been talking the entire flight, I hadn't really discovered what his passions were. He was a rather cheerful young man and, like one of our sons, he was a runner. I knew he was active in his school and church, but little else about him. So I asked him what his passion was.

He turned and looked at me and didn't answer for a moment. "I only have one real passion," he told me.

I sat up to take notice.

"Jesus Christ," he said. "I want to share what Christ did for me with everyone I meet."

I learned a valuable lesson from that young man: My life may be filled with passions, but none are as important as my relationship with my Savior.

> *Lord, thank You for the passions in my life,*
> *but don't ever let me forget that*
> *You are first and foremost.*
> —DEBBIE MACOMBER

THE GIFTS I'VE BEEN GIVEN

1 _____

2 _____

3 _____

4 _____

5 _____

6 _____

7 _____

8 _____

9 _____

10 _____

11 _____

12 _____

13 _____

14 _____

15 _____

October

16 _____

17 _____

18 _____

19 _____

20 _____

21 _____

22 _____

23 _____

24 _____

25 _____

26 _____

27 _____

28 _____

29 _____

30 _____

31 _____

November

Thou shalt rejoice in every good thing which the Lord thy God hath given unto thee. . . .

—DEUTERONOMY 26:11

🎗 GIFTS FROM ABOVE

Mon 1   *Let thy saints rejoice in goodness.* —II Chronicles 6:41

A GIFT OF HOLINESS

On All Saints Day our church celebrates the lives of those in our congregation who have died in the year just past. It's a service of songs and candles and kind words meant to honor those who have gone on before us. Yet, even in the somberness of the moment, our memories fill the sanctuary with the almost tangible presence of those who have passed through this place as they journeyed home.

To tell the truth, I don't need All Saints Day to sense their presence. The sun pouring in the windows on any day glows with radiance of Phoebe Greene, a true saint of Hillsboro Presbyterian, pure joy lighting up her face any time she walked into the church. The doors still have Gordon Smith's fingerprints on them, a reminder of all the years he served as Hillsboro's doorkeeper. And how could I forget Frances Faulkner standing in the chancel, reading a verse at our daughter Keri's baptism, or Kathleen Upham making sure everyone was welcome, or Sarah Burton putting out the doughnuts for coffee hour, or Claude O'Donnell playing his viola on Christmas Day, or Gail Swats belting out the Hallelujah Chorus on Easter Sunday. There's my friend Diane Schwartzman comforting a child, and Deanna Niblack lighting candles in the narthex.

A church is a perfect place to detect this great gathering of those we remember and those we can't recall, of those present now and those who are yet to come. Imagine a great banquet table where each person, past, present and future, has a place. Call it a church, or expand the vision and call it the world. Take your place, as one of those still here to use the good that others have left and to create good for those who follow after.

> *Father, I give thanks for those who showed me Your way.*
> *Let me use their gifts for good.* —Pam Kidd

Tue 2 *Give the king your justice, O God....* —PSALM 72:1 (NRSV)

Will your favored candidate win in the election today? While the outcome of today's election may not be at all certain where you vote, this one fact certainly is: Some of us will vote with the majority and others of us will not. There will be winners and losers today. And it's hard to lose.

That's why I'm using the advice given to me a long time ago, shortly after I became old enough to vote. I'll read Psalm 72 before I vote today. It refocuses me away from winners or losers, or which candidate thinks most like me, or even about seeking God's favor for the politics of the one whom I favor. It's a prayer of values, not victory. Its focus is not power for one but justice for all, especially for the powerless; prosperity for all, especially for the poor; and peace for all throughout creation. It is finally a prayer that the governments of the powerful protect and serve the legion of the powerless, not serve their own interests.

No matter how different my point of view is from someone else's, no matter what solutions I think are best for the challenges of society, on this Election Day the Psalmist again calls us to pray this prayer together for the well-being of all those created in God's image.

> *Grant me the wisdom and humility, God, to pray for our leaders*
> *and to work for my neighbors and to remember*
> *finally Whom we all serve.*
> —JEFF JAPINGA

November

Wed 3

I urge, then, first of all, that requests, prayers, intercession and thanksgiving be made for everyone.
—I TIMOTHY 2:1 (NIV)

If I hadn't been in such a rush, I probably would have taken time for my "good morning" to God at home. But life being what it is, I began my morning prayers at six o'clock on the subway. When I opened my eyes, I saw four pairs of work boots.

I don't normally notice shoes on the subway, unless five-year-old Stephen and I are playing I Spy. At this early hour, without caffeine, it took a minute to figure out that the predawn subway population is heavy on construction workers.

Curious, I looked around. Fully half the car wore work boots, blue jeans, a baseball cap and a sweatshirt with the hood up. The ethnic mix was broad. Most of the men were drowsing. I scanned my mental Rolodex to figure out who I knew in construction. To my surprise, the answer was no one.

I chose a sleeping worker at random and began to pray for his safety, his family, his soul. Done with that, I moved on to the next guy. I'm not usually on the subway at that hour. Who knew when I'd be there again?

Lord, it's a really good thing when I actually stop and think about people I don't know. Help me do that more often.
—JULIA ATTAWAY

Thu 4

Point your kids in the right direction—when they're old they won't be lost. —PROVERBS 22:6 (MSG)

I was five; my mother's birthday was the next day, so I decided I'd buy her a present. I put the thirty-five cents I'd saved into my pocket, slipped out of the house, and walked the dozen or so blocks to the five-and-ten-cent store. "I want to buy a present for my mother," I told the lady behind the counter.

"How much money do you have?"

I showed her my thirty-five cents.

Nodding seriously, she said, "I see." She showed me some things, but I only shook my head. Then she picked up a little blue glass jar with white bumps all over it and a powder puff inside. Wow! How could that lady have known that Mother had broken a jar just like this one!

"That's it!" Then fear. "What does it cost?"

"Uh . . . thirty-five cents. Would you like me to wrap it? Wrapping is free."

I carried the little brown sack with the gift-wrapped jar in it all the way home. I was so excited that it didn't seem far at all.

The next day while her friends were having birthday cake and coffee, I gave Mother my present. She was really surprised! Then she asked, "Where did you get this, Keith?"

"I walked to the store to buy it," I said proudly.

"You what?" Suddenly she looked frightened. "Don't ever do that again!"

I cried, and she picked me up. Hugging me, she said, "I love the present, but you shouldn't walk downtown alone." Then she wept and held me until I could wiggle free.

As I was running out, I heard one of her friends say, "How in the world did you teach him to do that?" Mother just shook her head. But I knew how. All my life I'd seen my mother giving presents to everyone she knew, and I wanted to be sure she'd get one herself.

Lord, thank You for a mother who lived the virtues she wanted to see in me. —KEITH MILLER

Fri 5

We . . . will lift up our banners in the name of our God. . . . —PSALM 20:5 (NIV)

When our son Chris was due back in North Carolina after his fifteen-month deployment to Iraq, my husband Gordon ordered an eight-foot-long, bright green plastic banner that said, "Welcome Home, Capt. Chris Barber!" On arrival day Gordon nailed the banner to two eight-foot poles of wood. When he and our son John lifted it up, I thought, *That's way too big. Gordon has gone overboard.*

As we crowded behind a rope outside the hangar at the airfield, the banner was so big that Gordon had to stand at the back of the crowd. I stood up front and cheered at the top of my lungs as our soldiers came down the aircraft steps. Suddenly, they began marching quickly toward the large hangar doors. Families rushed to cram through a single doorway behind the ropes; I couldn't see Gordon.

I was barely in the door when a loudspeaker began playing "The Star-Spangled Banner." I froze in place and put my hand over my heart, feeling lost. Two teardrops fell onto my hand. How would I ever find our family in the chaos when the ropes separating us from the soldiers were undone? Suddenly something big and green caught my eye on the far side of the room: the impossibly big banner!

The ropes came down. People swarmed everywhere. I battled the crowd over to the banner. By the time I reached it, Chris had found it too. We hugged and smiled and laughed.

As we left the hangar, it occurred to me that you can never really go overboard on signs of love. So lift up your banner as high as you can today so that those who are feeling lost and lonely can gladly gather 'round!

Dear Father, make my smile a banner that welcomes
everyone home to Your love.
—KAREN BARBER

Sat 6   *Don't be childish in your understanding of these things. . . .*
—I Corinthians 14:20 (tlb)

Retirement brought an abundance of pleasure-filled days and new activities. I had more time for Bible study and organ practice. I enjoyed attending our grandchildren's school and sports events. Dressing in a stomach costume and talking to grade-school children about nutrition was a blast. I was even thankful for time to clean the basement and fish tumbleweeds out of the window wells.

But several months after I left work, food and fuel prices started to climb. My retirement fund shrank by forty percent in the weak economy. Freelance work wasn't as consistent as I'd hoped. As my bank account dwindled, I began to wonder about God's provision for my future.

Then my husband Don and I stayed with our five-year-old grandson Caden while his parents attended a weekend conference. After his Saturday morning ice-skating lesson we had lunch at his favorite fast-food place. In the afternoon we went to his friend Noah's karate-themed birthday party. After that we spent two hours at Caden's favorite playground. "You guys are sure taking good care of me!" he called from the top of the monkey bars. But when it turned colder and started to sprinkle, he begged for more play time and hid in a tunnel to protest our decision to leave.

As I fished him out, God's truth hit me like the proverbial ton of bricks: *Caden wasn't the only one in the family acting like a five-year-old.* Retirement gave me the precious gift of time and freedom. I also had a warm house, nutritious food and an overflowing closet. Yet I complained that I might not have enough.

There is work for me to do in retirement: the vital task of maturing in faith and trust.

> *Loving and generous Father, thank You*
> *for using a child to help me grow up.*
> —Penney Schwab

November

Sun 7

When you received the word of God . . . you accepted it . . . for what it really is, the word of God, which also performs its work in you who believe. —I Thessalonians 2:13 (NAS)

We were harder on our first child, Jamie. I wish I'd been gentler and smiled more; I'd assumed that toughness and diligence made a good mother.

When Jamie was two, I punished her when she refused to use the big-girl potty. I eased up with Katie, our second child. Ten years after Jamie was born, Thomas came along and I relaxed quite a bit. He was potty trained at three, when he was ready.

Jamie's a gifted speller: She could spell *deciduous* in the first grade. I pressed hard, drilling her on spelling bee words. (What if she didn't get first place?) Thomas is seventeen and I've never even asked him if he's done his homework.

When Jamie was in the fourth grade, we insisted that she participate in Sword Drill, spending Sunday nights at church, learning to memorize Scripture. After a few weeks she could recite the names of the books of the Bible in order and locate Haggai in a flash. Katie and Thomas never attended Sword Drill.

At nineteen, Jamie's rebellion seemed to come out of nowhere. It lasted for years; I thought it would never end.

This Sunday, Jamie, now twenty-seven, sat with us in church. I stumbled around in my Bible trying to find First Thessalonians. I glanced at her, a little embarrassed.

"The *T* books are together," she said. In awe I watched her flip to the correct passage. My eyes blurred with tears as the pastor began reading.

"I'm so proud of you," I whispered as we shared my Bible.

> *Lord, Your Word alone covers my mistakes. It found a home*
> *in Jamie's heart and never left her.*
> —Julie Garmon

Mon 8   *The wise in heart shall be called prudent: and the sweetness of the lips increaseth learning.* —PROVERBS 16:21

My respect for words developed at an early age. Our elocution teacher at the convent school I attended in China emphasized the need for a good vocabulary and insisted that we learn to speak clearly. She had us contort our mouths like Eliza Doolittle in *My Fair Lady* and roll the vowels around until we pronounced the words right. That was no easy task—Sister Cecilia's English was tinged with a French accent.

She liked to tell us about the Chinese written character *Fu.* Its many forms relate to blessings and happiness. The one she drummed into us depicted happiness as "all that a person has, laid on the altar of God." The character for "all that a person has" was made up of two components: the *words of our mouth* written over a *rice paddy*, the symbol of our material possessions.

I was a smart-mouthed girl, quick with a quip that brought gales of laughter, often at the expense of the person I had targeted. After I'd been disrespectful to a teacher, my desk was put in Mother Superior's office until I repented and apologized. I sat there arrogantly for nearly a week before capitulating. Sister Cecilia took me in hand.

"Ma chère petite Fay," she said gently, "remember *Fu.* Happiness begins with the words of our mouth. They are a gift from God. Think about this before you speak."

I have thought about it ever since.

I rejoice that my ultimate happiness begins with the words of life
You have given us in the Scriptures, Lord. They celebrate
my joys and comfort me in my sorrows.
—FAY ANGUS

Tue 9

Calling the Twelve to him, he sent them out two by two. . . . —MARK 6:7 (NIV)

I sat on a splintery packing crate, struggling to get my feet into the hip boots our host Janet had just handed me. Janet had lived on this New Zealand oyster farm all her life; she'd put on both her boots by the time I'd wiggled and stamped my foot halfway into one.

Stretching out before us in the shallows of the bay were rows of oyster frames perched on posts. Between some of the posts Janet had strung fishnets. My boots on at last, we set out to see what the nets had caught for our dinner. The first part of the journey was easy, but with each step it got harder to lift my feet out of the clinging muck. Soon Janet was far ahead.

Don't fall, I kept telling myself as I wrestled one leg after the other from the deepening sludge. I didn't know how I'd ever get up, and the tide was coming in. Janet was still striding forward, but the mud was now almost knee-deep, and with every tugging step I came close to overbalancing.

And then, of course, it happened. I toppled backward in slow motion until I was sitting chest-deep in the rising water. Fighting down my pride, I called for help.

Janet turned, hurried back, gripped my hands and braced herself as I pulled myself up. She steadied me, too, all the slithery way back to the shore. While I showered in the farmhouse, Janet returned to her nets to bring in our dinner.

That evening I lay in the guest-room bed thinking that, in an age that exalts independence, I'd discovered why Jesus sent His disciples out "two by two." There's a lot of mud out there, waiting to catch any one of us and hold us captive, unable to get up by our own strength. But two by two—that's a very different story.

Grant me grace today, Lord, to ask
without shame for the help I need.
—JOHN SHERRILL

Wed 10   *The Lord . . . hath not pitied. . . .* —LAMENTATIONS 2:2

I have to admit that I sometimes give in to self-pity. *Poor Marion, who else suffers the way you do? Isn't it time to throw in the towel? Has God forgotten you?* I itemize my troubles like a grocery list: *My addicted son in prison doesn't write or want me to visit. I've been diagnosed with rheumatoid arthritis. I don't have any energy—physical, mental or spiritual. Some days I skip my Bible reading and prayer time. I can't remember when I last vacuumed. I'm months behind on correspondence. My office looks like a paper jungle.*

One November day I was dragging around the house, still in my pajamas, and flopped down wearily and dutifully for my morning quiet time. First I read from *My Utmost for His Highest.* Oswald Chambers didn't beat around the bush. (Did he ever?) "Self-pity is of the devil, if I go off on that line, I cannot be used by God for His purposes in this world."

I read it over and over, out loud, until the truth sank into my stubborn, sad self. Thirty minutes later I closed my journal, got dressed, made the bed, plugged in the vacuum and hummed: "My hope is built on nothing less than Jesus' blood and righteousness; I dare not trust the sweetest frame, but wholly lean on Jesus' name. On Christ the solid rock I stand; all other ground is sinking sand" ("The Solid Rock" by Edward Mote).

> *Father, today I praise the power of Your name as I vacuum.*
> *I forgot You are my helper.*
> —MARION BOND WEST

November

Thu 11

So I commended enjoyment. . . .
—Ecclesiastes 8:15 (NKJV)

I've always admired the ability of American GIs to find humor in the dark world of warfare. The TV series *M*A*S*H* illustrated this gift for handling pain with a well-phrased wisecrack or practical prank.

My Uncle John, who lives in Eureka Springs, Arkansas, was a gunner in World War II, stationed in the Philippines and New Guinea, where he served with honor. In his diary Uncle John recounts some of the lighter moments, like the time his trench-buddy was snoring so loudly that he drew enemy fire.

At Breakneck Ridge Uncle John had gone without a bath for a month, crawling around in muddy trenches in the same clothes every day. His shoes were lost in the mud, and his socks had rotted off, along with some of his skin. He lived on cold Spam and struggled to keep his mind from drifting into madness.

One day the battle eased enough that he could crawl out of the trench and read his mail, which included a care package from his home church. Hoping for some candy or a good book, he tore open the package to find a beautiful necktie. "I had no shoes," he said, "but I was the best-dressed man in the trench."

Thank You, Lord, for the men and women who have served
our country—and for the safety valve of humor,
a wonderful gift.
—Daniel Schantz

Fri 12

Nothing is perfect except your words.
—PSALM 119:96 (TLB)

I admit it: I'm a bit of an organization freak. I like to organize things and run them single-handedly. I've organized rummage sales, craft sales, writing workshops, teaching seminars, trips and, as a single woman, practically my whole life. Why did I do it all myself? As I said, I'm a bit of an organizing nutcase. I just figured I could do it best that way.

Then I came across this bit of writing my daughter-in-law Amy found on the Internet. It said:

Can yuo raed this? Sopspedluy msot plepoe can. Aoccdrnig to rscheearch at Cmabrigde Uinervtisy, it dseno't mtaetr in what oerdr the ltteres in a wrod are, the olny iproamtnt tihng is that the frsit and last ltteer be in the rghit pclae. The rset can be a taotl mses and yuo can sitll raed it whotuit a pboerlm. This is bcuseae the huamn mnid deos not raed ervey lteter by istlef, but the wrod as a wlohe.

After reading that, I decided everything doesn't have to be perfect. For my next project, an art, book and craft fair at the clubhouse in my neighborhood, I loosened up, asked for help, delegated and shared the workload. During my next work project, my friend Melanie and I shared the initial work equally, and then I turned the detailed decisions over to her. Both projects turned out much better than if I'd done them alone. Much better indeed.

*Lord, when it comes to searching for perfection, help me find it by sharing
both the workload and the joys of the finished project.*
—PATRICIA LORENZ

Sat 13

The four beasts and four and twenty elders fell down before the Lamb, having every one of them . . . golden vials full of odours, which are the prayers of saints.
—REVELATION 5:8

My house smells *so* good today. Around noon I put a hambone—thick with pink meat—into a slow cooker filled with pinto beans. Now the scent of ham and beans is filling the air. This dish was a staple of my childhood, one of my favorite meals. And I could always be certain that the aroma of beans cooking meant that soon another fragrance would be coming from the kitchen: cornbread. Later today I'll make a skillet of that too.

I just slid a marble cake into the oven. Its buttery, cocoa scent mingles with the other odors, and it all seems homey.

When, as a child, I first came upon Revelation 5:8, I was amazed to think that prayer might have a smell when it got up to God. Did prayers smell like incense? Roses? Fragrant spices? Fresh dewy mornings or crisp autumn nights?

I imagine my mother's prayers probably smelled like lilacs. Or maybe floor wax. (She loved to clean!) I'd like to think my own prayers smell like love, gratitude, trust—maybe a sort of grapey scent with a touch of freshly fallen snow. The thing I must be sure of is that my prayers never smell like stagnant water or dust or neglect, that they are fresh every day—just like God's mercies.

Those ham and beans and marble cake and cornbread smells have filled my house now. It's positively heavenly! And while everything finishes cooking, I have just enough time to offer a quick prayer.

Giver of all that is good, I praise You for Your love and grace. Accept this prayer. May it be a sweet-smelling offering fit for Your presence.
—MARY LOU CARNEY

Sun 14

Carry each other's burdens, and in this way you will fulfill the law of Christ. —GALATIANS 6:2 (NIV)

When my parents moved from New York City to Florida, they left me their spacious rent-controlled apartment a block from Central Park. I was living in the Bronx at the time and the lease on my apartment had a while to go, but I couldn't pass up the opportunity to live in Manhattan.

A young woman whom I knew and trusted was interested in subletting my Bronx apartment, and I wrote an enthusiastic letter to the landlord, who agreed to the arrangement with no problem. I breathed a sigh of relief and moved to Manhattan worry-free.

Some months later I was shocked to learn that the woman whom I thought I could trust owed thousands of dollars in rent and, without a word, had fled to another state. Since the lease was under my name, I was left holding the bill. I felt betrayed, foolish and terrified by the thought of having to pay the back rent. Because I didn't want my family to worry, I kept the problem to myself. Most of all, I felt alone.

The one place I did turn to was my church. I needed a shoulder to cry on and lots of prayer. As I expected, my friends listened to my troubles and prayed with me to repair the damage done. What I didn't expect was by the next day my church had cleared the debt. I couldn't believe it.

Grateful is a pale reflection of how I felt. By lifting my burden, they showed me that I was family. I had no need to feel alone.

Lord, thank You for teaching me to trust and depend on Your people.
—KAREN VALENTIN

Mon 15   *I am with you, saith the Lord.* —HAGGAI 1:13

I was having lunch with friends the other day, when one of them referred to an event in his life as *providential.* "We all have those watershed moments," one of the guys responded, and we all agreed.

I shared one such experience that took place while I was in the Army. After basic training it was discovered that I could type, so the military made me a clerk-typist (never mind that I had written for newspapers while in high school and college) and sent me to Hawaii for a year and a half of service. On our way to the islands, three buddies and I were waiting at a bus stop outside San Francisco.

"Shipping out?" a sergeant standing nearby asked. I answered that we were going to Hawaii. That was his last stop, he told us, inquiring about our assignments. When I told him that the Army had turned me from a writer to a typist, he laughed and told me that he was a newspaper editor. "When you get to Hawaii, call this number. Tell him the Gray Fox sent you." I took down the number but doubted anything would come of it.

I was wrong. That "chance" meeting at a bus stop and my subsequent phone call produced a writing job that suited my skills to a T and changed my whole time in the service. Providential? I think so.

> *Teach us, Lord, to trust Your hidden hand,*
> *Leading in ways we may not understand.*
> —FRED BAUER

Tue 16   *"His shoots spread over his garden." —*JOB 8:16 (RSV)

It was a sad little bromeliad, almost hidden behind healthier, showier plants on display in the grocery store. The "60% off" sticker slapped on the front of its plastic pot showed plainly what store management thought of it. My husband Keith reached down and picked it up.

"You've got a beautiful bromeliad at home," I said. "What do you want that one for?"

"It's got potential," he said.

I shrugged. "At least it's cheap." Taking care of the plants in our house was Keith's hobby, not mine.

When we got home, he put it on the windowsill over our kitchen sink, next to the beautiful bromeliad he'd been nurturing for months. The new one looked sickly, leaves discolored and drooping, stalk dry and dull. He peeled off the discount sticker and tossed it in the trash. I shook my head and left the plant care to him.

I don't notice the plants as much as I might, usually only when Keith points out something to me. So I didn't really look at the bromeliads for more than a week. Then I was putting some dishes in the sink and happened to glance up at the windowsill. The bromeliads looked almost like twins—firm, plump, shiny leaves, and each plant with a brightly colored bloom.

"What in the world happened?" I asked.

Keith smiled at me. "It just needed a little love."

God, let everyone who needs a little love find it and bloom.
—RHODA BLECKER

❈ THE GIFT OF SIGHT

Wed 17 *Their soul shall be as a watered garden; and they shall not sorrow any more at all.* —Jeremiah 31:12

EYES OF THE SPIRIT

My cousin Pam and I had coffee together this morning, and we both ended up crying. She asked about my eye, and I told her I could see only the big *E* on the eye chart, though it had been three weeks since my surgery. Pam's eyes started to water in empathy. Then I asked about her niece Shelley, who has stage-four cancer and is worried about her six-year-old daughter. "I'd gladly give up my life if Shelley could have hers," Pam said, "and if Skylar could have her mother." That was when I had to get out my tissues. We looked across the table at each other and realized we were crying in grief for the other. That was when we started laughing.

We both knew these were not laughing matters, but we'd held in our feelings for too long. We just needed someone to cry with and someone to laugh with too. Then Pam said, "I've been through so many painful times in my life, but right now I feel as though I'm in a state of grace."

How could that be, I wondered, *with all she has to bear?*

"Isn't it miraculous?" Pam continued. "When life gets hard, the spirit grows strong. Again and again I realize that the Holy Spirit has eyes that can see through all kinds of darkness!"

I always feel better after spending time with my cousin.

Thank You, Loving God, for good friends who pass on the state of grace You've given them. May I be graced with the ability to see with the eyes of the spirit and with ways to pass on that vision.
—Marilyn Morgan King

Thu 18

And God saw everything that he had made, and behold, it was very good.... —GENESIS 1:31 (RSV)

I talked to my mother today. "Now that I am at the cusp of my tenth decade," she said, and "You'd think your father would change his ways after sixty-five years of my advice," and "I remember going to village baseball games with my dad in the 1930s," and other pithy and wondrous things. Finally we got around to talking about the hip she just broke, which is around number fifteen on what she calls "the old-lady ailment list."

She admitted to feeling a little weary of being confined to bed and not being able to walk or cook or drive or use much of "the ancient machine the sweet Lord gave me for a body," she said, trying to laugh. As usual, she bent the conversation smoothly to my troubles. How does she do that so gracefully? And when I tried to get back to hers, she suddenly started listing all the great things she has "even now that I'm older than dirt."

"I have my husband, odd as he is, and five children who have never been arrested, yet, and I have the dearest of friends, and a whopping nine grandchildren, and my brain still works, and I make a mean meatloaf, and every day I hear the voices of people I love. Also there are great birds here in Florida and my tomatoes do surprisingly well in this soil. I just discovered two Neville Shute novels I never read, at least one of my children calls me every day, and the sun is out here when it's raining like the dickens where you are and snowing like the Arctic where we used to live, so what's to complain about? Soon enough heaven, and I'll see everyone I ever loved and ever loved me, and can talk baseball again with my dad. But what's the rush? This is a glorious world, the best one ever, don't you think?"

Dear Lord, what she said. Amen.
—BRIAN DOYLE

Fri 19
"In quietness and trust is your strength. . . ."
—Isaiah 30:15 (niv)

My daughter Kendall and her husband David had their first baby recently and spent the next several weeks both elated and exhausted by the reality of their new little miracle.

"Why don't you let me be your night nanny tonight?" I offered one afternoon. They readily agreed.

So that night I jokingly donned the hospital scrubs I'd worn during Kendall's C-section delivery and kissed my husband good-bye. As I drove to their house, I felt a twinge of smugness about the great gift I was about to give them, swooping in to swap my sleep for theirs.

When Kendall and David saw me all dressed up for my shift, they rolled their bleary eyes and took an obligatory picture. Soon they settled me into the guest room with my precious eight-pound charge, some diapers, pacifiers, bottles of formula and a bunch of instructions. "Don't worry about a thing," I told them as they disappeared down the hall.

I got ready for bed, checked my supplies and the sleeping baby beside me, and then turned off the light. In the darkness my own worries started filling my mind—upcoming health tests, financial challenges, new responsibilities—worries that always seemed to grow bigger at night. Then a new one struck me: I couldn't hear the baby breathing. I snapped on the light, saw his tiny chest peacefully moving up and down, and turned the light back off.

That's how the night went. Twice, I jumped up at his first stirrings to meet his needs—feeding, burping, changing—and rocked him back to sleep.

As the first light of dawn peeked through the bedroom curtains, I found myself watching him sleeping so calmly, so trustingly. I'd come here expecting to give my daughter a gift of sleep, but I received the greater gift: a tender reminder of the trust I should have that all my needs will be met.

Lord, a sleeping baby is a gift that reminds me of You.
—Carol Kuykendall

Sat 20

Write the vision, and make it plain upon tables, that he may run that readeth it. —HABAKKUK 2:2

*A*nna Karenina is a big book—840 pages in my hardcover edition—and it weighs a couple of pounds. It's a lot to lug around, but the best opportunity I have for reading is going from place to place. So I took Tolstoy's novel everywhere with me. I read it on the subway and the bus. I read it on the treadmill at the gym. I confess I even read it walking to work (without bumping into anyone).

But when I wasn't reading it, the characters were still with me. There was a dark-haired woman who looked just like Anna coming out of Lord and Taylor. The dashing Vronsky strolled right out of a brokerage on Fifth Avenue, walking down the avenue like he owned the place. At the farmer's market in Union Square, I was sure I spotted the earnest farmer Levin. He wore a floppy leather hat, a bemused expression, and he was carrying a bag of corn.

And then there were all the people I met who were great fans of the book. One man stopped me on the street and asked, "How do you like it?" Another time, I was reading the novel on the bus when I heard a woman's voice, "Where are you?" I looked up. "Has Levin proposed to Kitty yet?" she asked.

"He's proposed once," I said, "but I'm waiting for him to do it again."

Many would say that reading a book is a solitary activity. Perhaps, but I don't think a reader can ever be lonely. The best books—whether it's Tolstoy or the Bible—open us up to a whole world. Especially on the streets of New York City.

I give thanks for the world of books, Lord.
—RICK HAMLIN

November

Sun 21

Let us consider how to stir up one another to love and good works, not neglecting to meet together . . . but encouraging one another, and all the more as you see the Day drawing near.
—Hebrews 10:24–25 (rsv)

After church this morning, I stopped by the home of my friend Sandra. She handed me a cookie, and we quickly caught up on personal news—some frustrations but mostly blessings commensurate with Thanksgiving week. Before I left we prayed for each other: for traveling mercies and hospitality's graces, for fulfilling days and restful nights.

Then this afternoon, as I pulled a cookbook off my shelf, I remembered what day it was. In recent decades the Episcopal *Book of Common Prayer* has changed the set Scriptures and prayers for today, the last Sunday before Advent. But traditionally in the Anglican Communion, the priest says a prescribed prayer (here slightly modernized): "Stir up, O Lord, the wills of your faithful people, that they, plenteously bringing forth the fruit of good works, may be plenteously rewarded, through Jesus Christ our Lord."

And the Gospel reading? The feeding of the five thousand. The day came to be known as Stir-Up Sunday. And to dramatize the theme, cooks went home and started to whip up their favorite seasonal recipes—fruitcakes, plum puddings, confections—preparing for Christmas.

Later in the afternoon I made Thanksgiving pies, slipping one into the freezer for Christmas. And soon I'll head off to bed, mindful of my after-church conversation with Sandra, where we unwittingly commemorated Stir-Up Sunday by encouraging each other in our good and grateful works.

Holy Spirit, as we begin holiday preparations, stir up Your people—
including me—to good and encouraging works of service.
—Evelyn Bence

Mon 22

Devote yourselves to prayer. . . .
—COLOSSIANS 4:2 (NIV)

B aylor University has a wonderful new Student Life Center, including one of the best exercise facilities I've ever seen. Every night hundreds of students drop in to run on treadmills, ride stationary bicycles, lift weights, swim laps or play basketball. Three nights a week I join them.

Tonight I was running on a treadmill, feeling very much "the old man" amidst the students. I was amazed to see how seriously this emerging generation takes its physical fitness. A young woman was running effortlessly beside me as I labored away, and young men sauntered around the weight room, muscles rippling with vitality.

I was reminded that behind the beauty of youth is the adolescent fear of the unknown—of the future and how their lives will be shaped. They worry about what vocation they'll choose, who they'll date and marry, and how they'll perform in a critical world that measures them by grades, talent, industry, courage, "people skills" and a fair portion of sheer good luck.

As the minutes on my treadmill ticked away, I began to focus on some of the individual students around me. I found myself breathing short prayers for each one of them, for the gifts of encouragement, discernment, joy, maturity, love, intellect, self-acceptance, courage, graciousness, vision and a deepening sense of purpose.

Prayer is a gift, free to the giver but priceless in its spiritual value. And when I pray for others, it transforms me too.

> *Father, may my prayers for others be as constant and*
> *natural as breathing.* —SCOTT WALKER

EDITOR'S NOTE: *Join us today for our Thanksgiving Day of Prayer. Every day, Guideposts Prayer Ministry prays for your prayer requests by name and need. Visit us online at OurPrayer.org, where you can request prayer, volunteer to pray for others or help support our prayer ministry.*

November

Tue 23
When anxiety was great within me, your consolation brought joy to my soul. —PSALM 94:19 (NIV)

The call from my wife Julee came in right before 5:00 AM. She was in the Berkshire Hills where she was getting our house ready for a Thanksgiving family gathering. I planned to take the train up from New York City on Tuesday night, but now everything had changed.

"I fell down the stairs," she moaned. "The paramedics are here. It looks like I broke my collarbone. I'm going to the hospital."

"I'll be there as fast as I can."

"Call someone to come over and take care of Millie. She's hysterical." Our young golden retriever had never seen a commotion like this. Who were these strangers and why were they taking Julee away?

I threw some things in a bag, called our friend Chrissy to check on Millie and then go over to see Julee in the emergency room, and ran the few short blocks to Penn Station where I got a seat on the next train, due to leave in an hour's time.

What a long hour it was, pacing outside the station, too distracted even to focus on a coherent prayer. *What if Julee needs surgery? What if it's worse than just a fractured clavicle?*

"The what-ifs will drive us crazy," I recalled a friend once telling me. *What if,* I suddenly reminded myself, *God is in charge, and I just need to step out of the way and calm down?*

That's the what-if that mattered. Julee did break her collarbone, but she was going to be okay, and we had an interesting Thanksgiving with me doing the cooking. Millie was her joyous self once we were all reunited. *What if,* I reminded myself again a few days later as we waved good-bye to my family, *after all these years I just learn to let God take charge when I can't?*

> *Father, You never fail us in times of need. Next time I'll try to remember the most important what-if of all.*
> —EDWARD GRINNAN

Wed 24

Lift up your eyes on high And see who has created these stars . . . He calls them all by name. . . .
—ISAIAH 40:26 (NAS)

It was a predawn day in the snowy stillness of the Alaskan woods. Clusters of spruce trees huddled together beneath a vast black dome strung with stars. I twirled in circles, trying to see them high above me. *I wish there'd be a shooting star,* I mused.

Thanksgiving was nearing. Gratitude poured from me in praises to Father, Son and Holy Spirit. With upraised arms I called, "All that is within me, bless Your holy name!" Just then a shooting star split the sky. Wonder gripped me. It was as though God had written His name in the heavens just for me. Then a second shooting star flamed in the sky.

Despite the chill I couldn't leave. The Holy Spirit seemed to leap and laugh and exult in the cold with me. I looked toward the North Star. A third shooting star cut across the sky. My spirit soared.

As if God understood I needed to come back to earth, He shut down the show. Our star-conversation ended; it was time to go in.

Magnificent and awesome God, dwelling in far-flung splendor amid all that You have made, what a privilege it is to meet You in Your glorious creation! —CAROL KNAPP

READER'S ROOM

We feel that we have a Guideposts family like we have a church family. A few years back, as my own father had died, I asked Van Varner if he'd be my "proxy Dad." He was delighted. We came to feel extremely close to that beautiful man. I recently spotted a box of Barnum's Animal Crackers in a store and remembered that Papa Van had written about them. I had to buy them and send them to him. I received a card from a neighbor of his, advising us of his death. Through my tears, I thanked God for putting Papa Van into our lives. —*Lyle Archer, Mount Vernon, Washington*

Thu 25 *In every thing give thanks....* —I THESSALONIANS 5:18

When I was a girl growing up in Weirton, West Virginia, Thanksgiving meant my mother ripping up soft slices of Wonder Bread for stuffing, getting out the big tin roasting pan and putting the turkey into the oven, and sliding cranberry sauce out of a can. One year she had to thaw the frozen turkey with a hair dryer; another year we all came to the table to find the cat curled up in the bowl meant for mashed potatoes.

My great-Aunt Anne and her best friend Mary came for dinner, my father wielded an electric knife and said, "When Father carves the duck, potatoes fly amuck." And before we ate, there was always the prayer that, to hungry children, seemed to go on and on. My father thanked God for our many blessings, asked God to bless just about every family member who was and wasn't at the table, and ended with "God bless little children everywhere."

After I moved to New York City, I would invite up to twenty people to Thanksgiving dinner in my one-bedroom apartment. How I cooked in a kitchen the size of what today would be considered a closet, using an oven barely big enough to hold an eighteen-pound turkey, I'll never know. Later I shared a weekend country house with friends. Bigger kitchen, more people, much merriment. And still always the prayers.

Today I usually spend Thanksgiving at my sister's cabin in the woods outside Seattle, where a whole new cast of wonderful characters gathers. I make the stuffing, ripping up crusty loaves of whole wheat and rye and adding apples and fresh-rubbed sage. My sister and I are the great-aunts now (emphasis, as we always say, on the *great!*). And as we bow our heads before the meal, the prayer still ends the same way:

> *Dear God, bless every family member who is and isn't at the table.*
> *And bless the little children everywhere.*
> —MARY ANN O'ROARK

Fri 26   *Judge not according to the appearance, but judge righteous judgment.* —JOHN 7:24

I'd promised to bake gingerbread boys for my neighbor's twin sons, so the night before, I set out the flour, molasses and spices. I measured everything twice and then greased the pan. But I mistakenly used a recipe for cake instead of cookies, so my gingerbread boys spread over the cookie sheet and turned into gingerbread monsters. I tried to cut them into the right shapes while the tiny green candies I'd used to decorate them melted into shiny half-dollar-sized eyes. *I've ruined them!*

But when I heard the twins' familiar tap-tapping on my door, it was too late to do anything but serve my cookies. They looked nothing like the drawings in the storybook I'd planned to read, but the real-life boys loved them. "Gingerbread blobs!" Wasim and Kareem cried excitedly. I could barely get them to settle down for my reading of the gingerbread man story, but they got the idea. They spent half an hour racing around my apartment, laughing and calling out, "Run, run, gingerbread blobs!"

When their mom came to get them, she said, "Thank you, Linda, for this gift"—she nodded toward some of the gingerbread blobs, which I'd packed in cellophane for her—"and for the gift of an hour to myself."

Once the door closed behind them, I realized that I'd received a gift too. Maybe that too-short scarf I'd knitted would be a good doll's blanket. And the painting I'd done? I gave it a second look and had to admit that some things are just unsalvageable. *But not the cookies*, I thought, biting off a chewy arm. *Imperfect, like me, but good enough all the same.*

God, thank You for showing me that even if something isn't perfect according to my standards, it may be pure perfection according to Your even higher ones.
—LINDA NEUKRUG

✸ TWELVE KEYS TO THE GIVING LIFE

Sat 27   *And he that watereth shall be watered also himself.*
—PROVERBS 11:25

GIVE PRAYERFULLY

My mother was a generous giver. When she passed away, she left little behind in the way of worldly goods. Her only heirloom was a stately, walnut hall tree she'd bought on one of her yard sale expeditions.

Last fall my siblings and I heard that the historic Madie Carroll House, a museum in the Guyandotte community of Huntington, West Virginia, was looking for Victorian-era furnishings. We prayerfully decided to donate Mother's hall tree to it. Mother had taught first grade at Guyandotte Elementary in the 1940s and '50s, and we thought it would be a nice way to honor her.

I visited the museum when it was all decked out in holiday finery. Someone had hung a pine wreath from the top peg of Mother's hall tree. A docent was addressing a group of children. "Back in Victorian times, people didn't have closets," she told them. "They hung their coats and hats on hall trees just like this one." She pointed to a pair of curved arms at the center of it. "Right here's where they used to put their umbrellas. The metal dish at the bottom kept the water from hurting the wood."

A small girl with blonde pigtails reached out to touch the docent's hoopskirt. "I like learning about the olden days," she said.

Through our giving, Mother was still teaching. And like the gifts Mother gave while she was living, this one would go on and on and on.

> *Dear God, help me to place everything*
> *I own in Your capable hands.*
> —ROBERTA MESSNER

❦ THE GREATEST GIFT

Sun 28   *When his mother Mary had been engaged to Joseph, but before they lived together, she was found to be with child from the Holy Spirit.* —MATTHEW 1:18 (NRSV)

FIRST SUNDAY IN ADVENT: WAITING JOYFULLY

My mother was the one who brought Christmas. She kept the anticipation and, yes, the anxiety simmering from Thanksgiving weekend, when the first decorations were hauled from the attic to be modestly distributed in bedrooms and more lavishly laid in the living and dining rooms, to New Year's Day, when the tree came down.

Mom taught my sister Lori and me to give up candy with her during Advent to show that "we're waiting for Jesus," though my father was exempt from what seemed a monumental sacrifice. And she was in charge of the candles—not only the electric candles that glowed in each window, but also the Advent candles, the focus of our grace before dinner on every Sunday in Advent.

To appease my father, with his abiding fear of fire, no live greenery surrounded the candles; even plastic pine cones were unacceptable, "just in case." The four candles were set in a simple metal holder on the kitchen table. But unlike Advent candles in every other household and church in our community, Mom's candles were not purple and pink. Traditionally, purple candles are lit on the first, second and fourth Sundays in Advent to symbolize waiting for Jesus. The pink candle is lit on the third Sunday as a foretaste of our joy in His nearing birth. But my mother's metal wreath held four white candles.

There were two reasons for Mom's unconventional choice: First, she believed our whole time of waiting for Jesus should be joyful. And reason number two? Purple and pink clashed with the rest of her decorations.

Jesus, let the pure light of Your coming birth burn away my worries and distractions. —MARCI ALBORGHETTI

November

Mon 29

When my father and my mother forsake me, then the Lord will take me up. —PSALM 27:10

The small auditorium of the elementary school in the rural Ukrainian community two hours from Kiev was full of children anxiously waiting to welcome their guests from the United States. Our mission was to deliver Operation Christmas Child shoe box gifts and Knit for Kids sweaters.

Halfway into the distribution, our team leader began to worry that the children outnumbered the gifts. Mary, a veteran of countless mission trips, whispered, "Loaves and fishes, loaves and fishes. We need a miracle."

Randy stepped outside and prayed while his wife Rebecca went back to the van to look for more cartons of gifts. But she was certain that all of the boxes had been taken into the school.

John from Virginia was sure we'd be all right: "We'll have two cartons of gifts left over." We didn't pay much attention to him. The children were taking their gifts faster than we could unload them. The colorful sweaters they'd received brightened the dull auditorium. Finally the last child in line took a shoe box. We were relieved, delighted and, most of all, amazed that we had exactly two cartons of presents left over.

Before heading back, we gathered around the van for prayer. Rebecca told us that she'd found a carton underneath the chairs in one van and another box in the other.

Mary knew what had happened: "Loaves and fishes!" she said.

Lord, remember all the needy children of the world, and help me to be an instrument of Your love and generosity. —PABLO DIAZ

EDITOR'S NOTE: *For a copy of the Knit for Kids pattern, please visit our Web site at KnitforKids.org or send a stamped, self-addressed envelope to Knit for Kids, 39 Seminary Hill Road, Carmel, New York 10512.*

Tue 30 Therefore encourage each other with these words.
—I THESSALONIANS 4:18 (NIV)

It took me thirty minutes to write you that text message yesterday," Dad said.

I wasn't sure I'd heard him correctly over the phone. "Thirty minutes?" I asked.

"Yes."

"It was only two sentences long."

"Well, I am kind of new to this technology."

We both laughed.

Dad was new to cell phones; he and Mom had shared a mobile phone for a couple of years, but it was only for emergencies. Dad finally got his own phone last year, around the same time I moved from our home state of Virginia to California for graduate school.

I don't know how I would have gotten through those difficult days when I first arrived at school had it not been for the communication with my family that modern technology afforded me. Whenever I felt lonely or frustrated, I'd call or e-mail Mom or Dad, and they always had something encouraging to say.

I thank God that I live in an age when I can build relationships with my family no matter where my travels take me—and that it no longer takes Dad thirty minutes to reply to my text messages.

Thank You, Lord, for the people You've put in my life and for the means You've given us to keep in touch.
—JOSHUA SUNDQUIST

THE GIFTS I'VE BEEN GIVEN

1 _____

2 _____

3 _____

4 _____

5 _____

6 _____

7 _____

8 _____

9 _____

10 _____

11 _____

12 _____

13 _____

14 _____

15 _____

16 _____

17 _____

18 _____

19 _____

20 _____

21 _____

November

22 _____

23 _____

24 _____

25 _____

26 _____

27 _____

28 _____

29 _____

30 _____

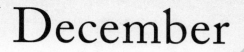

December

Every good gift and every perfect gift is from above, and cometh down from the Father of lights. . . .

—JAMES 1:17

❧ GIFTS FROM ABOVE

Wed 1 This woman was full of good works . . . . —ACTS 9:36

A GIFT OF HELPING

I had dragged two boxes of mail into the post office and trudged back out for more. Now I was in the long line, struggling with the heavy boxes as it slowly moved forward.

Finally I wrestled my boxes to the counter. The clerk weighed them and then shook his head. "I'm sorry, but you have three different-sized packages here. I'm going to put them into three containers and then you're going to have to put the correct postage on each piece." I went over to a table and arranged the stamps into three groups to match the parcels.

"What are you doing, honey?" a pleasant voice asked.

I looked up at a woman's smiling face and explained my chore.

"Well, I'm just standing here in line doing nothing. I'll help," she said.

I explained that the packages were going to people who had helped our AIDS orphans in Africa. "What a good cause," she said. "I'm so lucky to get to help."

She worked on and then stopped suddenly, looking back at the long line of mostly grumpy people. "Hey, come help us!" she called out. "It's Christmas, and we're doing something good." Soon others were pitching in, chatting together, laughing. The clerk was grinning from ear to ear as he delivered the last of the parcels to my amazing assembly line.

My new friend stamped the last piece, and before I could thank her, she was headed out the door. "Oh," I called, "wait! I don't know your name or how to thank you."

She laughed. "It's Christmas!" was all she said.

Father, thank You for the amazing woman who turned my Christmas around. As I have received, let me give. —PAM KIDD

⧗ COMFORT FOR THE HURTING HEART

Thu 2 "I am concerned for you and will look on you with favor; you will be plowed and sown. . . . I . . . will make you prosper more than before. Then you will know that I am the Lord."
—EZEKIEL 36:9, 11 (NIV)

TRUST FOR TOMORROW

Recently I met an out-of-town acquaintance I'd not seen in years. "Hi, Mary Lou," I greeted her. "Are you still writing newspaper columns?"

"No, the new editor fired me eleven months ago. Even though I take some comfort in knowing my work was good, I'm still grieving and feeling humiliated."

"What are you doing now?" I asked.

"Nothing much. I have no self-confidence left. Even God has let me down."

"Of course He hasn't!" I answered. "You know something? I was also fired by an editor. That editor's parting words, 'You're a pretty good writer. Go write for somebody else!' seemed tattooed on my brain. I couldn't erase my grief either.

"Then a friend came up with a thought. She quoted Ezekiel 36:9, 11 and added, 'God's concerned about you. So do as the man said: Submit your work elsewhere and see what happens!'"

I took her advice—and God at His Word—and sent my stories to another publication. That happened thirty-five years ago, and I've been writing for Guideposts ever since.

Dear Lord, help me always to remember that You're watching over me and that You will not allow anything to touch me that is not in Your will and for my good. —ISABEL WOLSELEY

December

Fri 3
*A cheerful look brings joy to the heart, and good news gives
health to the bones.* —PROVERBS 15:30 (NIV)

Every year my mom sends out Christmas cards featuring fun family updates, always with a positive spin. She highlights items such as Best Trip, Best Student and Best Athlete, but the much-desired top spot is Best News, and every year the family has a good-natured battle over who will get recognized in that category.

For the last few years I've been in the running with key life-changing moves like graduating from college or getting my first real job, but just as I started experiencing big changes, so did my siblings. Grandchildren started pouring in, and what's better news than a new baby in the family?

My mom has considered using vertical columns for everyone or doing away with the categories altogether, but she's been overruled time and again. This year I thought I might get the top spot for sure, thanks to my engagement, but then two new grandbabies swooped in. They're competing for the title and don't even know it!

As I sat wondering how I would do in next year's competition, having tossed my wedding into the hat, I realized how blessed our family is. How wonderful that we have so many good things happening that there are so many choices for the Best News spot!

*God, thank You for all of the blessings in my life and
the vision with which to recognize them.*
—ASHLEY JOHNSON

Sat 4   *Let the word of Christ dwell in you richly in all wisdom;*
teaching and admonishing one another in psalms and
hymns and spiritual songs, singing with grace in your
hearts to the Lord. —COLOSSIANS 3:16

On a gloomy day in early December, safe in the car's passenger seat, I pressed the satellite radio's Search button. Christmas music seemed to be on every one of the four hundred channels—not celebrating the birth of Jesus, but mixing merchandise and carols together into electronic jingles. The meaning of the season seemed to slip away, drowned out by the relentless message that Christmas is about gifts and food. Loneliness seemed to be speaking out of all the good cheer.

I pushed another button, and suddenly the car was filled with the glorious sounds of the last part of Ludwig van Beethoven's magnificent Ninth Symphony, known as the "Ode to Joy," which is also the music for Henry Van Dyke's great hymn "Joyful, Joyful We Adore Thee":

> *Ever singing march we onward*
> *Victors in the midst of strife,*
> *Joyful music leads us Sunward*
> *In the triumph song of life.*

Beethoven was only thirty-two and at the height of his career when he realized he was going deaf. He faced depression and loneliness. Yet some of his greatest music, including this passionate expression of joy and praise, was composed after he could no longer hear it performed.

As the music surrounded me, the irritations of the ceaseless electronic carols seemed very small. Beethoven believed in himself and in his God, and shared his gifts with countless millions of us who need to be reminded of the joy of faith.

Thank You for all the gifts given to us by inspired men and women
who brighten our days and deepen our faith.
—BRIGITTE WEEKS

❧ THE GREATEST GIFT

Sun 5   *"Here am I, the servant of the Lord; let it be with me according to your word.". . .* —LUKE 1:38 (NRSV)

SECOND SUNDAY IN ADVENT: LIGHT AND SHADOW

It was a crystal-cold December night. After dropping off my mother at the hospital to see my grandfather, my father had taken my sister Lori, seven, and me, ten, to see the lights on Hartford, Connecticut's Constitution Plaza. Though this amazing display was one of the state's main Christmas attractions, we'd never seen it.

That evening Christmas changed for us. My mother loved her father dearly, and we'd felt her anxiety when he grew ill as fall deepened. That worry overshadowed our happy anticipation of Jesus' birth. And when Grampa died, all the energy drained from my mother.

That year she didn't make her usual hundreds of Christmas cookies and candies. Instead of rearranging every decoration at least twice, she gazed at them, unseeing. There were no poinsettias, no elaborately set Christmas table. But underneath it all there was still a sense of peace: Grampa was with Jesus.

Mary's parents must have been anxious as they watched Joseph lead their daughter away, heavily pregnant, for the long, dangerous journey to Bethlehem. How Joseph must have worried when he realized the child would be born in a cave. But for them, as for us, Christmas tragedies are transformed into a Christmas miracle—the Savior—if only we can wait a little while longer.

> *Lord, help me reach out with hope to those who may be*
> *experiencing a Christmas tragedy this year.*
> —MARCI ALBORGHETTI

Mon 6   But these are written that you may believe that Jesus is the
Christ, the Son of God, and that by believing you may have
life in his name. —JOHN 20:31 (NIV)

Three years ago yesterday, following emergency surgery, I was diagnosed with stage-four ovarian cancer. Alone in my hospital room
with the doctor, I asked, "Give it to me straight. What does this mean?"

"About life expectancy?" she asked hesitantly.

I nodded.

"Two years, on average."

So today, three years later, I'm celebrating a miracle.

For a long time I resisted applying that word to my experience.
Miracles are mysterious. And they happen to other people, like the people in the Bible—and Skylar, the baby boy whose picture I put on my
refrigerator shortly after coming home from the hospital with my diagnosis. His mom is a friend.

Several weeks after his birth, Skylar was diagnosed with leukemia. He
was put on life support, and finally the doctors told his parents to prepare for the worst. His mother tearfully asked the nurses to pull all the
tubes when the end came near so that she could hold him until he died.

Meanwhile, across town at the family's church, a group gathered for
prayer and someone reported that Skylar was dying. A pastor suddenly
stood up and almost defiantly announced, "There are diagnoses and
statistics—and then there's God!"

Back at the hospital, little Skylar drew a few breaths on his own . . .
then a few more, slowly at first but then more steadily.

The Bible tells us that miracles are made known to us so that we might
believe that God is real. Today I look at the words written across the bottom of Skylar's picture: "And then there's God." I believe.

Lord, thank You for still sprinkling miracles into our days.
—CAROL KUYKENDALL

December

Tue 7

He giveth snow like wool: he scattereth the hoarfrost like ashes. —PSALM 147:16

The phone rang this morning; it was a friend calling from up North. "We got six inches last night," he complained. He didn't have to tell me six inches of what; I've shoveled snow out of a thousand driveways in my Ohio, New Jersey and Pennsylvania days. But now I'm in Florida during the cold half of the year and don't have to think about snow. "But," I can hear someone say, "you have hurricanes to contend with." And, of course, they would be right. There's no perfect paradise on earth that I know of.

Once a Florida transplant informed me that he was going North for one last winter to enjoy sitting around a fireplace. "It was wonderful," he reported later.

I know what he was talking about. With the first significant snowfall, my wife Shirley and I and the children would sit, warm and contented, around a fire, eating popcorn, reminiscing about vacations at the cottage in Indiana, sightseeing trips, visits to relatives, hiking, biking. The kids are all grown now, but those are indelible memories.

Further back, I can remember going to church on freezing Sunday mornings when only a few people showed up. But our family did; Mama insisted. And those who came worshipped just the same.

> *Thank You, Lord, for attending us in all kinds of weather,*
> *And for Your presence whenever we gather.*
> —FRED BAUER

Wed 8

Every good and perfect gift is from above . . . .
—James 1:17 (NIV)

My three-year-old grandson Frank and I were shopping for a Christmas present for him to give to his mother, my daughter Sanna. It was the last thing on my list, and I was tired. If I turned him loose to pick what he wanted, who knows what he might choose and how much it would cost. Guidance, I decided, was in order.

"Frank, your mommy needs pajamas," I said, steering him to lingerie. "What color would she like?"

"I don't know," he mumbled.

"How about these?" I held up a lavender set of pajamas that I knew Sanna would like.

"Okay," he said without much interest. We headed toward the checkout, the package under my arm.

Suddenly Frank stopped and stared at a big pot of yellow silk pansies.

"Flowers for Mommy," he said, touching them. I looked at the price tag and my heart sank. Not only were they expensive, they were also tacky-looking.

"But we already have pajamas for Mommy," I said, holding them up. "She needs pajamas."

"But Mommy loves flowers," he pleaded. Then I remembered that recently Frank's daddy had brought fresh flowers to Sanna, and Frank had witnessed her delight. We got the flowers.

On Christmas morning Frank proudly carried his gift to Mommy. Sanna carefully unwrapped the pot of pansies. She held them up to the light, turning them this way and that, as if they were the most exquisite thing she'd ever seen. "They're beautiful," she said, pulling a beaming Frank to her. And in the glow of love that sees through the other's eyes, they were.

Father, thank You that the joy of giving and receiving runs deeper than the gift itself and, in fact, is the best gift of all.
—Shari Smyth

Thu 9 "*Yours, O Lord, are the greatness, the power, the glory, the victory, and the majesty; for all that is in the heavens and on the earth is yours; yours is the kingdom, O Lord, and you are exalted as head above all.*" —I CHRONICLES 29:11 (NRSV)

When I first moved to Vermont a dozen years ago, people said to me, "Be careful when you drive at night—you sure don't want to hit a moose!" I'd reply by asking how common an occurrence this was, and they would invariably say something like, "It happens. And believe me, you don't want it to happen to you!"

Four years went by before I ever saw a moose. I was driving home from work in the early winter darkness. The moose was a teenager, so to speak, and yet he must have been seven feet tall. I had never seen anything like him outside a zoo. He was standing in the middle of the road, and I couldn't get around him. So I honked the horn. Big mistake. The enormous creature did not run away like a deer; he came toward me, so close that when he snorted, I was sure that I felt it. I've seen three or four moose since that first day, and the sight of each one reminds me to be respectful.

God is far mightier than any moose, and even though I don't feel God's power breathing on my neck, I know it through His acts recounted in Scripture. What I read in the Bible reminds me to give Him my respect—in how I think, in what I say and in my actions—as well as my love.

Holy and Powerful One, help me keep close to You today.
Whatever strength I possess comes from You.
—JON SWEENEY

❄ THE GIFT OF SIGHT

Fri 10   *Then a spirit passed before my face . . . an image was before mine eyes . . . .* —JOB 4:15–16

AN UNNAMEABLE SPLENDOR

As highly as I value seeing the faces of the people I love, vibrant colors, the beauty of the mountains and the mystery of night, there is one thing I love more. It's an unnameable splendor, a mystery far greater than I, not personal to me, and it lives in the heart of every being. Now and then I've caught glimpses of it in silent prayer, and I've come to know it as vast and boundless, all-loving and ablaze with the light of the Spirit.

Though I may someday lose my physical sight, I'll be okay, because I'll remind myself of Helen Keller's words: "The best and most beautiful things cannot be seen or touched. They must be felt with the heart."

And I'll pull up some of the many inspiring images I've stored in my heart to feed my soul when it's hungry for beauty. Often, as I'm falling asleep or waking up, images appear behind my closed eyelids—of wisteria flowers; or the sad-glorious stained glass window by Marc Chagall; or a twenty-foot-high rhododendron bush with my love smiling in front of it; or a sometimes flaming, sometimes softly glowing Nebraska sunset.

Sometimes I have even seen an image of Jesus holding a little lamb snuggled up against His cheek. That's when I remember my Aunt Alta's words as she was dying: "Oh! He is so beautiful!" Now I think I know Who she saw with her blind eyes.

Thanks be to God for the gift of sight, in all the many ways it manifests—physically, mentally and especially spiritually!
—MARILYN MORGAN KING

Sat 11

"Be strong and courageous. Do not be terrified; do not be discouraged, for the Lord your God will be with you wherever you go." —Joshua 1:9 (NIV)

It had been a difficult year for my husband Wayne and me. Our youngest son had received two DUI tickets. We'd poured out our hearts to God and prayed He would work in Dale's life. Once Dale entered rehab, we assumed everything would get better. Instead, everything seemed to get worse. Dale lost his job and took one personal blow after another. He was sober, but nothing else seemed to change.

I'm most comfortable writing out my prayers, and day after day I poured out my heart on paper to the Lord, praying for Dale. As his situation grew worse, I began to doubt that God was listening or that He even cared. Why was He allowing all this to come down on our son when he was trying so hard to get his life in order? It made no sense.

Then one morning after we'd received more bad news from Dale, my pen refused to work. I couldn't write out my prayers; it was as if God were tired of hearing from me. I must have mumbled something to myself because Wayne came to check on me. Shaking the pen in frustration, I told him it wouldn't write. Calmly, Wayne ran a glass of hot water and set the pen inside. When I picked it up again, the ink flowed smoothly. I stared at it for a long time, and with tears in my eyes I recognized what God was attempting to tell me: He was working in Dale's life. He put our son in hot water so that Dale could work out his issues. Everything was happening just the way God meant it to.

Thank You, Father, that You hear our prayers. Thank You, too, for the lesson that a little hot water is exactly what Dale needed.
—Debbie Macomber

❦ THE GREATEST GIFT

Sun 12   *"We observed his star at its rising, and have come to pay him homage." —*MATTHEW 2:2 (NRSV)

THIRD SUNDAY IN ADVENT: TRIMMING THE TREE

Our Christmas tree was a big deal. Mom whipped us into such a frenzy of waiting that when the appointed day came for the tree, we were beside ourselves. But what a day! Two Sundays before Christmas, after church, Christmas records were stacked on the record player and my father would wrestle the tree into our house.

Then the lights—gazillions of lights! We didn't touch them; Dad had to test them before stringing them on the tree. Then he would twine them deep inside the branches; Mom didn't like to see the cords. Finally, Dad, breathing relief, would retreat as the boxes were pulled from the spare room where they'd waited since Thanksgiving.

The big brown boxes were patched and ugly, but what treasures they held: angels, stars and miniature Nativities; homemade ornaments, store-bought ornaments, "Nana" ornaments my grandmother made, old ornaments from my mother's childhood; and some unclassifiable odds and ends. Mom, my sister Lori and I would get to work, putting them up as music filled the house. Then we had garlands of some gold-colored stuff to drape on the branches.

The short December Sunday flew by. We waited, breathless, in the darkened house for my father to plug in the lights. When he did, though it didn't seem possible, our racing pulses slowed and we breathed deeply the light and warmth.

In that glow was peace, the antidote to the frenzy that had gripped us, a taste of what would come with Jesus.

Jesus, let me seek and find Your peace in all my Christmas busyness.
*—*MARCI ALBORGHETTI

December

Mon 13 *Do not forsake your friend. . . .*
—PROVERBS 27:10 (NIV)

My job requires a person who's organized and thorough, with great communication skills. Unfortunately I'm not that person. My office resembles a garage sale caught in a tornado. So does my brain. I have little notes posted everywhere, surrounded by scraps of paper with mysterious phone numbers and no names. My e-mail in-box looks like the Manhattan phone book—but not in alphabetical order. If I had been planning D-Day in World War II, our capital would now be Berlin.

I've learned survival techniques to outwit myself. (Never underestimate the power of your cell phone's alarm feature. Now, where did I put my cell phone?) But of all the things that have gone AWOL in the chaos, only one missing thing bothers me: friendships.

Someone once said that if you have a handful of good friends by the time you're fifty, you're doing well. And I understand how it happens—a warm evening spent really talking, really understanding each other, followed by promises of getting together . . . but then life intervenes and the phone calls are less frequent, and soon it's down to the occasional e-mail, then . . .

Here's my Christmas wish: Believe in the cards you send. When you write "Let's get together," mean it. *Do it.* And while you're at it, you can work on the whole peace-on-earth-goodwill-toward-men thing too.

Which reminds me that I have yet to do my Christmas cards. I know I have a box . . . they were right over here somewhere. . . .

Lord, sometimes I feel like the living example of the second law
of thermodynamics: Whatever I do, the disorder around me
increases. Don't let me lose my friends in the process.
—MARK COLLINS

Tue 14

Jesus answered and said unto them, This is the work of God, that ye believe on him whom he hath sent. —JOHN 6:29

B*elieve.* It's a word that gets tossed around a lot this time of year. Sometimes it captions a picture of a jolly Santa and a charming child. Other times it stands alone, a solitary word on a cup or a sweatshirt or a holiday pillow: *Believe.*

But in what? Ah, that's not always clear. In Santa Claus? In the Spirit of Christmas? In the Incarnation?

For my birthday a few months ago, my friend Desila gave me a rhinestone pin that proclaims, in sparkly stick letters, *Believe.* As I pinned it on my coat at the beginning of Advent, I didn't even have to think about what it meant to me.

I am what my grandmother would have called "a believer." And she wasn't talking about men in red suits or a vague feeling of goodwill. To her, a believer was someone who accepted the whole Christmas story just the way the Holy Spirit dictated it to the Gospel writers. Angels, shepherds, wise men, smelly farm animals and an improvised crib made of rough planks and hay.

I think Grandma was onto something. Why play fill-in-the-blank with a verb as important as *believe?*

Thank goodness God is not only generous and loving, but also direct. *Hey, pay attention! I'm sending a Savior. Looking for something to give your life meaning? Seeking joy and peace? Believe in the Lord Jesus Christ and you will be saved. From your sin—and yourself.*

Yes, 'tis the season to believe. Thank God!

> *I believe. I believe. I believe.*
> —MARY LOU CARNEY

Wed 15 *A gift is as a precious stone....* —PROVERBS 17:8

I didn't want my son Jeremy to lose one inch of hard-gained ground. A recovering addict who struggles with bipolar disorder, he's come so far in the last year. But when he received a much-needed hip replacement, he couldn't attend his daily AA meetings.

Then on one dreary December day, the mail brought a small, heavy package from Texas. Someone named Betty wrote, "Marion, I've been praying for Jeremy daily. I'm sending him a few of the smooth stones I've been painting and giving away."

At the hospital Jeremy lit up like a Christmas tree when I put the stones on his bed. Betty had neatly printed a slogan on each stone, familiar messages from AA and Celebrate Recovery, like "One day at a time" and "Let go and let God."

After Jeremy wrote to Betty to thank her, she sent him another heavy box. The accompanying note said, "Jeremy, this time I'm sending blank stones with paints and brushes. You paint them, okay?"

When Jeremy returned to his meetings, he brought stones with encouraging phrases he'd painted on them and handed them out to his buddies. "You should have seen how excited the guys were to get the stones, Mom. I'm going to have to paint some more."

Thank You, Father, for the unbelievable kindness of strangers. And help me never to miss an opportunity to help those who are struggling to change their lives. —MARION BOND WEST

READER'S ROOM

Early one December morning, my eye caught a glint of vivid red gliding past the kitchen window. On the feeder, jaunty and splendid, sat a brilliant crimson cardinal. Each morning until Christmas, he perched on the feeder ledge, his scarlet coat shining brightly against the new white snow and the deep green pine trees surrounding our yard. His presence was a gift my heart treasures. —*Mary Jo McCarthy, Pequot Lakes, Minnesota*

✺ TWELVE KEYS TO THE GIVING LIFE

Thu 16   *Such as I have give I thee....* —ACTS 3:6

GIVE STEADFASTLY

When I was a girl, I earned extra money by helping my neighbor Alice with her household chores. All year long there was a table in her living room that was never to be disturbed; it held her gifts in progress.

What impressed me most was the way Alice tailored her gifts to the recipients. For a friend who was a sewing teacher, Alice wrapped a book on making doll clothes in gingham fabric. She used a yellow measuring tape in lieu of ribbon and a fat tomato pincushion for the bow.

Years later, when Alice moved to a nursing home a hundred miles away, what troubled me most was the thought that her wonderful gifts would stop. Her home had been sold to pay for her medical expenses, so she had no money of her own. But to my astonishment, when I arrived in Alice's tiny room on Christmas Eve, gaily wrapped packages were piled high on her bedside table and at the foot of her bed.

Alice couldn't wait for me to open my gift. She'd cushioned a rose-patterned cup and saucer with a square of clean gauze and packed it in a box that had once held latex gloves. The pièce de résistance was a bow she'd crafted from the twill tape the nurses used to secure her tracheotomy tube.

"Where did you ever find this exquisite china?" I asked. I turned it over, looking for clues to its origin. "Oh my goodness, it's antique Limoges!"

Alice's face lit up. "Won it at bingo," she said. "I've hooked up with one of the evening nurses, honey. She never fails to pick a winning card."

As it turned out, all the Christmas gifts Alice had won were donated by local people. Alice had recycled them and put her personal stamp on each one. And she taught me something I would forever carry with me: A generous heart will find a way to give ... always.

Dear Lord, teach me to give wherever life takes me.
—ROBERTA MESSNER

December

Fri 17

And the angel said unto them, Fear not: for, behold, I bring you good tidings of great joy. . . . —LUKE 2:10

I want the doctor to look at these pictures," the sonogram technician said as she left the room. I lay shivering on a gurney, half clothed, fighting off fear. I already knew I had a lump in the breast tissue under my left arm. My doctor thought it was a cyst. A mammogram the week before couldn't get to the exact spot.

The only difference between now and five minutes from now will be what I know, I thought. *My body will be the same.* It was weird to think that if I had cancer, malignant cells were at that moment silently multiplying. It was even weirder to realize that my day would change, not because of the disease itself, but because of my knowledge of it.

With Christmas so close, I wondered if what I was about to hear would ruin my holiday. In one sense, yes, of course; in another sense, not at all. Jesus Christ was still God made flesh, born for our salvation. Christmas itself would be the same, regardless of my feelings or personal circumstances.

The door opened, and the doctor strode in. "Show me where the lump is," she said briskly. With some difficulty, I found the spot. She squirted goo onto the sonogram probe and smeared it around my underarm. "Huh," she said, "I don't see a thing."

"How can that be?" I asked. "I felt it and my doctor felt it."

"Oh, cysts come and go," she replied casually. "Yours is gone."

Lord, whether I face happy or sad news this Christmas, help me focus on the good news that You've given us.
—JULIA ATTAWAY

Sat 18   *God sets the lonely in families . . . .* —PSALM 68:6 (NIV)

Every Christmas someone from our church family hosts a party for our pastor, staff members and members of the church council. Last year my wife and I participated in the White Elephant gift exchange. Each person draws a number and chooses a gift. (Maybe the word *gift* is a little misleading. The paper it's wrapped in is often worth more than the present itself.)

I drew a low number and unwrapped a Chia Pet, a present that doubtlessly disappointed its recipient and would have been discarded had White Elephants not been invented as a way of recycling useless objects like Chia Pets.

One of the rules of our gift exchange is that every participant can choose a wrapped package or "steal" something someone else has unwrapped. Nobody was interested in stealing my Chia Pet. A desperate thief with very poor taste would not steal a Chia Pet. "It's better than a pet rock," I said, hoping to pique someone's interest, but it was no use. I was left out of the game completely. To my surprise I discovered that being left out is just as painful at fifty-four as it is at fourteen.

After about a half hour of being ignored, a Good Samaritan snubbed all the other gifts and seized my Chia Pet as if he had longed for it all his life. And you know, I discovered that there's no age limit to feeling grateful for an unexpected kindness either; it's just as wonderful at fifty-four as it is at fourteen.

> *Dear God, thank You for the special people who place*
> *kindness above competition.*
> —TIM WILLIAMS

☙ THE GREATEST GIFT

Sun 19   *"The Lord is able to give you much more than this."*
—II Chronicles 25:9 (RSV)

FOURTH SUNDAY IN ADVENT: THE TREASURE HUNT

I'd love to say that presents weren't a big part of our Christmas. But they were, they really were. My sister Lori was particularly interested in—not to say obsessed by—presents.

I think it didn't matter what was in them, so long as she could gaze rapturously at them under the tree. According to my mother's schedule, presents would appear a week before Christmas, after she had vacuumed under the tree. Waiting for that vacuum cleaner just about drove Lori around the bend. Long before cleaning day, she'd start in. Couldn't we have just one present under the tree? Not even one of hers, though that would be a bonus.

No? Okay, then could she just see one, wrapped, of course? Refusals fell unacknowledged on her young ears; when thwarted in her attempt to view the presents lawfully, she'd search for hidden treasures. Mom couldn't do laundry downstairs without Lori having a quiet field day in our parents' closet. One thing Mom had on her, however, was height: Lori's presents always ended up on top of something, out of sight and out of reach. I was surprised, year after year, after the vacuum cleaner quieted and brightly wrapped presents nestled under the tree, that Lori didn't collapse from nervous excitement.

Lori wasn't a greedy child; she simply craved those colorful symbols of the love in our home. And what's wrong, really, with looking forward to Christmas presents? After all, didn't God give the world the most astounding, glorious present of all?

Lord and Savior, with all the presents I will give and get this year,
let me keep You, the greatest gift, first in my heart and mind.
—Marci Alborghetti

Mon 20

The light shines in the darkness, and the darkness has not overcome it. —JOHN 1:5 (RSV)

W hen my son Ross asked what I wanted for Christmas, I told him I didn't need anything—just having him home from college was present enough. Then my daughter Maria was hospitalized for treatment of a chronic health condition, and shopping was forgotten, along with decorating, baking and everything else. I felt particularly bad because we had promised Maria that this year we'd put up lights, something we hadn't done for years. But that wasn't going to happen. My husband Paul and I were struggling to keep things going at home and work while I spent nights with Maria in the hospital.

The Sunday before Christmas, Paul and I had spent the day at the hospital, and then I headed home to change clothes and pick up some things for Maria. As I turned the corner at the end of our street, I couldn't believe what I saw: Our house was covered with lights! Dozens of red, green, blue and yellow bulbs ran along the perimeter of the roof, across the top of the garage and through the bushes by the front door. Ross and his friend Sarah had spent the day hanging the lights, as well as putting up our tree and many of our favorite decorations.

It was the best present anyone could have given us, and it didn't cost a thing, except one entire Sunday afternoon when two teenagers could have been doing something else. Instead, they created the most beautiful light display I had ever seen. And when Maria returned home two nights before Christmas, she thought exactly the same thing.

Dear God, help me to give more of myself to those I love,
for often it's the only gift they want.
—GINA BRIDGEMAN

December

Tue 21

He casteth forth his ice like morsels: who can stand before his cold? —PSALM 147:17

Today is the first day of winter, and in New York City the season is letting itself be known—temperature in the teens, sidewalks glazed with ice, windchill below zero.

I've always been a bit skeptical about windchill readings. Why concoct a measurement for making it even colder than it already is? I suspect this is just another way to worry us into watching the TV weather report, like the heat index in the summer. Isn't ninety-five degrees hot enough?

My wife Julee buys into this hype. If she sees me going out on a cold night without a hat or gloves, she comes chasing after me until I'm properly covered. "It's minus twenty degrees!" she'll shout, quoting the dreaded windchill factor. I'll argue, but it's no use. Suddenly I'm swathed in scarves and hats and gloves so that I can barely see. I'll grumble about how this is nothing compared to the winters I grew up with in Michigan. Usually I end up declaring, "I love the cold!" By then I'm a mummy in Polartec and breaking into a sweat.

Tonight I preemptively bundle up to walk our dog Millie, who herself is impervious to cold. In front of a church up the block, homeless men and women crowd onto a school bus. Millie and I stop. Someone says, "It's a good thing the city was ready for this. They get all the homeless off the streets when the windchill hits zero."

All right, so I was wrong—again. There is a reason for that scary number, at least for the homeless in New York City. I walk Millie back toward our apartment, feeling the sharp wind on my face but warm inside—a good way to celebrate the first day of winter.

> *Lord, thank You for windchill factors, heat indexes,*
> *churches that help the homeless, nagging spouses*
> *and all the other ways You protect us.*
> —EDWARD GRINNAN

Wed 22

They shall call his name Emmanuel. . . .
—MATTHEW 1:23

The Christmas season was here once again and, as usual, I was running behind. It would be hours before I could leave the office. Then I'd have to fight the crowds in an effort to get my last-minute shopping done.

"Your mother is on line one," my assistant said. I already knew why she was calling.

"Mom, I don't have time to go to church," I said without even a "hello." It was Wednesday, so church was tonight and it was the last thing I had time for.

"Now, Brock, tonight's the live nativity scene, and if you don't go, I think you'll regret it." Most sons are familiar with the dreaded "you'll regret it" line. I had no choice now.

"Okay, Mom," I said, sighing, trying my best to let her actually hear me rolling my eyes. "I'll see you there." Even though I'm now thirty-six years old, I still find myself listening to my mother.

As I sat in the pew, next to my smiling mom, the children's choir sang "Happy Birthday, Jesus" a cappella in their sweet voices. I took a deep breath and felt a calm coming over me that I hadn't felt in some time.

"Silent night, holy night," my little winged-and-haloed niece Abby was singing. I looked around at my church family as she and the other children sang, "All is calm, all is bright."

Then I could feel it coming: Christmas, headed straight for my heart.

Dear God, Christmas calls. Let me be
smart enough to stop and listen.
—BROCK KIDD

December

Thu 23

Now the birth of Jesus Christ took place in this way....
—MATTHEW 1:18 (RSV)

Christmas is a time of miracles. The Christmas my youngest child was six years old, we had our very own.

We were on the way to get a Christmas tree. The backseat was packed with children, though I don't remember why. In the front with me was Phil, then eight. Little brother Blake was beside him, trying to get the car's heavy door shut. For some reason I was in a hurry and started up the car, managing to pop the clutch. Blake got yanked out and flung under, screaming in pain and terror. I froze. *Which way do I go? Forward? Backward?* Phil shot out of the car. "Forward!" he bellowed.

When I got to Blake, he was where he'd been tossed—head on the road, body under the car. The front tire was partly on the asphalt, partly on the shoulder of the road, bridging a shallow gully where our Northwest rain had washed off loose gravel. Blake's arm had miraculously fallen into this ditch. His coat and shirt sleeves were torn clean off; tread marks dug deeply into his reddened skin. Gravel was embedded in his neck where the tire had come up over his shoulder.

"Can he move his fingers?" the doctor asked when I called in a panic.

"Yes."

"His arm moves okay?"

"Yes!"

"He's fine."

"But his arm is as flat as a pancake!"

"It'll puff back up. His bones are still elastic."

Someone once asked me if I believe in miracles. Are you kidding?

> *Father in heaven, Christmas is so full of miracles,*
> *both old and new. And You are*
> *the Author of them all.*
> —BRENDA WILBEE

❦ THE GREATEST GIFT

Fri 24   *On entering the house, they saw the child with Mary his mother; and they knelt down and paid him homage . . . .* —MATTHEW 2:11

CHRISTMAS EVE: THE CRÈCHE

I have my mother's crèche, the one that was her mother's. It's missing a wise man, though I have a nattily dressed shepherd stand in for him. One camel loped away and hid somewhere. Two of the cows are plastic replacements. One sheep is missing a leg. Joseph's staff, a bent wire, disappeared long ago. I don't care. This is the crèche that lit my childhood Christmas eves with joyous anticipation.

After supper, after church, after baths and pajamas (new for Christmas!), after cookies for St. Nicholas, Mom would take my sister Lori and me to the crèche.

Set on a low shelf on a square of gauze, surrounded by greens, lit by electric candlelight, the crèche had been up for weeks, always the first sign of Christmas to appear. The wise men, banished to a nearby table, wouldn't officially arrive on site until January 6, and for nearly five weeks between Thanksgiving and Christmas something else was missing: Baby Jesus. Every evening we'd put a bit of hay in the cradle, preparing a bed.

Now, in the light of the window candles and the tree, my father ready with a big, blue flashcube in the camera, we would all three gently place the Babe in the manger. Mom's strong, slender hand, Lori's wee one, my nervous fingers, all but obscured the tiny figure. Our three hands hovered a moment over the manger after we set Him there, unwilling to let go. In that awe-filled moment, all worries about presents, food and visitors faded. Everything we waited for was right there.

Jesus, when I think about Your birth, let me be filled with wonder at what really happened to the world that holy night.
—MARCI ALBORGHETTI

☙ THE GREATEST GIFT

Sat 25 *The shepherds returned, glorifying and praising God for all they had heard and seen, as it had been told them.*
—LUKE 2:20 (NRSV)

CHRISTMAS: WORLD WITHOUT END

It's Christmas morning. My sister Lori and I sprawl on the floor amid torn wrappings, playing some game we've just opened. Mom carries a tray laden with a once-a-year treat—four tall glasses of Carnation Instant Breakfast, three chocolate and one vanilla for my father. The candles in the windows and the tree lights grow dim as the December sun rises higher. Slowly my father sighs, "Well, Christmas is all over now." And he bends to gather the crumpled paper and boxes for the trash.

What he meant, of course, was that the anticipation, the anxiety, of Christmas was over for him, well before 8:00 AM on Christmas Day. Almost everyone feels this letdown, whether it's on Christmas morning, after Christmas dinner, at bedtime or even the next day. For some, it comes with the Christmas bills.

Are we more attached to the hustle and bustle and the trappings of Christmas than we are to its meaning? Did Mary and Joseph feel let down when Jesus was born? Isn't it more likely that they felt a new kind of excitement? The waiting for this prophesied Child was over, and the rest—His life with them—was just beginning. For the shepherds, for the wise men, for the poor and lowly, for the frightened and sick and imprisoned, for all of us, Jesus' birth was—and every Christmas is—a new beginning. Today, when we "let down" and let go of the anxiety and busyness, perhaps we can pick up the hope and the joy.

> *Lord, today I celebrate the beginning of Your life. Help me*
> *to remember that You're always a part of mine.*
> —MARCI ALBORGHETTI

Sun 26

Come and hear, all you who fear God, and I will tell you what he has done for me. —PSALM 66:16 (RSV)

Last December I had open-heart surgery and that meant Christmas was mostly a time of recovery. No parties, no singing, no traveling, no shopping. One day, scarcely home from the hospital, I walked very slowly to the corner to get a gift certificate for my wife Carol. That was about it. On Christmas Eve, with the help of a few painkillers, I made it to church and then went to bed early.

Carol would just as well forget last Christmas. She took pictures of our celebration around the tree, but she's never let me see them. She says it's because I look bad. It wasn't much fun for her to have the holidays together with a half-functioning husband. Last Christmas is something she could just skip.

But there's stuff I vividly remember and want to hold on to: all the cards, all the food that people dropped off, all the visits and phone calls, all the prayers and e-mails. It's funny, I don't remember much about the pain in my chest and being tired a lot and never feeling warm enough and running a low-grade fever. What I recall is feeling loved and appreciated.

Please don't get me wrong; I hope your Christmas is full of abundance and good health. But if you're having a hard time, if you're worried about your health or your job or a loved one, let me tell you that there will still be something to treasure. The good stuff shimmers in the dark like tinsel in candlelight. Think of that first Christmas. It was one of the hardest on record. Look what came of it.

Even in the struggles, Lord, I know You are there.
—RICK HAMLIN

December

Mon 27

Shew I unto you a more excellent way.
—I Corinthians 12:31

Our ten-year-old Mary is the child I have the hardest time understanding. She thrives on lively companionship and physical activity; I yearn for a peaceful day of quiet reading. It hasn't helped that this year she seems to have had a jumpstart into preteen moodiness. Trying to find common ground hasn't been easy.

So I was surprised when, after a hectic period at work, Mary asked me to watch a movie with her—Fred Astaire and Ginger Rogers in *Shall We Dance?* Mary received a set of Astaire-Rogers DVDs for Christmas, and she'd been avidly watching them with her siblings. Somewhat reluctantly, I sat down in my blue reading chair as Mary eagerly put the DVD into the player.

Astaire and Rogers had never become a part of my mental furniture. When I was Mary's age, King Kong and Fay Wray had been my idea of a fun movie couple, and in all the years since, I hadn't given Fred and Ginger much of a chance.

Fred's character, Peter P. Peters of Philadelphia, has made a career as Petrov of the Russian Ballet. But while he's supposed to be practicing his *grand jeté*, he secretly nourishes a passion for tap, a passion he's able to express when he meets and falls in love with musical-comedy star Ginger. Mixing fabulous dancing, screwball comedy and such luscious George Gershwin songs as "Let's Call the Whole Thing Off" and "They Can't Take That Away from Me," the movie was wonderful—almost as wonderful as the grin on Mary's face as she shared it with me.

How many other misapprehensions, I wonder, have I carried through life? How many snap judgments have made my life a little smaller? I'll always have room in my heart for Fay and her simian admirer, but bring on *Swing Time* and *Top Hat*!

Lord, thank You for the people who prod me to widen my horizons.
—Andrew Attaway

Tue 28   *His children become a blessing.* —P SALM 37:26 (RSV)

I was watching television in the den when I saw the sleeping bag crawl across the doorway and into the room. I ignored the bag as it inched up to me and began to slide up my leg. But when it rose in the air and blocked my view of the screen, I became annoyed.

This had been going on since my son Andy had found the bag, a gift from his Grandma Jean, lying under the tree on Christmas morning. He had slept in it that very night (no problem there), but the next day he had discovered that it made a terrific mobile cocoon. For several days now he had been slithering around the house, bundled inside his bag, making weird chirping noises as he passed from room to room.

So far I hadn't minded very much. Having a giant blue slug in the house may not be everybody's cup of tea, but Carol and I were used to our children's antics. But invading the den and blocking the television? Enough was enough!

Just as I was about to lose my temper, Andy's glowing face, wreathed in a smile, poked out of the bag. "Merry Christmas, Dad!" he exclaimed as he wrapped the bag around me and gave me a big hug. What could I do? I hugged him back. After all, our own real-life family sitcom, filled with love, was worth missing a few minutes of the TV variety.

> *Lord, help me never to lose sight of the blessings of children.*
> —P HILIP Z ALESKI

December

Wed 29

The counsel of the Lord stands forever, The plans of His heart from generation to generation. —PSALM 33:11 (NAS)

Each night when my younger brother Matt and I were little, Dad would tuck us into our bunk beds and say a prayer. In those lingering moments of wakefulness, Dad would tell us stories about God's providence in his life and how God had a plan for our lives too.

But God's plan took a surprising twist when I was diagnosed with cancer at age nine. I spent a year on chemotherapy, and Matt had to live with different families from church while Mom and Dad were with me at the hospital.

Thankfully, I survived, and today I'm getting along well. So is Matt. In fact, last year he was elected student body president at Harvard University, where he is now a senior. I'd always been worried about whether he might feel that my illness overshadowed his childhood. There's no doubt that God has used my cancer to bring me surprising blessings: I have a great career as a motivational speaker and I had the opportunity to ski in the Paralympics. But what about Matt?

Matt and I had a late-night conversation this past Christmas while we were home. "That must've been really hard for you," I said, "having to stay with different families that whole year I was on chemo."

He nodded. "Yeah, it was. But I can see now how the ability to relate to so many different kinds of people came out of that experience. I think that's the main reason I was elected student body president."

Later that night, as we fell asleep in our old bunk beds, I closed my eyes, knowing that not only had God always had a plan to use the cancer in my life but that He had a plan to use it in my brother's life too.

Lord, thank You for the providence that
watches over each new generation.
—JOSHUA SUNDQUIST

Thu 30

*As arrows are in the hand of a mighty man; so are children of the youth. Happy is the man that hath his quiver full of them. . . . —*PSALM 127:4–5

When I was a girl, I dreamed of marrying and having nine children—enough that my family could field our own baseball team. They would make my house full or, as the Bible says, my quiver would be full.

My life didn't turn out as I dreamed. I have loved and married, but I'm single now. Instead of nine children, I have two who have become extraordinary adults. My son Chase and my daughter Lanea are both beautiful, creative, intelligent, civic-minded and God-fearing. Not long ago the three of us were sitting in a restaurant in Cincinnati, where Chase is studying opera. As we talked, I looked across the candlelit table at the two of them and smiled.

I used to think that to have a full quiver required many arrows. But lately I've been thinking that one or two finely balanced, sharpened and true arrows are sufficient.

When they were infants, toddlers and even teenagers, they gave me great joy. Now they inspire me, they support me and sometimes they teach me. I marvel at the people they've become. We can't field a baseball team alone, but my heart is full. Two is enough.

Lord, thank You for blessing me with Your precious son and daughter.
May they have joy and peace all the days of their lives
and may their quivers be full.
—SHARON FOSTER

December

Fri 31

Lord, Thou hast been our dwelling place in all generations. Before the mountains were brought forth, or ever thou hadst formed the earth and the world, even from everlasting to everlasting, thou art God. —PSALM 90:1–2

It's New Year's Eve. My wife Beth is accompanying twelve Baylor University students on a study abroad program in Hong Kong, Cambodia, Vietnam, Singapore and Thailand. My oldest son Drew and his fiancée Katie Alice are traveling in India. My youngest son Luke is teaching English in Bangkok. And my daughter Jodi is driving from Texas to school in South Carolina. I'm at home in Waco, with four golden retrievers to help me greet the new year.

It's more than a little disconcerting to have my family scattered all over the world. I'm lonely; worry about my family's safety has my anxiety level spiking. Like so many on the threshold of a new year, I face change in my life, an uncertain future and the dawning awareness that a chapter of life is closing for good. In an uncertain world I yearn for stability and predictability.

I find myself spontaneously humming a tune. It's a hymn, with words written by Isaac Watts three hundred years ago. I know of no better hymn to sing to bring us through the promise and the challenge of the coming year.

O God, our help in ages past,
Our hope for years to come,
Our shelter from the stormy blast,
And our eternal home.

Father, You have been through every year of my life to sustain me and supply my needs. Stay by my side as my loving Shepherd as we walk through this new year together.
—SCOTT WALKER

THE GIFTS I'VE BEEN GIVEN

1 _____

2 _____

3 _____

4 _____

5 _____

6 _____

7 _____

8 _____

9 _____

10 _____

11 _____

12 _____

13 _____

14 _____

15 _____

December

16 _____

17 _____

18 _____

19 _____

20 _____

21 _____

22 _____

23 _____

24 _____

25 _____

26 _____

27 _____

28 _____

29 _____

30 _____

31 _____

FELLOWSHIP CORNER

One of the gifts we're particularly thankful for these days is the fellowship of our Daily Guideposts family. They're waiting for you here with news to share about what they've been doing over the past year. And you can also visit them online at DailyGuideposts.org. They'll share their thoughts, favorite Bible verses, the music they love, photos and a whole lot more.

MARCI ALBORGHETTI has been gifted by God in countless ways this year, primarily with good health for both her and her husband Charlie Duffy. They divide their time between apartments in New London, Connecticut, and the San Francisco Bay area. Marci's novel *The Christmas Glass* was published by Guideposts last year. "This book was what I would call a joyful challenge! It spans three generations of a family from 1940 to 2000, and covers an incredible amount of geography from Italy to New England, Florida to California. It gave me a chance to write about places I've lived, and that was a treat."

FAY ANGUS of Sierra Madre, California, writes, "I'm vicariously living with my son and his family in Colorado through e-mail videos of grandkids snowboarding off homemade ramps into their acres of meadowland and phone calls telling me there was a herd of elk at the wire fence. On my first visit, the vista of the Rockies was breathtaking, the Red Rock Amphitheater an incomparable canvas from the palette of our Creator, but for me the greatest joy was arms around my neck and endless cuddles—the gift of being there to actually feel the presence of love."

"It's been a year full of gifts," says *Daily Guideposts* editor ANDREW ATTAWAY of New York City, "including a few I'd never have put on my wish list. But the end result has been a lighter, fitter, happier me. And then there are the gifts that keep on giving: five astonishing, exasperating, exhilarating, almost-impossible-to-keep-up-with teens, preteens and littler folk, their mother—through whom God has given me gifts beyond measure—and all the members of our *Daily Guideposts* family." You can keep up with the Attaway family at DailyGuideposts.org.

"The children are growing up quickly," writes JULIA ATTAWAY of New York City. "It used to be that we had little ones swirling around us when we walked down the street, but now we're mostly a family of almost-adult-size people, with one or two kids tossed in for symmetry. Having a high schooler and a kindergartener requires a bit of a stretch, but the bigger challenge this year has been balancing work and family life. Somehow we muddle through, and I'm sure that's not due to me but to the infinite grace of God."

"Gordon and I were blessed with the gift of a safe homecoming from Iraq for our son Chris," writes KAREN BARBER of Alpharetta, Georgia. "He's out of the service now and working on an MBA. Another gift came from our son Jeff and his wife Leah—and our very first grandchild! With our youngest son John off at college, I worried that I wouldn't know what to do with myself. Thankfully, God had something in mind: starting a nonprofit called Prayer Igniters International whose purpose is to encourage and increase prayer via a Web site where everyone can share helpful ideas on prayer."

ALMA BARKMAN of Winnipeg, Manitoba, Canada, writes, "My husband Leo and I thank God for the gift of health. I'm thankful that God made each of us a do-it-yourselfer, because many of the things we now enjoy doing for others, like quilting and writing, gardening and baking, required honing of latent skills neither of us knew we had. Our desire to learn new things these days has waned considerably with one exception: We are always eager to learn what's new with our four children, their spouses and our ten grandchildren."

FRED BAUER and his wife Shirley make their home in Englewood Beach, Florida, and State College, Pennsylvania. In addition to church work, they find time to volunteer. Shirley, a retired elementary school librarian, still stacks books at school occasionally; Fred's favorite is the Salvation Army. Fred and Shirley keep close tabs on their four grown children and three grandchildren. Of this year's theme, Fred says, "We're all blessed by God with many special gifts. Think of all the talents people have to share—woodworking, sewing, drawing, singing, writing, teaching. Whatever your race, gender, occupation, location of faith, the Lord has given you a way to express His love."

EVELYN BENCE of Arlington, Virginia, notes, "In my professional life this year I've been privileged to broaden my historical perspective. I've read Augustine, John Calvin, John Wesley. I also researched the life of James Madison, 'Father of the Constitution.' A new awareness of the concerns, trials and triumphs of past generations has helped calm some of my current fears. The future may be uncertain, but God is here, offering His peace to my spirit. I pray I can, in turn, lead others to the gift."

"We received so many gifts this year that I wouldn't know where to start," says RHODA BLECKER of Bellingham, Washington. "Keith and I have the richness of our love for each other as a basis for our lives. Our community is stronger and more central to us this year than before. The science-fiction anthology I edit had its second annual volume and is being well received. Though we were snowed in for days in December, the kindness of neighbors and friends kept us warm. And, of course, every day we have is a gift, bright with promise, generous with beauty and filled with sunshine, even when it's rainy."

MELODY BONNETTE of Mandeville, Louisiana, writes, "I was shopping the other day and came across three beautiful ceramic figurines by Claire Stoner, representing Faith, Hope and Love. Faith is a meek and humble angel, hands clasped together in prayer. Hope is an angel reaching upward, hands embracing a white dove above her head, and Love is cradling a soft pink heart in her hands. They now reside on my windowsill just above my kitchen sink and remind me daily that faith, hope and love are indeed the greatest gifts I have been given."

"It's easy to see the good things as gifts," says GINA BRIDGEMAN of Scottsdale, Arizona. "The challenges are tougher, although they've taught me a lot about prayer." Gina is working full-time as a communications specialist at the school from which her son Ross graduated and where her daughter Maria attends ninth grade. Ross is now studying music in Nashville and loves performing around the city with various bands. Maria experienced the summer trip of a lifetime: she visited six European countries as a People to People Youth Ambassador. Gina's husband Paul continues his work as technical director for Arizona Broadway Theatre.

Fellowship Corner

For MARY BROWN of East Lansing, Michigan, this year abounded with gifts. "Our family labeled this our 'triple milestone year.' A month after our son Mark's 16th birthday, my husband Alex turned 60 and our daughter Elizabeth turned 21. We held a huge party and relished celebrating with many special people." Mary has found her new career tutoring dyslexics extremely rewarding. "Alex and I were honored to become godparents to baby Gus, the grandson of close friends. Spending time with Gus, his sister Ava, 3, and their wonderful parents is an absolute joy!"

"Gifts—I love giving them!" says MARY LOU CARNEY of Chesterton, Indiana. But it's Mary Lou who has received the best gift this year. In August, son Brett and wife Stacy will welcome a new baby. "With their daughter Isabelle Grace and my daughter Amy Jo and husband Kirk's three sons, that will make five grandchildren . . . and counting!" You can read about Mary Lou's family—and her spiritual journey—on her blog at OurPrayer.org.

"One of the biggest gifts of my life has been the opportunity to see so much of the world as a journalist," says JEFF CHU of Brooklyn, New York, who is an editor for a business magazine. Jeff grew up traveling—the son of immigrants from Hong Kong, he has relatives in at least eight countries—but when he became a reporter, it meant someone else would pay for it. The most memorable subjects "are always the normal, nonfamous people," he says. "The biggest gift for a writer is to be trusted to tell someone else's story."

"This has been the most difficult year of my life," writes SABRA CIANCANELLI of Tivoli, New York. "My sister Maria died unexpectedly in March, and I've been coping with grief and sorrow. During dark moments and sleepless nights, I've found comfort in my prayer book and watching the sun rise. My sons Solomon and Henry continue to brighten my life as I enjoy the daily gifts of being their mom. My husband is busy with the final renovations of our house, fixing the shutters and front porch, and I just ordered my seeds for this year's vegetable garden."

"By the time you read this, my wife will be a doctor," says MARK COLLINS of Pittsburgh, Pennsylvania. "While trying to complete a PhD in religion, she worked and kept the house together. I don't know how she did it. Maybe all those years of studying biblical heroines helped Sandee raise Hope, 17, Grace, 13, and college freshman Faith, 18," muses Mark. "They were strong, independent women—and that's what we have, although sometimes they make me nuts."

"In 2001 we returned to the East Coast from California and moved to Carmel, New York, an hour-plus drive from New York City," says PABLO DIAZ. "Our plan was to move to the city after our son Paul graduated from high school. Gradually and surprisingly, we discovered that Carmel's beauty, peacefulness and scenery were gifts from God for our family. Today we are head over heels for winding and crooked roads, the hills and streams and country living—even if they make my allergies worse. We've purchased a condo and become contented small-town dwellers. Sometimes God's gifts come in small packages."

BRIAN DOYLE, the editor of *Portland Magazine* at the University of Portland in Oregon, writes, "As regards being ridiculously slathered by gifts from the Profligate Maker, I still roll over in the morning and am astonished to find my stunning wife there again—a miracle! And for all that I moan and growl about the rude sneery teenage kids in our crumbling house, I don't forget that they are the greatest graces any man in the history of the universe ever received."

ERIC FELLMAN and his wife Joy made a major move this year from Washington, DC, to Fort Worth, Texas. Eric took a new job in Bible translation and publishing, and Joy continued her work as a nurse practitioner, helping to plan and provide clinics in rural African countries. Both of them, however, most enjoy their new role as grandparents of Ella Grace, born to son Nathan and his wife Jessica. Youngest son Jonathan married Beth this year, so the Fellman clan is greatly increased.

"Whenever I think of gifts," says SHARON FOSTER of Durham, North Carolina, "my first thought is always my children. Lanea is doing fabulous work as a community organizer. Chase has completed grad school with a degree in opera performance and is singing this summer with the Cincinnati Opera. Most of all, I'm grateful that they've grown to be good, loving people. My *Daily Guideposts* family is a precious gift, and I appreciate each note and e-mail. You can check my Web site sharonewellfoster.com for opportunities to meet me and share a special hug."

"This December my husband Rick and I celebrated our thirtieth anniversary," says JULIE GARMON of Monroe, Georgia. "We were high school sweethearts and married at eighteen and nineteen. Last Saturday, during the two-hour drive to the mountains, I remembered. I replayed the best days and the most difficult ones. As we wandered through our favorite store, the one that sells apples and Christmas ornaments, I said, 'Thank You.' 'For what?' Rick asked. 'For the years. For faithfulness. For honesty.' We held hands and sipped our cider. Maybe time brings two gifts: the gift of wisdom—a deep, almost unspeaking understanding of what matters most—and the ability to let go of the rest."

"The gifts we were given this year," writes OSCAR GREENE of West Medford, Massachusetts, "were so unexpected." A pen pal from Oregon visited Oscar's home. It was only the second time they had met, although they had exchanged letters for thirty years. A former co-worker Oscar hadn't seen for years visited from Florida. Then a former Sunday school pupil called from Montreal to thank Oscar for lessons taught forty years ago. These visits have inspired Oscar to thank those who have touched his life and to pray in thanksgiving for those who are no longer here.

"At the beginning of Thanksgiving week," writes EDWARD GRINNAN of New York City, "Julee tripped over a dog toy in the middle of the night and fell down the stairs." Julee ended up having two surgeries to fuse the bone. "The interesting thing was, I not only learned to take care of Julee, I learned a little more about how to take care of myself." And that infamous dog toy? It belonged to golden retriever Millie, now 2. You can catch up with Millie and Edward at Guideposts.com. "Check it out. I love it when people post comments."

RICK HAMLIN and his wife Carol, of New York City, became empty nesters when their youngest son Timothy went off to college this past year. Their oldest son William graduated from college in 2009. "I figured he'd come back to roost when he was out of school," Rick says, "but Will got himself a job in San Francisco and has moved there with some buddies. It gives us another place to visit in California." Carol, writing under the name Carol Wallace, has a new book out later this year about the death of Vincent van Gogh called *Leaving van Gogh*, and Rick is a regular blogger on both Guideposts.com and OurPrayer.org.

"I'm sitting here thinking of the gifts I've received during my lifetime," writes MADGE HARRAH of Albuquerque, New Mexico. "I thank God for the gift of two loving, kind parents who gave me a happy childhood filled with books, art supplies, piano lessons and a strong faith in God. I'm grateful for the gift of a younger brother who taught me how to play baseball. I'm grateful for my lifelong companion Larry, whom I met in eighth grade and married when we graduated from the University of Missouri. We are grateful for the gift of two children, five grandchildren and two great-grandchildren. Riches indeed!"

"If you'd told me a year ago that Carol and I would be empty nesters again, I would have been very skeptical," writes HAROLD HOSTETLER of Poughkeepsie, New York. "But midway through the year our daughter Laurel and granddaughter Kaila decided to move to Arizona, where Laurel lived when Kaila was born. We miss them a lot, but we've been spending more time with our other daughter Kristal and her family, and leading Bible studies and prayer at our church. Grandsons Konner, 6, and Brennig, 5, are a constant amazement to us. The other day Konner even allowed me to beat him at chess! And Brennig has thrown himself into soccer."

How is growing older, with its arthritic knees and thinning hair, a gift? Because it also meant that JEFF JAPINGA of Holland, Michigan, could watch his son Mark graduate from college and take on his first job, and see his daughter Annie, now in high school, continue to grow into a wonderful, poised young lady and a wickedly good volleyball player. This awful recession? It hit especially hard at McCormick Theological Seminary where Jeff works and teaches, but he says, "It also gave us the opportunity to focus on what's most important. That's a gift, even if it's one we didn't ask for."

This year brought a heaping pile of gifts and blessings for ASHLEY JOHNSON of Birmingham, Alabama. She welcomed a niece and a nephew into the world (that makes six total!), shared one last visit with her 97-year-old grandmother before she passed away, and joyfully replied "Yes!" when Brian Kappel, her boyfriend of five years, proposed to her. By the time you read this, Ashley will be married.

BROCK KIDD of Nashville, Tennessee, writes, "My life seems to be overflowing with gifts this year. My son Harrison and I have found someone to make our family complete. We recently asked a wonderful woman to marry me. I say *we*, because Harrison actually beat me to the punch. The three of us were driving together when suddenly Harrison burst out, 'When are you gonna marry my dad?' Harrison is greatly anticipating his role as best man."

"What a pleasure it's been to take time to consider the gifts I've been given," writes PAM KIDD of Nashville, Tennessee. A few years ago my daughter Keri went into real estate to support our Zimbabwe habit; now we are feeding nine hundred hungry children every day with our earnings! For years we've dreamed for a perfect life-mate for Brock; now he's engaged to marry a woman we all adore! Keri and Ben's daughter Abby continues to sing and dance through our days and is anticipating being a big sister soon. And grandson Harrison remains our family naturalist. My mother and near-father Herb continue to thrive, and soon my husband David will be retiring from our beloved Hillsboro Presbyterian Church and we'll discover the mystery that waits ahead!"

MARILYN MORGAN KING of Green Mountain Falls, Colorado, received a new appreciation for her gift of sight this year when she had surgery for a detached retina. Her vision in that eye is still distorted, and macular degeneration is attacking her right eye. So why is this a gift? "I can still see!" says Marilyn. "I can see my husband's cute pixie smile and my children's and grandchildren's beloved faces. This morning I saw the sun rise over the mountain. What a glorious display it was! For as long as I have eyes that see (whether blurry or clearly), I'll continue to thank our Creator for the blessed gift of vision, worth more to me than diamonds."

CAROL KNAPP of Lakeville, Minnesota, writes, "Two more grandchildren, Matthew and Grace, make an even dozen for my husband Terry and me. Most live in Alaska, so I made two trips there last year—and a wonderful summer visit with my 86-year-old mother in north Idaho. I raked pine needles, delighted to find a small speckled bird's egg safely cracked, its occupant flying free—a metaphor for my life as I have wrestled to break free from old 'safe' confines and soar into Galatians 5:1 (NAS): 'It was for freedom that Christ set us free.'"

CAROL KUYKENDALL of Boulder, Colorado, writes, "I heard a quote once: 'One of the gifts of getting older is that we get to keep all the ages we've been.' I agree! The passing years have given me treasured memories to savor and the perspective to see the unique gifts of each season. I'm cherishing the gift of grandchildren (five, with a sixth on the way!) and the joy of adult friendships with our three children and their spouses. My daughter Lindsay and I combined efforts this year to create a new ministry at our church called Stories . . . , which gives me the opportunity to mentor others in telling their stories. And my husband Lynn and I continue to thank God for the miraculous gift of good test results for our cancers."

PATRICIA LORENZ of Largo, Florida, writes, "I am delighted every day with the gifts I've been given. I have joyful work that includes writing books and speaking to groups around the country. My eleventh book, *The 5 Things We Need to Be Happy and Money Isn't One of Them* (published by Guideposts), is doing well. I'm blessed to be living in a warm, sunny, happy-making climate. My four children, their spouses and eight grand-children are healthy and enjoying their lives in Ohio, Wisconsin and California. Life is full of little adventures, leisurely bike rides, wonderful swims in the Gulf of Mexico and in the pools across the street."

Whether DEBBIE MACOMBER is sharing her faith with her eight grandchildren in her creative annual "Grandma Camp" or writing her new nonfiction book *One Simple Act*, she endeavors to inspire others to pursue the dreams that God has placed in their hearts. Debbie continues to serve on the national board for Warm Up America! and actively supports Knit for Kids and World Vision. She and her husband Wayne serve on the Guideposts National Advisory Cabinet and look forward to splitting their time between Port Orchard, Washington, and their new winter home in Florida, where the dolphins and manatees visit them daily.

"There are more than one thousand references to *giving* in the Bible," says ROBERTA MESSNER of Huntington, West Virginia. "Giving is very much God's idea." This past year found Roberta simplifying life at her historic log cabin. "I experienced the most amazing sense of freedom in giving away many of my personal possessions. What a pleasure it has been to see others use things I've enjoyed over the years." Now, instead of collecting old treasures, Roberta finds joy in collecting stories of the giving life.

KEITH MILLER and his wife Andrea live in Austin, Texas. Last year Keith received a very special gift, an honorary doctor of humane letters bestowed by the Seminary of the Southwest (Episcopal), recognizing his impact on American Christian life and thought. Keith and Andrea are completing a book tentatively titled *Square One*, due to be published this year. Several of Keith's earlier books, including *The Taste of New Wine*, are scheduled to be released by Thornton House. You'll find a summary of Keith's life and work at keithmiller.com, where you can also sign up for his free weekly e-mail devotional.

LINDA NEUKRUG lives in Walnut Creek, California. This year she adopted a cat named Prince Westley, an eighteen-pound gray male longhair larger than her Thanksgiving turkey. Linda will be cooking a pie a week and bringing it to a local homeless shelter where there is a sign posted: "To him that is joined to all the living, there is hope"(Ecclesiastes 9:4). She got the idea from Lorraine Sylling, who passed away in 2008. Lorraine began writing to Linda several years back and was unfailingly cheerful and always busy—baking pies and cakes for others, knitting for soldiers, making quilts for babies. Even though Linda never met her, Lorraine is missed and she serves as a God-inspired—and inspiring—example of giving.

This year gifts have rained down abundantly on REBECCA ONDOV of Hamilton, Montana. After the unexpected death of her dog, a golden retriever puppy wiggled its way into her heart. And if that wasn't enough, a stunning paint horse joined Rebecca's herd. "It's been a year sprinkled with gifts, and I even have a new book coming out. The tentative title is *Horse Tales from Heaven*."

MARY ANN O'ROARK keeps traveling—to Arizona and Ohio to spend time with family and friends, to Spain's Barcelona and Madrid to "sacred sightsee," to Seattle and Pittsburgh to lead workshops in sacred journaling. And maybe, best of all, she's stayed home to enjoy New York City and her furry kitty Sheila.

DANIEL SCHANTZ is enjoying his forty-second year teaching at Central Christian College in Moberly, Missouri. His wife Sharon is retiring from public school work. One joy in their life is watching the grandchildren, as their gifts become more and more obvious. Abram, 10, loves to garden, like Dan. Rossetti, 11, enjoys church and missions work. Silas, 13, is good at piano and guitar. Hannah, 16, excels in drama. She left home-schooling behind to enter the New Franklin Public School, where she is doing exceptional work.

GAIL THORELL SCHILLING of Concord, New Hampshire, continues to teach at NHTI, Concord's community college, and to work as a docent at the Canterbury Shaker Village. She says, "Our family will be together when daughter Trina and her beloved Steve marry in June. They'll exchange vows on the waterfront of my mother's cottage on Merrymeeting Lake, where I've done belly flops since age 6. Recent milestones include Mom's 90th birthday, my 60th and a trip to Quebec City for its 400th. How could I possibly feel old in an enchanting city 340 years older than I am?"

"The best gift of retirement is time," writes PENNEY SCHWAB of Copeland, Kansas. "My husband Don and I visited grandson Ryan at Texas Tech; watched grandkids David, Mark, Caleb and Olivia in plays, choir performances and multiple sports events; and attended 5-year-old Caden's hockey games. I've had more time for church activities and organ practice. And I've had lots of outdoor time with my dog Tarby. Most important, I've spent more time in Bible study and prayer, getting to know the greatest gift, Jesus."

As the stairs in their house in Chappaqua, New York, became longer and steeper, ELIZABETH (Tib) SHERRILL and her husband John made the reluctant decision to sell the home where they've lived for more than fifty years. "It's astonishing," Tib says, "how many *things* a house can hold." Most daunting was clearing the accumulation of half a century from the attic. Their three children—Liz from Boston, Donn from Miami, John Scott from Nashville, Tennessee—came to help. "It was hard, slow, dusty work, but as memories surfaced, the clearing-out became a celebration of a family's life shared in this place."

"Everyone warned us that selling our home would be traumatic," says JOHN SHERRILL of Chappaqua, New York. "But one loss I couldn't have imagined—fifty years ago, when Tib and I bought the house—was that I would have to give up *cooking*." At their new home, however, the main meal of the day will be supplied by the community. "So it's good-bye to spatula and measuring spoon. But in my experience, when one treasure is taken away, another will take its place. I wonder what that new treasure is going to be."

SHARI SMYTH of Nashville, Tennessee, writes, "I've passed another mile marker this year: I'm now on Medicare and celebrated by having a complete physical. I'm fit and fine—and for that I'm grateful. In fact, my gratitude cup is full and running over. Our grandson Frank, who just turned 4, stays with us several days a week while his parents work. I also enjoy gardening, both at home and at church. I continue to teach Sunday school; I never tire of presenting Jesus to the little ones. 'We are His sheep,' a child whispered to me recently. It's true—we are."

JOSHUA SUNDQUIST writes, "I've certainly been blessed with my fair share of gifts this year. After finishing my master's degree in communications, I moved back home to McLean, Virginia, and started traveling the country full-time as an inspirational speaker. The best gift I was given this year was a book deal with a major publishing house for a memoir about my battle with cancer and my ski-racing career. I am truly blessed!"

JON SWEENEY of Woodstock, Vermont, writes, "My article on the serious ways some people take Jedi religion has been read by more than a million people at explorefaith.org. My books? I wish! Not as much." Jon's books include *The St. Francis Prayer Book* and the new *Cloister Talks: Learning from My Friends the Monks*. He has two teenage children, Sarah and Joseph, who "are God's greatest gifts to me."

"Months shy of my son's first birthday, I found out that I was pregnant with number two," says KAREN VALENTIN of New York City. "I worried about juggling another baby along with the rest of my responsibilities. Then, after a frantic day, my son snuggled into my arms and gave me a kiss. My next child will bring double the workload, but the blessings and love will be multiplied as well."

SCOTT WALKER of Waco, Texas, writes, "In June 2008 I resigned as pastor of First Baptist Church in Waco to focus on writing, teaching and helping university students. My book *The Edge of Terror: The Heroic Story of American Families Trapped in the Japanese-Occupied Philippines* will be published in October. My wife Beth continues her work with international students. Our son Drew has graduated from law school and will be married to Katie Alice Cox in August. Luke has returned from ten months of teaching English in Thailand. Jodi is a college senior majoring in English. She'll spend two months this summer teaching English in Japan."

"Our son Ryan graduated from Belhaven College this year," writes DOLPHUS WEARY of Richland, Mississippi. "Our daughter Danita continues to practice medicine as a pediatrician in Natchez, Mississippi, where she has also been serving as chief of staff at the hospital. Little Reggie is 5 years old and is in kindergarten." Dolphus' wife Rosie now serves as vice president of REAL Christian Foundation; Dolphus serves as president on a part-time basis and is now president emeritus of Mission Mississippi.

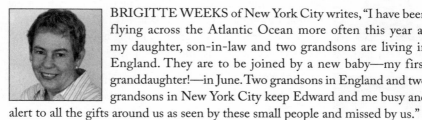

BRIGITTE WEEKS of New York City writes, "I have been flying across the Atlantic Ocean more often this year as my daughter, son-in-law and two grandsons are living in England. They are to be joined by a new baby—my first granddaughter!—in June. Two grandsons in England and two grandsons in New York City keep Edward and me busy and alert to all the gifts around us as seen by these small people and missed by us."

"I didn't expect to be so needy this year—physically, mentally and spiritually," writes MARION BOND WEST of Watkinsville, Georgia. "I didn't like it one bit. God, in His gentle way, suggested I put to use some of His gifts that I'd not fully received. In quiet desperation, I agreed. I decided to 'be anxious for nothing' (Philippians 4:6, NAS). I determined to 'trust in the Lord with all [my] heart' (Proverbs 3:5). I believed that 'a joyful heart is good medicine' (Proverbs 17:22, NAS). Finally, I experienced 'when [I] lie down, [I] will not be afraid; when [I] lie down, [my] sleep will be sweet' (Proverbs 3:24, NAS)."

"It's been a crazy year," says BRENDA WILBEE of Birch Bay, Washington. "On the upside I finally found a full-time job. On the downside I was let go within months and replaced by someone just 20 years old. So the struggle for financial security remains a challenge. Interestingly enough, I learned two days after I'd been laid off that I'd won first place for inspirational writing at the Pacific Northwest Writers Association.

'A divine moment,' a Hollywood screenwriter told me. So surely if Hollywood can recognize God's direction, I can."

TIM WILLIAMS of Durango, Colorado, writes, "My wife Dianne retired from teaching this year. Our schedules once revolved around daily work, appointments and needs. Now our needs seem almost seasonal. Do we have enough firewood cut this fall? Do we have extra shear pins for the snowblower? Do we need to pick up more seeds and starter plants for the garden this spring? And my favorite question: 'Shouldn't I go fishing one more time this summer, so we can put a few in the freezer?' We are never too tired to attend church and never too busy to visit our family and friends. I'm grateful for every spare hour in the day."

ISABEL WOLSELEY of Syracuse, New York, writes, "One of my fun highlights of the past year was an eightieth birthday surprise for my husband Lawrence. Friends who winter in Florida had often invited us to spend a few days with them, so he suspected nothing when I suggested, 'Let's do it this year,' even though the date coincided with his birthday. Lawrence's four daughters—three from Oregon, one from Switzerland—were also invited. When the girls emerged from their hiding spots, it took several minutes until he realized they really were his!"

PHILIP ZALESKI of Northampton, Massachusetts, says, "This has been another year of change and thanksgiving. Our son John is graduating from college and will be spending a year at home before going on to graduate school in medieval studies. Andy, meanwhile, is entering high school and continues to enjoy baseball, skiing, reading and Latin. Needless to say, Carol and I are overjoyed at the prospect of having both boys at home together again, filling the house with their infectious energy and humor."

Authors, Titles and Subjects Index